THE
RECOVERY
OF RACE
IN AMERICA

THE
RECOVERY
OF RACE
IN AMERICA

Aaron David Gresson III

UNIVERSITY OF MINNESOTA PRESS
MINNEAPOLIS
LONDON

Published by the University of Minnesota Press
111 Third Avenue South, Suite 290, Minneapolis, MN 55401-2520
Printed in the United States of America on acid-free paper

Library of Congress Cataloging-in-Publication Data

Gresson, Aaron David.
    The recovery of race in America / Aaron David Gresson.
        p.   cm.
    Includes bibliographical references and index.
    ISBN 0-8166-2446-1 (alk. paper)
    ISBN 0-8166-2448-8 (pbk. : alk. paper)
    1. United States—Race relations—Psychological aspects. 2. Loss
(Psychology) I. Title.
    E185.625.G672   1995
    305.8'00973–dc20   94–19162
                                                                 CIP

The University of Minnesota is an
equal-opportunity educator and employer.

For LaFrances, Jerry, Barbara, and Pat;
to the memory of
George Houston Bass;
and especially for Ariane Isabella

Contents

❖

PART IV
The Rhetoric of Recovery: Theory and Practice

Preface

❖

This book is a rhetorical study of loss and recovery. It explores the rhetorical structure and dynamics of the response to two particular losses: white Americans' loss of moral hegemony and Black Americans' loss of the myth of racial homogeneity. The first of these losses has been recently encoded in such notions as the "loss of cultural literacy in America," the "recovery of excellence in education," and the "white male as victim of affirmative action." The second loss has been expressed in the rise and nonresolution of the "Black sexism debate," the Who is Black? movement, and the "Black conservative as new Negro controversy." The convergence of these two loss-recovery agendas was played out around President Bush's nomination of a self-avowed Black conservative judge, Clarence Thomas, to the Supreme Court of the United States.

This book is about the perceived losses and recovery efforts that underpin such events as the Thomas confirmation hearings in the U.S. Senate. Although the original manuscript predated the nomination of Clarence Thomas and the sexual harassment accusation by Anita Hill, its topics anticipated both the nomination and the controversy it generated among Blacks, females, liberals, and conservatives. I consider these basic questions: How does a powerful group regain or recover the moral right to dominate other groups when the reigning cultural myths negate the direct use of supremist ideologies? How does the most visible and vocal oppressed group renegotiate its relationship to itself and the dominant group when the liberation struggle has run its course without achieving its liberation goals? How do contemporary African-Americans manage the rhetorical task of self–Other liberation in a postmodern society? What myths, discourses, and rhetorical strategies are employed in the tasks of white and Black recovery?

To explore the issue of loss in contemporary interracial life, thought, and speech, this work develops and applies a theory of rhetorical recovery inherent in the human condition as contradiction and choice.

Toward this end, I have pursued a special reading of the emergent literature on Black literary theory and fiction. I have also pursued a reading of several narratives taken as part of a psychology study of racial commitment attitudes and behavior (Gresson 1985b). In this way, I attempt to answer this still larger question: What is the contemporary nature of racial recovery discourse, and how does it bear on the general issue of rhetorical theory development?

Recovery is the concept that I have employed to organize the material in this book. Recovery is a human necessity: whenever and wherever there are losses, we must respond. This response is a recovery response, an attempt to gain back something of the balance — whether good, bad, or different — that we once knew. We have come to understand from scholars of the fairy tale, for example, that the fantasy of Christmas is more important to parents than to children: children often know "the truth about Santa Claus" long before parents want them to; it is the parents who remember and desire to recover the wonder and innocence of the small child on Christmas morning.

So it is with things racial: the inherited racial fantasies and myths die hard. Most notable are the myth of a monolithic Black race committed to a common and collective liberation from racism, on the one hand, and a myth that says powerful white men and women do not continue to use race and racism to maintain their privileges in American society, on the other. This brings me to another point I wish to make about the message of and audiences for this book.

I have called this book *The Recovery of Race in America* because it emphasizes the new feature characterizing American intra- and inter-racial relations. This new feature is symbolized by Clarence Thomas and Anita Hill. The original manuscript was completed two years before the famous Thomas-Hill affair; yet it foretold that drama. It anticipated the surfacing of a clash between Blacks who held on to and those who rejected the traditional beliefs — both fact and fiction — regarding the persistence of racism in America and the need to remain racially chauvinistic in defense against it. Thomas as a Black conservative and his Black opposition, the traditional civil rights groups, represent this clash at the communal level; Thomas and Hill, as individuals, represent it at the personal or intimate level.

The manuscript of this book also foretold the role of whites in the new conflicts among Blacks. It anticipated that certain white feminists would emerge as the dominant critics of the stereotypic Black male. It also suggested that white males — experiencing themselves as the new victims of public critique (read as oppression) — would use their power to manipulate the legitimate differences among Black liberation-seekers. Both the Democrats and Republicans graphically displayed this: first, the Republicans as they struggled to influence "what kind of Negro" would replace the late Thurgood Marshall as Supreme Court justice; later, the Democrats as they manipulated Anita Hill in a desperate effort to bar Thomas's confirmation.

Although I deal with white recovery as well as Black recovery, I do not want to give the impression that I consider the recovery efforts of equal weight. On the contrary, today there is an insidious insistence (often by well-meaning and humanistic individuals) that any allusion to past inequities as relevant to contemporary discourse and politics is "reverse" chauvinism. I disagree. The relative and absolute power held by white Americans in relation to Black Americans does not invite this "let the past be forgotten" mentality. Indeed, my purpose is to draw attention to the fact that these various recovery efforts have all contributed to an unprecedented racial irony: one where racism may persist — often viciously — even as one hears clamors of *No mas!* (No more!).

A Note on Reading This Book

I hope readers will want to proceed through the chapters sequentially. However, because of the rich variety of material and themes covered in the book, some may wish to read certain chapters out of sequence. The following is intended to suggest one way to do this.

This book develops a theory of how people try to recover things they lose yet value. I develop this theory using many complicated and often unfamiliar ideas. Usually it is possible to say what one wants to say without getting into a long, drawn-out theory; but this is not the case, I feel, with the new challenge of racial identity and consciousness in America. Most of us have been shocked and horrified by the ethnic strife in the former Soviet Union; but America is facing its own economic and social crises and is witnessing its own racial and ethnic turmoil. There have been many changes in racial relations during the past thirty years, and it may not be feasible to communicate emerging intergroup problems with the same old ideas and language. The theory I have developed tries to clarify these problems in a new way.

But for some readers, my theory, as interesting and important as I feel it to be, may not be the first thing of interest in this book. In doing research for the book, I conducted interviews with an extraordinary group of Black women. Because the interviews were a strong influence on my writing this book and show the feelings and attitudes I held while writing it, I have presented excerpts of these prior to stating the theory. These excerpts appear in part III. Readers interested largely in reading the interviews that focus on Black female, Black male, and racial liberation issues might prefer to treat chapters 2–6 as a unit. From this view, the three narratives may be viewed as elaborations of the ways three individual females have struggled with the developments described in chapters 2 and 3.

As I point out in chapter 1, Black male and female liberation discourse over the past two decades is a part of a larger liberation discourse. We have come to call this larger discourse "postmodernism." This word, however, has tended to mystify rather than enlighten in many instances. Thus, by presenting the Black American predicament first, it is possible to describe in more familiar terms much of the larger social plight and discourse. Chapters 7, 8, and 9 differ from the earlier chapters by the emphasis placed on theory development and illustration. In chapter 7, I present a theory of recovery; in the two subsequent chapters, I illustrate the various elements of the theory and show how it may help explain more fully and meaningfully contemporary racial and identity politics in America. Chapter 10 presents my concluding thoughts.

Acknowledgments

❖

I would like to thank some of the many people who contributed to the completion of this project. First, there are the many women who encouraged me during various phases of the earlier study inspiring this work. These include Carole Watkins, Jean Baker Miller, Carole Cartwright, LaFrances Rogers Rose, Lena Wright Myers, Patricia Bell Scott, and Barbara Morrison. Here I would also like to mention Beverly Brandon Finley, Gaytra Lathon, and Tyleta Howell, who inspired me to undertake the earlier study on Black female racial commitments and who have continued to support my efforts to understand and transform my own sexist upbringing and proclivities.

During my writing of various drafts of this work, Tyleta Howell and Robert Haskell were more than good friends and confidants: they shared their own inspiration with me. James Stewart and Deborah Atwater were kind enough to read drafts of this book and to make important suggestions. Rhett and Alegra Jones and John and Cordelia Swinton were valuable emotional supports during the dark days associated with this project. Carroll Arnold and Richard Gregg have been distant but powerful influences on my continued fascination with rhetorical theory and analysis, and I thank them yet again. A special thanks to Thomas Benson, who got me to take on this project seriously. Richard Brown, Gerald Platt, and Fred Weinstein have remained generous critics and supporters throughout my scholarly career, and I continue to be in their debt. Thanks also to John Swinton and Jill Brighton, who helped with the preparation of the manuscript; their editorial and secretarial support is greatly appreciated. I would also like to acknowledge my colleagues at Penn State University; their kindness and support provided me with "a room of my own" that was all the difference between success and failure in this project.

During the summer of 1993, I participated in the University of Pennsylvania's Ford Foundation Summer Seminar entitled "History, Content, and Method in Afro-American Studies," conducted by the Center for the

Study of Black Literature and Culture. I can only begin to express my great gratitude to the center's staff, notably Houston Baker, Jr. (director), and John Roberts (seminar leader). They helped provide an exciting and stimulating intellectual climate, and the seven other scholars they brought to Philadelphia to participate in the seminar had a profound effect on my work. To my fellow seminar participants and the invited scholars who came to share their time, interests, insights, and inspiration with us, I owe a debt that can never be repaid. Although this work was already largely completed at this time, I was able to strengthen it in important ways because of constructive and compassionate criticism of this group of scholars. Members of the seminar included Frank E. Dobson, Dianetta Bryan, Dorothy Denniston, Lillian Ashcraft-Eason, Pearlie Peters, Alma S. Freeman, and Hoda M. Zaki. Thank you all!

I remain always thankful for my first mentors at the University of Waterloo in Canada: Palmer and Nancy Lou Patterson, Walter and Ruth Klausen, H. D. and Ruth Kirk, Sally and David Weaver, Leo Johnson, and Thomas Abler. John and Nancy Oliver, Barbara Morrison, Jerry Salters, and Pat Fortson, along with my family, have helped me keep my sanity when I have been most vulnerable to insane places and practices. Thanks.

We are all occasionally fortunate enough to know one or two great human beings. For me, George Houston Bass was such a man; I miss him as I know many others — his widow and three children first among them — do. In his life he seemed always to me to make communal and compassionate personal choices, and I continue to draw strength from the memory of him. And finally, I thank Ariane Isabella Gresson, my daughter. Although she is only a little more than three years old, she has, perhaps predictably, profoundly influenced my writing and my desire to be a better human being: I thank her for her vitality, freshness, creative self-assurance, and compassion. All of these have sustained me and helped me to believe in a "Promised Land."

PART I

Loss and Recovery 1: Race Hegemony — The American Context

═══ ❖ ═══

The New McCarthyism atmosphere of self-censorship will continue to collide with massive alienation and anger among white victims. The solution to this question is both simple and difficult: talk about the issues. As has been demonstrated in this book, widespread talk can be a potent instrument of change. The huge variations in income, education, and family styles among Blacks should be kept in mind. These variations contradict simplistic all-Blacks-are-poor and inequality-equals-discrimination assumptions and raise questions of any categorical race preference.
— Frederick R. Lynch, *Invisible Victims: White Males and the Crisis of Affirmative Action*

1

Race, Rhetoric, and Recovery

❖

*The problem of mankind today ... is precisely opposite that of
men in the comparatively stable periods of those great coordinating mythologies which now are known as lies. Then all meaning
was in the group, in the great anonymous forms, none in the self-
expressive individual; today no meaning is in the group — none in
the world: all is in the individual.*

— Joseph Campbell (1968)

Joseph Campbell claimed contemporary men and women differ from
their ancestors in that the individual, rather than the family, group, or
society, determines what is real, valuable, and necessary. I take Campbell's observation as a central assumption, arguing that this shift in the
locus of meaning from the group to the individual creates a special rhetorical situation: the individual must both make meaning for the self and
convince others of its integrity. No doubt this task has to some degree
always existed, but it takes on a special urgency in contemporary society with the individual at the center of meaning at precisely the time
when society is reconstructing its own sense of morality and purpose. In
this circumstance, the individual makes meanings for the self and offers
these meanings as useful collective alternatives to the lost "coordinating
mythologies" that Campbell discusses.

I call this task of individual and collective persuasion "the recovery project," by which I mean that people must recover ways of
being related and connected to something and someone larger than
"I" and "me." My focus is this recovery project, and I intend to
identify the implicit theory of rhetoric within that project by examining the form and function of recovery themes in the contemporary
American racial liberation discourse. I make a second assumption:
the social- and cultural-change movements of the 1960s inspired several competing yet complementary liberation movements. To varying

3

degrees, these racial-ethnic, intergenerational, gender, and sexual liberation movements converged with and "encouraged" the recovery project
of Western man.

The Concept of Recovery

Recovery is generic to the story of humankind. For instance, in the
Christian version of salvation history — humankind's fall from God
and its recovery through Christ — the goal is to recover a lost oneness
with God. Much later, Freud saw birth as a separation from the oneness with mother — a loss people try to recover through allegiance to
a group leader. A core theme in sociology, from Georg Simmel in the
1890s to Ernest Becker in the 1970s, has been that social life implies an
individual loss, a loss the individual seeks to recover in various ways,
including even social deviance.[1] In each of these domains of human response — the spiritual, psychological, and social — recovery equates to
the reclamation of an original or ideal state of being.

From this perspective, we can see recovery as the reconnection to, or
regaining of, a prior and privileged position or relationship. The notion
of the Black apocalypse (see below, pp. 16–17) incorporates these two
forms: (1) recovery of a collectively shared set of ideals by which to con-
duct civil relations; and (2) recovery of a mutually binding interracial
code of morality. Recovery discourse articulates these twin recovery
motives.[2]

Recovery Discourse and Rhetoric

"Recovery discourse" refers to conversation about self–Other liberation.
It implies a prior awareness, recollection, or avowal regarding oneself
and others. This discourse is the source of the particular justifications
or persuasive themes (*topoi*) associated with liberation rhetoric. It is
talk about recovery. One may also consider recovery discourse as both
specific rhetorics of recovery and a generic rhetorical form.

"Rhetoric" is broadly defined here to mean persuasive speech or
nonverbal communication. Implicit in this term is the presence of certain
shared values, beliefs, concerns, and so on that may be used in the effort
to persuade or influence others. Specific strategies aimed at legitimiz-
ing a particular recovery strategy usually focus on a given *topos*. These
strategies are called "recovery rhetorics." Christopher Lasch (1984), for
instance, sees the individual "turning in on self" as a result of societal failure: attempting to manage the anxiety, confusion, and pain of
frequent and often contradictory shifts in social values, an individual

makes personal choices, choosing to be what Lasch calls a "minimal self." To rationalize this emphasis on self, an individual adopts a "rhetoric of survivalism" and a "logic" particular to the "cult of narcissism," a belief in self above all else. Lasch's message, a fulfillment of the visions of Campbell and Wilson Moses (1982), tells us that when society fails the individual, the individual tries to take care of self. I contend that the individual tries to persuade the Other that this personal focus, an apparent selfish gesture, actually provides the Other with guidance.[3] But this edification may fail, and the failure may generate specific recovery rhetorics.

For example, I have suggested (Gresson 1982) that failure can inspire "rhetorics of betrayal and consolation" that persuade one to accept the need to act as one's own advocate, defining alone who one is and to whom one is committed. Observing modern medicine's inability to console patients, Arthur Frank (1989) described cancer self-help groups as creating a "rhetoric of self-healing," a critical tactic in reclaiming the right to define what their illness means and how they can maintain a sense of selfhood within the technocratic and often insensitive world of oncological care.

The Rhetoric of Recovery

Rhetorics of betrayal and consolation (Gresson 1982), failure (D. Payne 1989), and self-healing (Frank 1989) illustrate "recovery rhetorics." What I call "the rhetoric of recovery" is a configuration of elements shared by all of these "recovery rhetorics": (1) a motive to recover something perceived as lost through violation, failure, or betrayal; (2) the use of narrative to describe a discovery with inferred relevance for both one's own and the Other's ability to deal better with duplicity and uncertainty; and (3) an implicit invitation to identify with and accept the liberative powers of that discovery.

Recovery and Power

Power plays a central role in recovery rhetorics, mainly evident in the right to name, to define, and to self-validate choices affecting others as well as oneself. Liberation discourse became recovery discourse through such power. The power is both political and moral, and it appeared at the nation's ethical beginnings with its peculiar and ambivalent posture toward Blacks and to a much lesser degree toward other disenfranchised groups. Accordingly, recovery in America largely depends on the power to control others or the power to escape this control. In either case, race is a pertinent factor.

Recovery and Race

Campbell's conclusion that humankind has lost its unifying beliefs is shared by others. For instance, the African-American historian Wilson Moses (1982) "Americanized" this argument regarding loss, contending that the American sense of manifest destiny, embodied as a social messianism, was America's unifying myth, with the Vietnam War as its death spasm. Moses noted that African-Americans have shared in this loss of vision and that their various liberation ideologies have, like the call for manifest destiny, lost their persuasive power.

I suggest that the mythic vision was weakened but never fully lost, and efforts to recover it are everywhere evident on the American landscape. It is primarily evident in the renegotiated meaning of liberation. Through the 1970s and 1980s, recovery for the powerful and the less powerful gradually converged, then parted in an obverse irony that currently portrays the white male as victim and the Black male as villain. This reversal occurred as a result of a peculiar process of rhetorical identification I call the "deconstruction of the oppressed."

The Deconstruction of the Oppressed

According to *Webster's New Collegiate Dictionary*, "nigger" means simply any member of a dark-skinned race; the dictionary adds that the term is usually taken to be offensive. In spite of this definition, the fact is that the enslaved African was called a "nigger" and took it to be offensive only because the masters intended it as such. Later, because of its pervasive negative connotation in American society, "nigger" became a broader metaphor for America's non-dark-skinned victims of oppression in the 1960s and 1970s. From white college students and white females to children and the elderly, the notion of "nigger" became an empathic metaphor for the low status and plight of various non-Black-skinned groups in search of equity and equality.

Table 1 depicts this enlarged use of the term "nigger" as a compelling, collective metaphor. Several points must be stressed regarding this expansion of the "nigger" metaphor. First, its power encouraged women and students, two weaker but nonetheless significant segments of the white population, to associate themselves emotionally and politically with Blacks. It was an important coalition, one that persists as the "Rainbow Coalition" metaphor (Gresson 1987).

Table 1
The Deconstruction of Oppression

Date	Group	Metaphor
1600s	Africans	NIGGER
1960s	White Students	Student as Nigger
1970s	White Women	Woman as Nigger
1960s	Blacks	BLACK POWER
1970s	Homosexuals	Gay Power
1970s	The Elderly	Gray Power
1970s	Children	Kid Power
1980s	Whites (Male)	White Power

NOTE: The association of the word "nigger" with gays, the elderly, children, and white males without power came to be subsumed in the concept of "power." Thus, it is no longer necessary to specify "nigger." Moreover, too much resistance from Blacks weakened the metaphor narrowly applied. Ironically, an inversion occurred from this: NIGGER = POWER.

Second, the crossover of white women and students encouraged the recovery of white moral indignation at the loss of face the 1960s liberation movements effected. This moral indignation found expression in the 1980s in the rhetoric of White Power. Although received as a response to the strident Black Power rhetoric, White Power rhetoric pointed more toward the recovery of hegemony. White recovery efforts have been largely successful. Even some contemporary Black scholars have chosen to emphasize the idea that Blacks have abused and victimized whites by exploiting their guilt for their racist past. For this finally to occur, however, the differences between Blacks and other "nigger" groups must first be reforged.

Third, students and women as white "niggers" became the occasion for the disenchantment with Blacks and the eventual portrayal of Black men as villains. The well-documented battles between Black and white student liberation groups illustrate this: for example, clashes between Black Panthers and some Jewish groups gave rise to the rhetoric of "Jewish racism" and "Black anti-Semitism" (Gresson 1978; 1982). But the pivotal clash has been between white women and Black men, a clash that set the stage both for white recovery of moral indignation and for the eventual isolation of Black men as the villains of the liberation movement.

A classic instance of this conflict between Black males and white females occurred in September 1970 when *Psychology Today* published an interview between two prominent psychologists, a white female, J. A. Gardner, and a Black male, C. W. Thomas. Their debate about the "woman as nigger" metaphor is instructive:

> CWT: I doubt that the feminist movement will go anywhere unless it finds a form, a communion of its own and stops trying to be a carbon copy of the Black movement, which only leads them into ridicule. I just don't agree with the idea inherent in the article "woman as nigger." The analogy breaks down too quickly.

> JAG: We have a coalition organization and do a program together over a Black radio station — but some Black males are acting like white sexist bastards, or worse. Dammit, you think we're just clubwomen on an ego trip, when actually feminist demands are more threatening to the existing system than Black demands. (Gardner and Thomas 1970, condensed from 49–53)

Notice that Thomas "invited" Gardner and white women to disidentify; he emphasized real differences; and symbolically, he expressed behaviors that would eventually be stereotyped and employed by various groups of previous allies — Black and white women, Jews, gays, and so on — as "Black male narcissism." (In 1991, Clarence Thomas enlarged this gulf by refusing to take a profeminist stand on *Roe v. Wade*; as a result, white women led the feminist effort to discredit Thomas as competent even as another white woman, his wife, sat beside him in the hearings.)

C. W. Thomas's rhetoric also invited Gardner to introduce the "Black male as villain" ideology: she first likened Black men to white men as "sexist bastards"; she then implied that their behavior is possibly worse than the behavior of white male sexists. In just this way, Black men became isolated as the real enemy of both Black and white women. But Gardner actually said something more in this passage. She introduced the ideas that Blacks generally are less than they appear to be, that Blacks are just opportunists who want a better position in the current pecking order, that white women by contrast seek to change the entire system.[4]

In this manner, Blacks became villains. Two public ritualizations of Blacks as perpetrators rather than victims of oppression occurred during the early 1990s. One was a book by a Black man, Shelby Steele. This book, *The Content of Our Character* (Steele 1990), has won a National Book Award and has been described by some critics as the most important and compelling work on race in America in twenty-five years. Although the book makes many cogent points, its most provocative theme is that Blacks — having massively and effectively exploited white guilt regarding racism — now oppress whites.

The other ritualization of Black villainy was the televised clash between Clarence Thomas and Anita Hill during the confirmation hearings for Thomas's nomination to the Supreme Court. Thomas, a Black Republican under fire from the Senate Judiciary Committee, claimed that he was a victim of a "high-tech lynching." Although some felt that this tactic was clever, few gave credence to his claim. For example, on nationwide television, Senator Ted Kennedy said:

> Quite frankly, I hope we're not going to hear a lot more about racism. The fact is that these points on sexual harassment are made by an Afro-American against an Afro-American. The issue isn't discrimination and racism; it's about sexual harassment. I hope we can keep our eye on that particular issue. (*USA Today* [October 14, 1991])

Some Black women, historic defenders of Black men against real lynchings, showed no more sympathy than Kennedy for Thomas. Shawn Kennon, a thirty-two-year-old Black lawyer, told *USA Today* (October 14, 1991), "I'm appalled at his emotionalism in trying to diffuse the issue by talking about lynch mobs."

But how does the white male's recovery figure in all of this liberation activity? To answer this question, we must first understand that the racial liberation movement and its companion liberation movements represented losses for white men as moral heroes; the emotional and symbolic aspects of this loss, moreover, were greater than any material loss the American dominant majority sustained. These symbolic losses combined with the loss of faith in government and "authority" to ensure a peculiar form of "white privatization": whites' refusal, if not inability, to identify with their racial past. Increasingly, whites experienced themselves as oppressed victims of an uncaring authority and cited efforts on behalf of Blacks, Hispanics, Native Americans, and other ethnics as "reverse racism" — the birth cry of modern white racial recovery rhetoric.

As this rhetoric began to develop, the ominous ambivalence white Americans feel about the presence of Black Americans resurfaced (Katz and Hass 1988). This ambivalence first reappeared in the late 1970s as white ethnopolitics. As Harold Isaacs wrote, Americans were "refragmenting and retribalizing ourselves to deal with the massive upheavals of the 1960s across racial and ethnic lines" (Isaacs 1977, 2–5). But this incisive observation failed to signal the larger picture: although typically considered an expression of ethnic awareness and pride, ethnopolitics was really the vehicle for grappling with the larger recovery agenda, the recovery of the lost myths of supremacy and specialness.

Because the traditional racism-dependent myths of social messianism and manifest destiny lost persuasive power, recovery became a privatized pursuit. Discussions of racism now pertained to particularistic instances. With racism officially dead, any future manifestations would have to be seen as more or less private matters (Klumpp and Hollihan 1979). Clear instances of a turning back to past ideologies provided means to recover a felt loss.[5] "Reaganism" is the name for this recent period of recovery. Its significance as a rhetorical recovery movement can help clarify the nationalistic and racial aspects of the white recovery project.

The White Recovery Project: The Significance of Reaganism

In "The Rhetoric of Denial and Alternity," Richard Gregg contended that the nation's thrust toward an enlightened foreign and national policy ended with the defeat of Jimmy Carter and the rise of Ronald Reagan. For Gregg, Reagan's inaugural address captured the essence of this shift in national mood:

> It is time for us to realize that we are too great a nation to limit ourselves to small dreams. We're not, as some would have us believe, doomed to an inevitable decline. I do not believe in a fate that will fall on us no matter what we do. I do believe in a fate that will fall on us if we do nothing.
>
> So with all the creative energy at our command let us begin an era of national renewal. Let us renew our determination, our courage and our strength. And let us renew our faith and our hope. We have every right to dream heroic dreams. (cited in Gregg 1989, 392)

These, Gregg suggested, are images of denial — I call this Reagan's recovery rhetoric. Gregg associated the recovery theme in Reagan's rhetoric with the traditional emphasis placed on rugged individualism and the heroic quest:

> Here is the heart of Reagan's message. It is an unabashed accolade to individual opportunity, individual challenge, individual commitment, and individual courage. The values heralded in Reagan's accolade are deeply embedded in American thought. Reagan rejects the thinking that the nation had achieved the height of its power and was on the way down. Rather, he would return to the "American compact" and "long standing American spirit." His rhetoric harkens back to rugged individualism, an ideal that became enthroned early in the American experience and made mythic heroes of pioneers and frontiersmen, loners like Daniel Boone who kept moving beyond civilization, cutting trails through the wilderness as they went.

In Reagan's rhetoric there is not even much hint of changing context. There are still frontiers to be won, natural resources to be exploited, individual opportunities to be taken advantage of, the role of a chosen people to be played out. (ibid., 393)

Joseph Campbell saw contemporary men and women seeking to recover a set of myths to live by and a series of heroes to bring forth the message. Wilson Moses saw the white American as hero embodied in the "social messianism" of the myths of manifest destiny and the chosen people, and, presumably, these myths were "dead." But we see they were not. Even before Ronald Reagan took office, some scholars realized those myths merely slumbered (Klumpp and Hollihan 1979). With the ascendance of Reagan to the presidency, many others started to wonder what was happening. How could this B-movie actor use faulty facts and even weaker logic and still grow in mythic power? Finally, we largely agreed it was his rhetoric, his storytelling, his narrative style that propelled him so unexpectedly forward (Fisher 1987; and W. F. Lewis 1987).

Reagan's rhetorical power has yet to be described in sufficiently heroic terms, although Klumpp and Hollihan (1979) and Gregg (1989) have come close. Without connecting the rhetorical situation to heroic recovery, however, we will find it difficult to explain or appreciate fully the mythic linkage between contemporary Black and white conservatism in the United States or this conservatism's link to the larger recovery project Campbell envisioned. To make these associations we must first see the so-called white backlash as itself a recovery project for individual whites. Only then can we see how Reagan's rhetoric took the form it did when he described the average American (a white) as the "real hero," one whose birthright included imagining himself or herself as destined by God to grow indefinitely and to rob death of its sting: "We have every right to dream heroic dreams."

The present book presents a way of understanding the white recovery project implied in the exercising of this "right to dream heroic dreams." Once we see the form this project has taken, the aggressive and hegemonic underpinnings of contemporary racial discourse will stand forth more clearly. In particular, we will begin to see how racism has become a problematic *topos* and how it may be characterized as a deteriorating rhetorical situation. As Lloyd F. Bitzer said,

A situation deteriorates when any constituent or relation changes in ways that make modification of the exigence significantly more difficult. The audience may grow tired of the speaker or of the exigence and turn its attention away, or may drift away for other reasons. The immediate situation may be upstaged by a competing situation. The audience may lose its capacity to modify the exigence. The exigence may become nonrhetorical. (Bitzer 1980, 34)

I will show that white political and economic recovery efforts in America have resulted largely in judicial, occupational, and symbolic losses for Blacks and others previously targeted for so-called mainstreaming. I will show also how the perceived need for this recovery of White Power is the exigency, in Bitzer's words, that has silenced Black Power and its progeny, the Rainbow Coalition. In short, white recovery accounts for the diffidence of racism rhetoric. But other forces are at work here as well; whites have not been the only opponents of seeing systemic racism as the lens for understanding human relations in America or as the primary force blocking various groups from achieving greater human rights. Nowhere, in fact, is this dampening more evident than in Black-on-Black conflict and communication.

A major aspect of racial recovery rhetoric now centers on conflict among Blacks. In fact, the presence of Black sexism and classism threatens to compromise the feasibility of discussing interracial conflict solely, or even predominantly, in terms of race. This loss of a historically core exigency is most notable in Black women and Black men's relational rhetoric.

Recovery and Gender

The gender component of recovery receives its most explicit expression in the stories and struggles of white women. White women, after all, were empowered, more than other disenfranchised groups, by their positions as the mothers, wives, daughters, and sisters of white men. Despite the urgency of their plight and their determination to change their "second-class gender" status, however, white women have not typically been viewed as a serious problem to the white man, and thus they can share in his recovery of hegemony.

Black women were perceived and treated differently than white women by both white and Black men during the liberation struggle. For one thing, Black women became the scapegoats for the male dread of and rage at strong, assertive womanhood. In the late 1960s, the familiar notion of the Black matriarch aided the recovery effort of white men. In the late 1970s this view of Black women faced challenges, as is evident in the historic 1979 Black sexism debate.

> In the late 1960s, many Black men castigated Black women as dominating, domineering, emasculating. In a sense, then, it is merely "turnabout" that in the late 1970s some Black women are mounting assaults upon

Black men as weak, irresponsible, indecisive, and inadequate. (H. Edwards 1979, 59)

Harry Edwards, a sociologist and co-organizer of the Black athlete protest at the 1968 Olympics, contributed these words to the debate over Black male sexism vis-à-vis Black women. Edwards acknowledged that Black males had inflicted serious wounds upon Black women and that the wounds had not healed. Nor did the 1979 debate accomplish any healing. Rather, it revealed the breadth of the schism. It also served symbolically to acknowledge that Black recovery pertained to more than Black liberation from white racial oppression. Black liberation discourse, joined by the other so-called oppositional discourses (enumerated in table 1), constituted a semiotic of nonessentialism: everything and nothing, everyone and no one, was "black." "Black" was a social construction: liberation was now the transcendence of constructionism. In an ultimately perverse manner, Black male recovery ideology exposed both the possibility and pathos of nonessentialism.

Black Male Recovery: Personal Choice and Postmodernism

For Blacks, recovery as a postmodern agenda began largely with the civil rights and freedom marches and advanced into Black Power (often armed) skirmishes with whites. But other aspects of recovery gradually grew out of these pivotal activities. For example, a pursuit of "the good life" became a major recovery theme. "The good life" meant various things to Blacks, but ultimately it meant the pursuit of material and cultural riches: cars, well-paying jobs (often, whites sniped, as pimps, "poverty pimps," and "professional Negroes"), and, for many, such fruits of integration as the freedom to fall in love with whites.

Black males, especially, embraced the latter form of recovery. To rationalize it, these men often turned to a personal-choice rhetoric: "It's my life." This very stance was dually problematic. First, it rehearsed the historical racial secret: "Race is a social construction." Second, it prophesied a racial fear: "We ain't ever gonna get 'the Man' offa our backs."

Personal-choice rhetoric, coming from a few well-situated — if not a multitude of — Black men, was deadly. It conflicted with the collective aspects of recovery and found a powerful yet problematic ally in the postmodernist discourse that, by the 1980s, had become an ascendant vision of life.

Postmodernism rejects historical events and definitions of reality as unreliable and unnecessary; the individual, in the concrete present, is the source of meaning; reality is socially constructed rather than an inevitability. The characteristic skepticism about established or historically recognized facts renders language and concepts inadequate, problematic tools of persuasion. Thus, postmodernism has a special attraction for those whose lives once found definition almost totally through a "master's" definitions of reality. Postmodernism also provides an enticing enlargement of the ideology that Blacks must be one and cannot be conservative or prefer whites to other Blacks. Personal-choice ideology resonated with this characterization of postmodernism. And it was the de-essentialized Black male who "sold the race" to postmodernist selflessness (hence, racelessness).

Personal choice as a postmodernist ideology exploded the historical race myth that American Blacks had forged during and after the journey from Africa. Unwittingly and unintentionally, the recovery of the 1960s exposed Blacks to a painful "liberation possibility": Black liberation may never fully occur; only a few Blacks may escape the wretched stigma of "Blackness." Because they cannot honestly or pragmatically demand exemption from the stigma of Blackness, many Blacks rely on postmodernist rhetoric to negotiate themselves beyond the arbitrary oppression of racial relatedness and the constricted opportunities this identity implies for those fortunate enough to find escape through skill, fame, and interracial acceptance.

Although Black men were first and more prominently identified with this personal-choice and postmodernist orientation, Black women soon adopted it as well. That is, Black women countered the Black male abandonment with their own personal-choice rhetoric. Exposed to the humiliation of Black male abandonment and abuse, whatever the dimensions of these phenomena may have been, many Black women reacted with now-familiar signs: first grief and withdrawal, then anger, and later, attempts to recover by discovering alternative visions of themselves and their personal choices. Recent writings by Black women largely relate to this task of recovery. These writings often seem apocalyptic; they expose the Black male and female as natural allies who are now alienated. This apocalyptic stance has also revealed certain impediments in the works and lives of the major Black artists and critics.

Black Apocalypse as Recovery Crisis

Two impediments have been particularly prominent. The first is isolation. The preferred, or most evident, expressions of Black recovery have enjoyed only slight favor in the so-called Black community; the discursive elite remains significantly separated from that community (Gates

1988; Hogue 1986; O'Neale 1987; S. A. Smith 1985). The second impediment is the conflict among Blacks over the fact that personal-choice and postmodernist thought in the Black liberation struggle appears to advance white male recovery by intensifying intragroup hostility.

This intragroup conflict is generic to the recovery process. In South Africa, for example, the Black factions fight only in part at the white power elite's instigation. In fact, the instigation succeeds, to the extent it does, only because of an inherent possibility of disidentification and nonrelationship among various African tribes. Similarly in the United States, Black heterogeneity — the very real differences among African-Americans — often motivates responses that serve the interests of white supremacists. For instance, this tension recently coalesced around the nomination of Clarence Thomas for Supreme Court justice. His nomination to a court now overwhelmingly conservative and considered hostile to the past liberation achievements of women, Blacks, and the masses illustrates the recovery of white male hegemony in its ability to define what is real and relevant. Meanwhile, compelling personal needs and collective visions predispose many Black persons to collude in this white recovery project so that, perhaps for the first time, America entertains a Black presence similar to that found in some postcolonial African and East Indian nations.

Unfortunately, too few Black leaders and scholars have addressed this inherent heterogeneity and its inevitable consequences in a pluralistic, transitional, and narcissistic society. It is, moreover, precisely this refusal to address Black heterogeneity that brings Black Americans to the threshold of apocalypse.

Black Heterogeneity as Apocalyptic

Although recovery concerns permeate life, they do not always mesh in a tidy, benign way. By conforming one's private needs, beliefs, and aspirations to the Other — God, society, or family — an individual may feel loss rather than gain or recovery. That is, identification with a particular Other may decrease one's capacity to stand alone as merely a human being. This fact has special relevance to Blacks as individuals and humans. As Kenneth Burke wrote,

> Striving for freedom as a human being generically, he [i.e., a Black] must do so as a Negro specifically. But to do so as a Negro is, by the same token, to prevent oneself from doing so in the generic sense; for a Negro could not be free generically except in a situation where the color of the skin has no more social meaning than the color of the eyes. (Burke 1968, 193)

The givenness of certain "inalienable rights" is, for Americans, a collective belief and national concern. But some Americans have been denied their "inalienable rights" by other Americans. These disenfranchised Americans, notably Blacks, have had to share a common plight and have used this plight, in part, to forge a racial liberation agenda. These Americans face a dual task: (1) to recover rights as human beings and (2) to recover rights as members of stigmatized groups of human beings. As Burke observed, Black individuals cannot achieve freedom as humans without addressing their freedom as Black Americans. Nevertheless, many Blacks try to ignore their racial status and pursue the recovery of their "inalienable rights" purely in terms of their status as human beings. Burke understood this temptation, or perhaps this necessity, and he referred to the situation as "a dialectical one." I have used the phrase "paradox of liberation" in a related way to emphasize that individual recovery concerns do not necessarily parallel collective recovery interests (Gresson 1982). The prospect of this clash of recovery interests figures prominently in the rise of Black racial recovery discourse. This divergence of discourse takes on apocalyptic[6] dimensions as the private and collective recovery agendas clash and sides form over the perceived need to define one or the other as primary.

The "Black apocalypse" refers to the split of Blacks into camps over their recovery visions. History shows that Blacks have always differed over liberation strategies. Malcolm X characterized this difference in terms of those Blacks who loved the master more than themselves: "house niggers" as opposed to "field niggers." Malcolm naturally preferred the "field nigger." But the 1980s saw a new entity emerge as a predominant rather than aberrational type: the "privatized Black" seeking to revise racial motive. Among other prominent examples, Julius Lester comes first to mind. Lester seems willing to fight both Black and white America to be himself. He thus gives voice to the problematic fact that we can expect some Blacks to be as oppressive as whites if they want strongly enough to go their own way.

Audre Lorde, reflecting on the failures of many Black men (like Lester) to avoid the "personal choice pitfall," declares that the "collusive bond" between Black male and female has been broken, and the Black male is now "the ex-comrade."

The Black apocalypse, then, is the clash between Black privatization and Black collusion. The pull of privatization places the individual at the center of meaning; the demands of collusive bonding, collective vision, and liberation struggle place the group at the center of meaning. Meanwhile, within the soul of the individual we see the necessity of both demands and the resultant effort to resolve the paradox in a personal way that has collective value. This need reveals the dynamics of recovery as a collective matter. Rhetorical theory helps reveal the logic of the persuasive strategies employed in this process, but to be used this way, rhetorical theory must be atypically applied to race relations. Hence, a brief discussion of the theory and approach of this study may be helpful at this point.

Rhetorical Theory and Racial Apocalypse

In the late 1960s, Elliott Rudwick and August Meier examined the rhetorical aspect of racial apocalypse and offered instructive findings on Black racial violence in the twentieth century:

> It would appear that both in the World War I period, and today — and indeed during the ante-bellum era and at other times when manifestations of violence came to the fore — there has been a strong element of fantasy in Negro discussion and efforts concerning violent retaliation. The Black Muslims talk of violence, but the talk seems to function as a psychological safety valve; by preaching separation, they in effect accommodate to the American social order and place racial warfare off in the future when Allah in his time will destroy whites and usher in an era of black domination.... Du Bois and others who have spoken of the inevitability of racial warfare and Negro victory in such a struggle were engaging in wishful prophecies. And Negroes have been nothing if not realistic. The patterns of Negro behavior in riots demonstrate this. In earlier times, as already indicated, those who bought guns in anticipation of the day when self-defense would be necessary usually did not retaliate. And Negro attacks on whites occurred mainly in the early stages of the riots before the full extent of anger and power and sadism of the white mobs became evident. (Rudwick and Meier 1969, 412–17)

Rudwick and Meier's observations point to that aspect of Black behavior reflecting the rhetorical situation: Black realism in the face of white sadism. For if it is true that Blacks have been realistic and adaptive, then presumably individual Blacks have seen the limits of contemporary "white pacifism" and racial tolerance. They have likewise come face-to-face with the growing ambivalence and duplicity among African-Americans with respect to mutual racial support. (Although downplayed by the press, most of the fifty-five people killed in the 1992 Los Angeles race riots were Black males; thus, the trend has not changed as we approach the twenty-first century.)[7]

Indeed, "realistic" Blacks have seen the writing on the wall for some time now; they are likely to direct their discourse toward intragroup issues, toward real but safe contradictions within the race. Also, except for fleeting, blatant, and outrageous events caught on camera, realistic Blacks will shrink from interracial conflict. In fact, many Blacks will start to lose their certitude over the presence and meaning of racial hostility. Like their white counterparts, they may find it more useful to call racial conflict "human conflict."

This reluctance to find racial meaning in oppressive acts played out in the larger social context is an additional aspect of Black privatization. The tendency toward privatization is also both the source of and a constraining factor in the emerging recovery rhetorics of Black Americans — an idea that can be illuminated by a brief review of recent rhetorical theory of racism.

Rhetoric, Narrative, and Privatization

Rhetorical theory remains sensitive to individual and public dimensions of social change (Condit 1987, 79). Extensions of this concern have led to the recent emphasis on the role of narrative as rhetorical event requiring an enhanced theoretical sensitivity. Closely associated with Kenneth Burke's (O'Banion 1992) and Walter R. Fisher's (1987) work, the realization that narrative perspectives help clarify certain types of communications issues, transcending the limits of traditional modes of argument and persuasion, has attracted many scholars in recent years. Generally, they agree on the value of a narrative perspective of rhetorical discourse and criticism. Their disagreement revolves around the generic nature of the perspective: Is it a paradigm? If so, what are the criteria for assessing narrative discourse?

A related criticism focuses on the privatization aspect of the narrative perspective. We know that traditional modes of rhetorical analysis often fail to detect the shift toward private definitions of self and Other ("privatization"), and several scholars have attempted to address this "privatization of morality." Notably, the privatized view of morality, where everyone determines her or his own moral responsibility based on personal experience, has been incisively challenged by scholars like Celeste Michelle Condit: "If our understanding of morality is bound by such models, I think our rhetorical theory will be impoverished by the lack of long-term perspective, of public participation, and of action" (Condit 1987, 88).

Condit advanced the possibility and preference of a theory that "recognizes collective discourse as the source of an active public morality" (p. 89). In her study of the rhetorical history of race relations, she emphasized the interplay of individual and collective arguments in constructing a collective morality: "Looking at the rhetoric produced in the situation gives us a means to understand this moral problem in historical perspective. Simply put, when racial slavery was instituted, Anglo-Americans had not yet crafted a public moral code that included Afro-Americans in the demands of 'equal justice.' It is taking hundreds of years to modify that original relationship" (p. 89).

Additionally, focusing on the political and media re-creation of the image of Blacks as being like whites, Condit observed that

> across two hundred years or more, therefore, new rhetorical structures of great importance have been created. Blacks and whites are now publicly identified, not only as human, but also as essentially similar. Moreover, a strong moral code that demands human equality has gained currency. The original Anglo-American moral code of "justice" has thus evolved into a broader "American" code that belongs to and includes persons of all descents and skin colors. (p. 92)

Condit correctly challenged the usefulness of "conversational" discourse for deciding matters of public morality. Further, she rejected the conversational model of discourse and its emphasis on private resolutions of moral issues:

> Therefore, because it leads us to expect the wrong kinds of results in the wrong places, a conversational model feeds pessimism, despair over the public realm, and the wrenching alternative of private morality in an immoral social world. If it can be constructed, a model that explains how public advocacy crafts a viable collective morality will lead us rather to understand the possibility of slow, painful, moral resolutions in the public realm. (p. 81)

Condit's discussion of "justice for Afro-Americans" provides an enlarged rhetorical analysis of race relations. Still, there *is* an individual dimension to the public discourse. Richard Brown (1987) described this private feature in terms of the individual as ironist and rule-breaker, a characterization both informative and instructive: in the narrative mode we may not solve the public or collective matter, but we may begin to apprehend the person's separateness. This understanding of the Other promotes a mutually useful and morally fair exchange. Condit's stance approaches the conservative stance of the group trying to force identification and cooperation, and in a transitional society, characterized by competing loyalties and cultural contradiction, this view of rhetorical exchange may distort the meaning forged by the individual.

Beyond the individual's importance in rhetorical creation and criticism, we confront the matter of racist behavior and institutions, however defined. While a reduction in the blatant, brutal racism of the past signifies a welcome change, Condit's reconciliatory analysis overlooks the destructive forcefulness of subjective racism, along with the ways "authority" sustains it. James Klumpp and Thomas Hollihan offer a perspective that retains Condit's insight into the changing moral vision while recognizing that racism persists even as the "official" moral code changes.

The Persistence of Racism and Ritualistic Rhetoric

In their study of the rhetoric surrounding the firing of Earl Butz for his racial slurs against Blacks, Klumpp and Hollihan observe that

> viewed sociodramatically, . . . the sacrificial ritual blurs the pervasiveness of racism. [M.] Edelman describes a political process of arousal and quiescence which begins when organized political groups are aroused to pressure for governmental action. Government then responds with new programs and processes that, while yielding some progress, ultimately serve only to rob the aroused group of its energy and thus to re-create the original disorganization and apathy. A better explanation of American racial history would be difficult to find. The efforts of the last two decades are hardly the initial efforts to end racism, but each earlier effort has led to quiescence that later exploded once again in violence and momentary government action. The governmental actions of the 1960s now threaten to become the next in this succession of rituals that achieve quiescence and halt progress. The ritualization of Earl Butz's resignation demonstrates this. (Klumpp and Hollihan 1979, 9)

This focus on the dramaturgical aspect of the public punishment awaiting whites caught in racist behavior holds implications for both rhetorical theory and interracial relations. More precisely, Klumpp and Hollihan imply that we must do more than merely identify broad historical developments as a sign of new moral perspectives. In fact, they consider it possible for one to adopt a new ritual (rhetoric) even as one maintains the infrastructures that perpetuate racism. My intention here is to relate this understanding to the white recovery project and to the evolving reenslavement of the Black voice.

An Approach to Recovery Analysis

What, then, is the central set of rhetorical issues within recovery discourse? The rhetorical situation of heroic recovery is one of anomie, societal regression, and transition. The rhetorical task is to make personal meaning and to embrace the constructionist role of the colluder: to make new bonds with old enemies and tentative, new bonds with old friends. This is the creative, exhilarating, and critical task of recovery of a believable story by which one can live one's life in civility.

In suggesting that "racism" is a nearly defunct *topos,* I do not mean that the behavior called racist itself has ended. Rather, I intend to suggest that the meaning of the behavior has become renegotiable. One can now call that behavior something other than what was typically understood to be racism. This possibility has a number of nuances and implications. One nuance is that both Blacks and whites may disavow connection with things racial. One implication is that both Blacks and whites (in disavowal) may dismiss traditionalists — those who retain the language and imagery of racism as a morally forceful weapon — as violators of the individuality of the person and the unique moral force that inheres in the individual's story or narrative. The Black apocalypse, to repeat, is the split between those who think traditionally and those who disavow the traditional in favor of a private vision rooted in the experience of problematic but personally satisfying choices. The narrative is the rhetorical vehicle for expressing choice and disenchantment with tradition. The rhetorical power of narrative in this recovery task derives from the various concrete forms narrative takes.

Narrative and the Rhetoric of Being

Communication theory increasingly acknowledges the relevance of mutuality between speaker and listener, writer and reader. This reciprocity, while essential to the social sciences, appears less formally in the field but is clearly there in a number of recent works (E. E. White 1980; Benson 1974). I find one of the most important formulations of this reciprocal or mutual relationship between context and actor in the work of Eugene White, whose theory and method of rhetorical analysis emphasize a complex historical dialectic:

> The most important characteristic of any event, especially one we would consider rhetorical, is the fluidity and movement that give it vitality. Life is always development and flow. Without exception speech acts, like all human junctures, involve antecedents that envelop, mix with, and change with human responding events in such a way that consequences sequentially emerge that are in fact merely modified statuses of the antecedents. To deal with the contextual, processual, and correlational features of rhetoric, it is necessary to find some way to rationalize the complexity of the

rhetorical act with its historical linkage to time and change, development and flow. (E. White 1980, 13–14)

White affirms here that the person who acts does so in space and time, both past and present. Moreover, the interpretation of this event in time and space must be true to the agency of the historical flow of the event. From this view, privatized Black female and male behavior as over against traditional racial expectations cannot be wholly received as mere personal choices or private decisions. Recent psychological studies support this view (Sloan 1987), but we have earlier intuitions of White's understanding of the "narrative being." In an important study of the rhetorical dynamics of autobiography (in this case the autobiography of Malcolm X), Thomas Benson shows how Malcolm X's life became persuasive precisely because, when viewed through the lens of his autobiography, we entered his experience and saw "how early mistakes led to later enlightenment" (Benson 1974, 3). Benson used the phrase "dialectical rhetoric" to characterize his reading of Malcolm's life:

> Malcolm's life is a drama of enlargement. In this view, Malcolm is a gifted but flawed man whose natural powers and sympathies undergo a gradual but powerful opening up to embrace wider scenes of action and larger groups of people. What makes Malcolm's life a drama — an enactment of conflict — *rather than a mere growth is the presence of racism, the agency of constriction, domination, and injustice.* We reject the figure of growth because it is essentially passive, suggesting the involuntary fulfillment of a destiny. . . . He is a man in conflict with a condition whose nature he comes to understand and transcend as motive passes from his environment to him. Malcolm's readers [followers] are not reduced to admiring him; they can pick up where he left off. (Benson 1974, 9)[8]

Benson provided a conceptual clue to the task of self–Other representation as rhetorical recovery, or personal growth as separation and reconnection. His emphasis on the dialectical orients us to a particular type of narrative: the dialectic. Others too have supplied clues to this task. For example, John Louis Lucaites and Celeste Michelle Condit offer important guidance in the discussion of narrative form and function. Identifying three major narrative forms, they address function this way:

> [R]hetorical narratives develop in response to the specific purpose of the larger discourse and context in which they operate. While poetic narratives invite an audience passively to observe the "transformation relations" among characters, rhetorical narratives describe a set of relations

contributing to a conflict or problem and ask the audience to participate actively in the interest of the discourse to bring about the desired
transformation. (Lucaites and Condit 1985, 100)

"Voice" pertains to the substance and style of persuasion. Univo-
cal narratives tend to close off interpretation (choice of meaning and
actions) and advocate for a single view. These are called "rhetorical
narratives." Multivocal narratives are poetic and dialectical: they allow
for various interpretive meanings and advocate, as a rule, themselves,
rather than courses of action beyond themselves. As Lucaites and Condit
conclude, "Dialectical and poetic narratives must portray a logically or
aesthetically complete vision, creating a whole world or a whole truth.
Rhetorical narratives can never achieve such independence and com-
pleteness, for they speak of only parts of a whole and of a changing
world" (Lucaites and Condit 1985, 101).

Although treated as separate, these two forms combine in narrative as recovery discourse to serve a paradoxical function: self- and
Other-persuasion. The self-persuasion entails, at least initially, a closed,
nonnegotiable story around the idea of "forced choice." This is the poetic and dialectical quality of recovery narratives. But since the narrator
also aims to persuade the Other, he or she must simultaneously gain
support for having exercised the choice and show that the choice is gra-
tuitous since this telling, too, is a choice. Here we have the rhetorical in
the recovery narrative.

These qualities converge in recovery narratives to be expressed as
the "narrative of being," or what Thomas Benson called the "rhetoric of
being": "Insofar as rhetoric is a way of being, it is ideally a collaboration
between speaker and listener to find a mutually satisfactory notion of
themselves as interacting agents" (Benson 1989, 318).

The narratives of Black women typically exemplify this rhetoric of
being in that they attempt to engage a listener in a shared vision of each
other as sensible and sensitive Blacks. The sensible appears in the urgent
concern for personal survival and well-being; the sensitive appears in an
acknowledgment that one is, after all, "Black" and therefore ought to
do something for someone in need — some oppressed Other — somewhere in the narrative. For Black narrators, this dual concern within
the rhetoric of being presents a constant, though not always continual,
tension.

Some scholars, like Molefi Asante, have labored toward a conceptual
resolution of this tension: "Orature is the total body of oral discourse,
styles, and traditions of African people. It is the metaphoric discourse

of reintegration." He goes on to clarify the relationship of orature to rhetoric: "Thus, rhetoric is a transforming power, a mythic discourse in the midst of a plethora of symbols" (Asante 1988b, 97, 170). This statement posits a holistic African vision, one where the diversity or heterogeneity of African visions apparently converges toward a mythic union.

Asante has gone far toward clarifying the challenge inherent in the rhetoric-of-being tension. Yet metaphor remains a complex and dynamic tool of reintegration, and it often fails because it ultimately recapitulates the existing rhetorical crisis rather than transcending it (Gresson 1978). This impasse is rooted, moreover, in the understandable but futile desire to speak for the Other. Neither Asante nor I can tell another's story; at best, we can find (or co-construct through intertextuality) points of connection, convergence, communion.

The chapters that follow identify individual solutions to this apparent impasse. The narrators presented here employ metaphors to resolve their crises and to assume a persuasive perspective on the shared racial plight. I found it useful, therefore, to ask myself if the metaphors they employed seem to work. The central focus in this regard is the relation of the narrative constructions to the larger reality, a concern deriving mainly from the privatization as self-validation in the narratives. In this regard, Michael McGee and John Nelson offer the following observation:

> Myths take accounts and give accounts of our world. The elements of myths are the epistemological equivalents of money; the characters, events, settings, and symbols of myths are the coins of our consciousness: earned more than given. The order of myths is narrative order, and the order of stories is the sequentiality of counting. Myths recount characters, events, rhythms, settings, and symbols in order to structure their significance. (McGee and Nelson 1985, 152)

Because metaphor and myth are central to self–Other persuasion, I paid close attention to them in the stories I was told. Likewise, I listened to how the narrative voice unfolded in these various stories. My main line of analysis in this study followed the concept of *rhetorical reversal,* or persuasion through reversed meanings. This concept allowed me to research the recovery rhetoric for clues to the implicit theory or persuasion (rhetoric) being employed in the narratives. I detected rhetorical reversals by remaining alert to emphases on narrator characterizations of self and of others, particularly Blacks and whites, male and female. By examining reversals I show how this rhetorical tactic becomes central to recovery by ironic inversions or a "twisting" of reality. This use of language and fact may not be unique to recovery, but it is a uniquely recovery-focused activity familiarly associated with the Black trope known as "signifying." Elaborating upon Gates (1988) and others, I suggest that "signifying" is ultimately a trope of the "helpless" and is, as such, a special instance of rhetorical reversal. Accordingly, that most potent of impotent significations, "Yo' Momma," would be, in the mouth of the historically powerful white man, a rhetorical reversal. Its use symbolizes the postmodernist world where, as Malcolm X once observed, the villain can be made to seem a victim, and a victim may be pictured as a villain.[9]

PART II

Loss and Recovery 2: The Black Apocalypse

❖

What we have not done accurately since the sixties is to assess the problems created within and by the Movement, the psychological contradictions with the very successes of desegregation. . . . We have not yet isolated the psychological failures of the Movement, not analyzed why the struggles for desegregation stopped far short of achieving a genuine social revolution.
—Manning Marable, *From the Grassroots: Social and Political Essays Towards Afro-American Liberation*

She might be willing to fight for the white man, endure insults and stares just to be with him, and she defends her right to love a white man. She says she is not prejudiced, and falls back on the same explanation that the Blackman has adopted: that her particular whiteman had nothing to do with slavery — that was before his time. . . . She feels no guilt in being a traitor to the Blackman by accepting another race over him. She sees guilt as an outdated hangover which has no business in her modern "do what I wanna do" system.
—Shahrazad Ali, *The Blackman's Guide to Understanding the Blackwoman*

2

Black Male Recovery:
Personal Choice and Breaking
the Collusive Bond

❖

*Norman Mailer came up with an interestingly accurate idea about
a peculiar phenomenon — the intersection of the Black man's and
the white man's fantasies, that is to say, their frustrations. As a
result, I think he had a profound effect on such Black leaders as
LeRoi Jones and Eldridge Cleaver.*

*Black male hostility to Shirley Chisholm exploded any illusion
that Blacks might actually be able to sustain a notion of themselves
apart from America's racist-sexist influence, a notion essential to
their autonomy and inner direction.*

— Michele Wallace (1978)

The world may not have always been dominated by men; class differences have not always impressed themselves upon society as they now do with such embarrassing consequences; and white heterosexuals have not always enjoyed the privilege of defining gender, race, and sexuality with near-totalistic agency. In short, there is every likelihood that once "being" and "becoming" were less categorical, less constructed, less contextually problematic.

Still, at some point in the past, something like "racial essentialism" reigned: Black men and women, thrust together into slavery, forged a collusive bond, both similar to and different from the bond found within other patriarchal, heterosexually dominated communities. While racism differed in different times, places, and circumstances, something monolithic in its nature did promote the illusion, if not the reality, of "Black unity." Thus a particular historical situation enlarged and strengthened the natural bond that might form between any other man and woman.

29

The dominant liberation ideologies of the 1960s sought to intensify this bond, and the hope of racial liberation became reclothed in an ideology that held the Black man to be a regal warrior and the Black woman his queen, the mother of future generations of "revolutionary babies." "Black is beautiful!" became the affirmative slogan of the period. Yet the euphoria of the age could not suppress a congenial dis-ease within the racial family. Michele Wallace identified a widely held perspective on the root cause of the illness: a Black male increasingly subverted and sickened by the values — patriarchalism, whiteness,[1] and capitalism — of American society, a preference that produced self-hatred rather than self-love.

Whatever the problems with this perspective on Black men, some Black women identified with it. To gain a fuller grasp of the contemporary texture of racial recovery discourse, it is critical to understand how Black women have come to view the Black male role in the movements of the 1960s and 1970s. In the previous chapter, I argued that recovery discourse resonates around a vortex defined by Black male and female self–Other understanding. This chapter clarifies this connection. It first addresses Black males' personal-choice rhetoric as a racial and relational violation in the eyes of Black women, who have identified themselves in terms of the race and Black male self-concept. Then it shows how Black male autonomy issues become imbedded in Black female narratives and particularly in the themes of loyalty to Black males and the traditional racial uplift ideologies — all of which provides a context for examining both the structure and argument of Black female recovery discourse. My purpose in this chapter is not to essentialize or totalize African-American representation; however, I do insist that a particular set of racial images or representations has dominated the mass media and popular imagination. It is against these representations that the emergent recovery discourses resonate.

Blacks and the Identity Crisis

The immense, scientific destruction of human life in World War II had a devastating, numbing impact on humanity's view of itself. The gas chambers, the nuclear bombing of Japan, and the trials for crimes against humanity all served as signs that the world was indeed, as Friedrich Nietzsche had declared, godless. This spiritual exhaustion contributed to the rise of existentialist thought, literature, and lifestyles, and it raised skepticism about traditional human values and a certain ambivalence about what humankind had become. In America, we called this uncertainty an "identity crisis."

Orrin Klapp observed a more particular challenge for African-Americans within the context of this national identity crisis:

> The American Negro is in a parallel predicament as he struggles toward equality, though, in his case, the question is more pertinent because he is moving directly in the very situation where identity problems seem to thrive. No doubt his answer would be, "Give us the Thunderbirds and split-level homes, and we'll worry about the identity problems later." Moreover, it must be admitted that to trade a stigma on identity and menial status for a mere confusion about identity may be a bargain. (Klapp 1969, 5)

We now know that these Black aspirations to the mainstream were more than a "mere confusion about identity." Indeed, Wilson Moses has argued that the very moral and rhetorical bases of Black liberation struggle accompanied the losses that brought forth collective confusion:

> The erosion of traditional Black messianism is parallel, of course, to the disintegration of the myth of destiny that once flourished at the center of American consciousness. The loss of direction experienced by Black America since the deaths of Malcolm X and Martin Luther King is symptomatic of the loss of purpose experienced by the entire society since the debacle of Vietnam. (Moses 1982, 15)

The rise of what I call recovery discourse and rhetoric correlated significantly with some of the events begun during the 1960s and extending into the 1970s. Expressions of personal needs, exercised during this period by some Black males, became central rationales for recovery themes among Black women. To provide an understanding of the rise of recovery narratives among Black women, I intend to examine certain rhetorical choices Black males made during this period.

The Hunt for a New "Middle Passage"

During the "middle passage" — the journey between Africa and the Americas — more than eleven million Africans died in chains. Those Africans who survived the journey were both strong and lucky, but their survival in the New World would require more than luck and strength. Driven by fear and sustained by mutual care, the different but mingled African tribes adopted each other. Children whose parents had died in enslavement found new families: new persons bestowing love, understanding, and support in a hostile world. African-American unity, in short, began with the middle passage.

Over the centuries these bonds of kinship remained a more or less firm buffer against racism and segregation. But the trends toward racial integration and an increased tolerance of racial and ethnic diversity stimulated changes in this traditional African-American unity, particularly in the increase of the precise interracial intimacies prohibited by the Jim Crow laws of the late 1800s. Interracial intimacy is, however, only one indicator of a more elemental process affecting many African-Americans: the renegotiation of self-identity.

Whereas it was once clear that anyone with any African ancestry was de facto and de jure Black, today many African-Americans choose to define themselves in other terms. They may accept their racial heritage, but an apparent increase in racial tolerance enables them to adopt an enlarged self-identity. The experience of Black author Julius Lester is instructive here. The Black literary community criticizes Lester for his divisive public and private behavior: publicly, he champions the idea that Blacks treat Jews unjustly and perpetuate "Black anti-Semitism"; personally, he shows a preference for white women. To one Black female critic who used his book *All Is Well* as an occasion to criticize both his politics and his private life, Lester responded:

> The challenge *All is Well* makes to the reader is...to confront the many facets of identity as they exist in one person. I am Black, but Blackness is not the totality of my identity. I have the freedom to define myself as I think best (after all, who's living my life?) and if I have to fight white and Black America to retain that freedom, so be it. Blackness is not my identity but an aspect only, which I do not denigrate in racial self-hatred, nor elevate in panegyrics of narcissistic racial self-love. To do either would be childish. (Lester 1982, 82–83)

Lester illustrates, in short, how a Black person may come to experience Black and white critics as equally oppressive and may then take a personally comforting but politically problematic position. Lester fails, of course, to acknowledge that as compelling as one's personal liberation needs and requirements may be, satisfying them does not necessarily change the collective social reality. Nor does the claim that his behavior sets an example for others who want to be free of race consciousness dismiss or reduce anyone's accountability for his or her choices and their possible damage to collective liberation.

Still, Julius Lester's experience does illustrate the oppression of the group, and it seems wrong for the group to denigrate the personal injury and alienation Lester and others feel and express. We pay too little attention to the personal needs of oppressed group members when the fulfillment of these needs appears to clash with a group need for sacrifice. Consequently, and more generally, we misunderstand how individuals experience and rationalize their efforts to fuse individual choice and collective sacrifice.

As noted above, during the middle passage, Africans of various tribes and temperaments found themselves thrown together, and they became "one." Blackness became a monolith, a homogeneity. Lester's stance is problematic for this mythic monolithic Blackness. It may also signal the end of a four-hundred-year voyage. During that time many stories documented the trials, mortifications, and triumphs of the Black African monolith and "its" descendants. But those were stories of then. This is now. The old stories have lost their power to unify and to transcend the differences of tribe and temperament. The journey is not quite over. In fact, we may need a new middle passage: a new basis for kinship and mutual care.

To extend the metaphor, the Black recovery activity of the 1960s and 1970s resembles the end of the one voyage and the start of a new one, and this perspective can help us understand the particular form and structure of the Black identity crisis inherent in the relationship of Black men and women. Many Black men have failed to describe this crisis accurately and address it adequately. Thus, hardly out of the harbor, the new voyage has been blown off course. Given the historical understanding of the importance of the voyage, this loss of direction is doubly ironic, as the Black sexism debate of 1979 illustrated.

Black Male Choice as Privatized Recovery

In 1973 Robert Staples concluded his book *The Black Woman in America* by observing that Black women had remained steadfast and committed to the race despite a Black male sexism and abandonment exemplified by those Black males who chose non-Black women. He also predicted that "the well" — of Black women's care and commitment — might someday run dry. "While some black men have abdicated their responsibilities, deserted their families, and abandoned black women for white women," Staples wrote, "black women have generally kept the faith. But there may come a time when wells run dry, patience runs thin, and black men may overdraw on the supply of the black woman's goodwill" (Staples 1973, 214).

Yet Staples himself became a symbol of the betrayal desiccating the goodwill of Black women. Addressing several female critics of his essay on Michele Wallace's *Black Macho and the Myth of Superwoman*, Staples said:

The response to my article . . . was not unexpected [but] that it was so sharply divided along gender lines was not what I expected — or wanted. The men, whether they agreed with me or not, discussed the issues I raised. The women chose to attack me as a male rather than deal with the flawed work of their sister in arms, Michele Wallace. From reading their responses, one would think I had advocated a classical male chauvinist position, of dealing with women by keeping them barefoot and pregnant. It almost appears that Michele Wallace's anger, confusion, and logic has infected the Black female body politic. Her views are held by an increasing number of Black women and are reflected in the same anger and confused logic expressed in her book. (Staples 1979, 63)

Staples is, from a certain perspective, correct. From another, he is grossly in error. Most males reacting to his essay probably did handle the material differently than most of the female respondents. But this differential response to the material should alert Staples to the need for a new discursive arena and a new relationship among the voices. Instead, Staples's discourse ("women as irrationality") reflects a sexist perspective in language and logic, if not intention. Terms like "flawed," "female body politic," and "infection" suggest that he, at least symbolically, advocates the kind of discourse and ideological context that generated the "barefoot and pregnant" expression and image in the first place.

Meanwhile, the many Black men who steadfastly chose Black women as mates proved the superficiality in the notion of personal choice. For them, the ideas of personal choice and "Black" (as race, mate, offspring) remained unified, and self-assertion through racial separation remained repugnant.[2] Rejection of personal-choice logic was voiced by such Black male traditionalists or Afrocentrically oriented men as Sterling Plumpp:

[I]f we were not powerless we would just simply set up certain guidelines concerning marriage and those individuals bucking our will would get fucked and that would be all there was to it. You don't see any other ethnic group in America talking about who is one of them. They all have rules which they must respect. If one of them becomes bold or foolish enough to break the rules, then the group acts to enforce some kind of sanction, either ostracism or death. But there is never a lot of rhetoric about what should be done. (Plumpp 1976, 96)[3]

Plumpp is here speaking to "Black heterogeneity." It has always been an aspect — perhaps inevitably — of Black cultural life. The unrealized desire for collective agency Plumpp laments indicates that, on the one hand, Blacks have long recognized the importance of racial essentialism — as a group political weapon, if nothing else — and, on the other hand, Blacks have resisted, for various reasons, definition into essentialism.[4] (Within the narratives presented in part III this resistance to essentialist definition is very apparent and serves as the basis for the creative bonding employed by the women in their negotiation with the implicit critiques of my research questions.)

A refusal to accept collective Black rules — modulated by a need for such rules in a racist society — necessitated a recovery discourse all oppressed Blacks could understand if not indulge: personal choice. Two important features of this male rhetoric stand out for comment. First, it was unwise to choose a "validational logic" that revolved around reason and personal choice to explain the increasing incidence of Black male and white female intimacy. It would backfire.

Second, personal-choice idioms clearly failed to address the existing collective crisis and required the users (rhetors) to isolate and insulate themselves with esoteric rationales like "mysticism" to conceal the obvious contradictions in the exercising of personal choice. Listen to Julius Lester:

> [*All is Well* is] the first autobiographical statement by a Black mystic. The mystical experience is as incomprehensible to the non-mystic as the Black experience is to non-Blacks. *All is Well* is the story of a Black man living with and mediating the tension between the racial reality and the mystical reality where always and forever, all is, indeed, quite well. (Lester 1982, 85)

The mystic and mysticism have a place in recovery rhetoric, but they may be less persuasive of a counterstance than effective as self-justification. As I observed elsewhere, Black mysticism is too esoteric a liberation (rhetorical) *topos* — it appeals to individualistic arguments rather than to those grounded in mutuality and involvement (Gresson 1985a). Black mysticism can connect and persuade only by modeling or reflecting a private-choice and *privatized* way out of "Blackness." It offers no suggestions for the plight at hand: the collective liberation of the group.

Personal Choice and Emergent Black Women's Narratives

The critical point Lester confronts — inadequately, I believe — is the very one W. E. B. Du Bois, Kenneth Burke, and Erik Erikson, among others, have identified: Blacks are human and must act like humans despite the artificial categories that define and constrict their lives. Still, for Blacks to act as if the historical stigma — "You are Black" — exerts no influence on that behavior is to engage in denial and self-deception. Lester, and many contemporary Black Americans like him, refuse to face squarely the immense burden of being labeled and held accountable, by both the oppressing and the oppressed, as a "brother's keeper." Like the Cain of Genesis, they propose a rhetoric of nonaccountability: "Am I my (Black) brother's keeper?" But in the present instance, the query, while fully rhetorical in intent, is aimed not only at those who demand that Blacks "stick together" and pursue their liberation under the same ideological umbrella. (The debate over the acceptability of the Black conservative Clarence Thomas as a Supreme Court justice is illustrative here.) This rhetoric also exercises a self-soothing and self-persuasion function, much like the rhetoric of personal choice.

In the 1960s, when Black men and white women became publicly linked first romantically, then politically, many identified this alliance as the Black male's and white female's chance to grasp what had once been denied them: the chance existentially to experience each other as mate. But few went far enough in their analyses, and even fewer associated this type of event with its recovery impetus. Yet students of history and psychology had already observed that

> at the conscious level these wishes codified as ideology will serve as explanation, justification, rationalization, and legitimation for whatever action becomes necessary. In this way such wishes and fantasies themselves become systematically routinized as conscious modes of expression, serving to take the place of the previously internalized patterns. (Weinstein and Platt 1969, 68)

For this reason, moreover, this rhetoric became the precursor to Black female recovery discourse. But to understand Black female choices in terms of Black male choices is not to suggest that the female sense of self is mainly reactive. It is to say rather, as Joyce Ladner wrote in the foreword to Robert Staples's *The Black Woman in America,* that Black women's sense of themselves has always been tied to their relationship with the Black man and especially to his sense of his own manhood.

The definition of oneself in terms of another is hardly unique to Black women. Psychologists tell us that generations of women have been raised to see themselves, their value, worth, and esteem, in their caring for others. Such behavior helps define woman, and Black women certainly share this conditioning. Thus, defining themselves in terms of Black men — fathers, sons, brothers, lovers — was only natural. This general definition notwithstanding, however, the actual behavior has never proceeded so predictably. In fact, many women generally, and Black woman especially, are woman-centered and woman-identified, valuing and caring for each other in remarkably sensitive ways. Nonetheless, a major assumption here is that, by and large, Black women have relied upon Black men for emotional and racial stability through much of their shared history in America and that this bond suffered a severe rupture during the 1960s and 1970s.

Black Men in Black Women's Narratives

In the following pages, I present excerpts from two narratives. The first narrator, Rhoda, reveals how the presence of a sensitive and strong father can affect self-perceptions, build a love for Black men, and shape a narrative ideology that perpetuates the traditional values of racial self-love. The second narrator, Andria, reveals the limits of a "ruptured" racial vision; she expresses the Black postmodern idea: that racial love is suspect as a basis for defining oneself and one's choices. She asserts that Black love is no longer sufficient to overcome the personal pain and despair that, for many Black women, challenge the possibility of a "collusive bond" with Black males.

Rhoda and Andria also illustrate the implicit strain between Black males and females in terms of race and gender roles, and they offer insights into the importance of Black fathers for their daughters (a topic that has received surprisingly little scholarly treatment)[5] and the way in which a father's absence or distance can influence the story in the narrative. The first narrative excerpt depicts Rhoda, a woman who has felt blessed by her parents' love, courage, and resources. For her, the invitation to talk about Black men presented an opportunity to tell a story of how parental modeling of conjugal loyalty encouraged her to view her own growth in conjunction with the Black mate she might expect to find.

Rhoda: Beloved Daughter
and Keeper of the Racial Narrative

Rhoda is a thirty-two-year-old, college-educated university administrator. She comes from a solid middle-class New England background and has one younger sibling. To a question about her father's place in her life, she responded this way:

> My father had a way of always making me feel good about myself as a female person. I had an interest in cars, and that is something that he helped foster and develop, and I see that as somewhat progressive in that I was a female child. I liked cars, and it wasn't something that he said: "Girls don't like cars, girls don't do that." It was something that he helped me develop: buying cars, buying car magazines, and sitting down with me and talking about the mechanics of cars. So that was a very positive experience. There

was also the sense of being daddy's little girl which was, in some ways, in juxtaposition to this nongendered kid who liked cars. Being daddy's little girl was actually a very healthy balance I think.

Rhoda became animated when she discussed her father. In her narrative, he approached mythical patriarchal proportions, even though Rhoda could see his many sides:

I think that my father is conservative. I think that he is sensitive. I think that one being sensitive allows one to have more feeling and be aware of other people's feelings and might tend to [allow one to] interact with people in a way that is less threatening. I think one of the things that affected me in a positive way is that my father was well-respected in the community. People looked up to him, and that was different than the fathers of some of my friends. My father was a community leader. There were three Black Baptist churches in the city, and he did get the recognition that allowed me to stand up and take notice *that my father is somebody!* This is something that I had sensed all along but something that I associated with the church.

In this frame of mind, Rhoda reminded me of the women in Susan Contratto's (1987) study of middle-class white females who see their fathers as strong, loving, and special. But Rhoda differs from Contratto's women in one respect; she also saw her mother as a powerful and positive force:

I think I looked at my mother as my first role model with respect to being a strong Black woman . . . a very strong role model. My father is a minister who worked two jobs. My mother also got in there and pitched in, too. She was trained to do hair but she couldn't stand hair because of the gossiping in the shops. I think that she is a much more private person, she buys into being a minister's wife, yet she's truly herself. When men would act inappropriately, she would say, "Wait a minute, there's women here now" [Rhoda laughed]. She serves in the choir, she is very supportive of him at the same time that she is herself.

I see my mother as a very strong individual with her own strengths and weaknesses. There is a lot of giving and taking in that relationship between both of them. She has been extremely supportive of my father and of his career. I mean she has laid back and has made sacrifices so that he could move along. When I say that, I see the inside of her; the church people see only the outside, and I know that there have been places where things stopped. But there have been times when my father has gotten called in at night and would do some counseling, and my mother would get up and say, "I am not going to let you go to that house by yourself." And we would get up out of the bed and go and sleep in the car and she would be with him because she was concerned about his safety.

I asked, "Would you do that for your man?"

> First of all, I love Black men. I do. I think Black men have had a very
> hard struggle and will continue to have a very hard struggle. Black women
> have been able to move ahead faster than Black men for a number of so-
> ciological reasons. So therefore, I am behind Black men 100 percent. If I
> were going to get into a relationship with a Black man, insofar as who was
> going to be the leader and who was going to be the follower, I think times
> are very different now. Some of the blatant limitations have been stripped
> away, but some of the subtle ones remain in terms of career development
> and educational opportunities. But I would like to think that my relation-
> ship would be open, that I could say — if I am making a sacrifice, or a
> compromise I don't want to make — "Can we work something out?" And
> hopefully something could work out. I think I would make any number of
> sacrifices. Career is important to me, having it and developing it is impor-
> tant to me. But I realize that if I were in a situation with a man who was
> offered a job at XYZ and he thought it was the best opportunity for him
> and I had a good job, I would be willing to pack up and go, even though
> that sacrifices my development, because I am positive enough to think that
> I will find something and start back developing.

Rhoda's allusion to her resilience, the willingness to "start back developing," points to a recovery feature characteristic of the narratives.
This is the theme of the "Superwoman" many professional Black women
identify with. (It is also the theme Michele Wallace treats satirically in
Black Macho and the Myth of Superwoman.)

I had taped the interview before Rhoda and I ate dinner at my home.
We had been colleagues for several years, but the interview marked
our first real social association. Thus, one should understand the next
remark as Rhoda's appraisal of me as a potential intimate, both my
question and the response reflecting some mutual attraction. The question was: "How would you define a man who would be willing to adjust
to your needs?"

> I think it would be wonderful. I think it would be an extraordinary sit-
> uation. I have a male friend who I think would make the perfect house
> husband. Although he is ambitious, he is not good at focusing and direct-
> ing his energy so that he can accomplish tasks. At the same time, he is very
> creative and he would be very good at being at home. In this case I think
> that he would be a good house husband in that he would be content to
> stay home and to raise the kids and cook the dinner and be extremely sup-
> portive in terms of, "If you want to go do that, fine. Go do it and I will be
> here when you get back." I don't think that I would necessarily be bored
> with that kind of person, but I am looking for someone who is equally as
> ambitious as I am. He would be a rare, rare individual, very rare, and I
> feel that when you come across somebody who is rare you want to keep

him and treat him as *this is somebody who is very special.* It is not to say that others are not special in their own way but that quality is extremely special.

The quality of family life, particularly the ways in which various family members have played certain roles, can strongly affect how children choose to identify themselves. Rhoda's affection for and pride in her father are evident in her description of both his concern for her and his role in the community. It is helpful here to recall a previous point: how Black women define themselves has largely been determined by how Black men define their own racial and gender roles. Rhoda's sense of racial and gender identity clearly reflects her father's and mother's influences. This kind of parental influence will emerge later in the narratives of Monique, Eartha, and Akia where mother-father relationships contextualize how these women view Black men and particularly how they characterize Black men as aids or hindrances to personal growth and psychological well-being.

The next excerpt depicts a paternal and familial story in stark contrast to Rhoda's. Notice how Andria describes and contrasts her family of origin and family of identification. Notice too what kinds of events seem to prepare her to adopt her lover's father, a white male, as her own father figure. This observation is especially significant since Andria did not yet identify herself as a "real" lesbian. In fact, Andria suggests that she based her choice of a partner on factors other than sexual attraction — namely, the desire for respect and her sense that Black males would withhold this respect.

Andria: An Ambivalent Relinquisher of the Racial Narrative

Andria is a tall, dark-skinned Virginian. At the time of the interview, she was thirty-three years old. Her lover, Julia, is a white woman who is approximately the same age and is from the Northeast. They both work in the mental health field, and I met them while doing clinical work in a northeastern health center. This excerpt begins where I asked Andria if she had told her lover about our earlier interview. Andria burst into an infectious laugh:

She [Julia] kind of laughed. She was a little leery of you and your motive and one of the things she wanted me to be sure to ask you is how I was selected out — that is, How was it my name came up to be interviewed? Because so often you will get caught in the double bind, and I said, "I think he is on the up and up because I signed the papers and everything." I said that usually when you go to that length you talk about confidentiality, and that is what it is about, and I felt comfortable with it. So, she was a little leery because I'm late in confessing my homosexuality. She and I talk about stages that we all go through in terms of wanting to tell the world. She often thinks I may be running through that stage and wanting to confess to everyone that I am. And so she becomes a little leery when I just say it without knowing people, in terms of professionally here [at the job].

It is natural enough that one's lover would share one's concerns and interests and want one to be safe from harm. But there is a disjunction here: I am a Black man; Julia is a white woman. I observed much earlier that the deconstruction of race has generated, among other things, postmodernist portrayal of the Black male as villain (see Butler 1993). Andria addressed this theme as she told me how her lover, a white woman, felt the need to protect her from me. Once the relationship between Black man and woman was such that Andria, as a bisexual woman, would not have had to explain her intraracial loyalty and connection. But if the Black man gives her no respect and the Black woman is homophobic, then she has, in fact, a restricted set of options. One implication of the biracial gay option is that I, as a Black man, can no longer be seen de facto as "comrade." Thus, Andria must explain to Julia her connection to me, her concern for me and my motives, and, finally, her trust of me. I am truly the "ex-comrade" in Audre Lorde's formulation, and Andria must rest her "residue of Black care" on her trust in my integrity as a scholar who protects his subjects and informants. The question implied here is: What enables the two women to share a vision of Black men that sustains their intimacy beyond the essential attraction to each other? Andria offered a clue when she expressed her vision of Black men:

[M]y dealings with Black men are, "We [Black men] will share but it is our option to share. You are really supposed to do that, and you are really supposed to be grateful to me for doing your job." It is not done from a sharing — maybe you'll do it this week 'cause you have the time to do it, and I'll do it next week.

It is from [a perspective of], "This is what you are supposed to do. But if you really need help, you should thank me for getting in there." And this is what I see more of than anything else. I would not use the word "sexist," but I think that I can empathize in terms of it being sexist because Blacks have so little, at times, to hold on to.

Maybe sexism, from a male's perspective, is one of those strong features they need to have in order for that self-image to be up; whereas women have kids, they have other things that they can do — which men could do as well if they saw that as a valuable sharing in terms of parenting. But I don't see where society or our culture sees that as valuable from a male perspective. I mean, the male takes care of the kids only because the male is out of a job.

Andria tried to be fair.[6] She offered an "apologia" for Black male sexism. But her fairness did not deter her from doing what she felt to be in her own best interest.

I. Boszormenyi-Nagy and G. M. Spark wrote extensively about the "invisible loyalties" within families, generally, and among African-Americans, in particular. They argued that "loyalty commitments" are central to the nature of groups and families and that they operate differentially from person to person, but, nonetheless, powerfully — and subconsciously — across generations:

> The unconscious attempt to retain one's parents through the magical device of undifferentiation and eternal immaturity leads to a symbiotic possession of one's children. The state of undifferentiation of personalities and the state of consecutive overcommitment to the relationship go hand in hand. Yet overcommitment of a symbiotic type does not require visible interactions or overt acts of loyalty. Seemingly meaningless self-destruction, unfounded violent attacks on the parent, delinquency, or psychosis in the offspring may all result from inalterable, fateful, unconscious devotion to the parents. (Boszormenyi-Nagy and Spark 1973, 162–63)

This acute observation extends our understanding of the psychodynamics that propel individuating activity. It also hints at how critically a warm recollection of and devotion to parents can affect the way one relates in adult life. The process of intimacy extends over a lifetime, and as an aspect of intimacy, sexual attraction lasts just as long. How one chooses one's intimates cannot be charted simply. Still, for Andria, the experience of Black men led to a broadened sexual identification.

Women seeking to separate themselves from family patterns that threaten to engulf them in pathological dynamics tend to explore novel political, social, and sexual possibilities. The women I interviewed for the commitment study I discussed earlier (Gresson 1985b) often verged on such explorations, which they generally expressed as a "letting go" of the Black male as psychoemotional intimate. The women differed, however, in their capacity to be alone and their willingness to welcome woman-centered sexual intimacy into their lives. Andria revealed a part of this dynamic in her story, and she described her lesbian "coming out" as just such an exploration:

> I was at State University, and I don't, I can't say definitely that I have always been attracted to women and so forth. I just can't. I can't say that with a lot of strong conviction. It just kind of happened. I was at the

University. I was teaching there. I met Julia, her family in fact, while I was bowling — that was my biggest pastime — and they invited me to come to their Fourth of July party. And they said, "We don't care" — I mean these were just some crazy people; "We don't mind no mixed groups" — is the way her father came on. Her father did not know that I knew Julia, and I did not know that Julia's father was her father. I did not know any of those connections, but I just went. And things just started happening after that time. In terms of coming out, I'm still not out as far as my parents are concerned. I think [she laughs] that there are strong assumptions. My mother doesn't . . . is the type of person who would not like to hear. But she knows.

Julia's family is very supportive and have been very supportive. A couple of things really stand out, and we kind of joke and laugh about it, [like] when we invited them over and they wanted to know whose bedroom is this and whose bedroom is that, and Julia said, "This is the main bedroom and this is the second bedroom." And her mother went home and started asking dad questions, because dad knew and her mother was really hurt that she didn't just tell her. And what happened after that point was that Julia and I had to go to her and say, "This is the way it is." And everything kind of turned out all right.

Julia knew that she was lesbian. I didn't. And I went through a lot of . . . of . . . I was getting ready to teach my second year at State. All I knew was that I had really, really strong feelings for Julia. I had been dating males. . . . I had gotten to a point where I did not feel I was going to find a man who was going to respect me. I felt that the higher I went up the socio-economic level and in terms of education, there were going to be fewer and fewer Black men to whom I could relate. My dealings with white males is limited. I really didn't have a preference one way or another, but I wasn't really drawn to white men.

And that is where I was: I enjoyed my solitude. I had my apartment alone for a year while I was at State University. I enjoyed my privacy; it was something we never experienced in [the South]. We lived in a three-room house: my sister, myself, my mother, my father. So I enjoyed that part of my life. And when it did happen, and we finally got down to basics — 'cause we had hemmed and hawed — and I went over, and we played cards, we did a number of things together. I did a number of things with the family. And for me it was like a game. I was trying to figure who was the center of this whole thing because just her family alone was something I had never experienced, because [sigh] her sister and she have a house and her parents have a house. But a lot of people you could see were coming and going, and I was trying to figure out sociometrically who all this was revolving around. And I was so curious about that whole dynamic that I kind of stuck with it. She was having problems with her former lover, and I just kind of happened along. She said that she was attracted to me when we first met and that still didn't mean a thing to me. We just did a lot of things and from that point it just grew. We have been together for five years now.

I ended up going to my adviser and my supervisor, who were two women — who I suspected but they never really said it in any form or fashion; they were white — and so I went to them and I said, "Look, I'm having all these kind of emotions coming out, and I'm thinking about having a roommate. What do you think?" And they said, "Well, these are the trade-offs: You've got to think about this and this and this." Never once did we talk about it being lesbian! Never once did we talk about it being any type of... uh... it was kind of just understood, you know, and we still never said it. We never said what they were; we never said what I was going through. But they understood it, and I appreciate that. I appreciate being able to deal with it from that perspective.

The experience of racial or sexual oppression in the larger environment partly explains Andria's continued identification with her family and race. She revealed this dynamic in her distinction between white and Black homosexuality. At one point she lamented the absence of a Black lesbian community in the city where she lived. When I described to her the presence of such communities in New York City, she showed serious interest in visiting them.

Andria's identification of a white male as her surrogate father and her choice of a white female as her mate may not have been a direct result of the lack of respect she received from Black men. But we get a hint that Andria's surrogate father was different from her biological father; she compared Julia's mother to her family and characterized Julia's father as showing the class and civility she associated with her two white female supervisors. What is important in Andria's narrative is her portrayal of a woman alone, content in her uneventful life. Then one day out bowling, she found an exciting new world. This new world was unfamiliar, but, intrigued, she followed its unfolding plot. Then one day things seemed to fall into place.

This is essentially a story of the archetypal heroine who, trapped in the confusion and perseverations of the group, ventures out, happens upon the truth, and is transformed by it. The significance of lesbianism and interracial intimacy in such stories is seldom related to physical or romantic love. Most often, these choices seem to represent a break with the old ways, an embracing of something radically different that satisfies an emotional need, and an enlargement of the person's sense of self.[7]

Together, the excerpts from Rhoda's and Andria's narratives illustrate the central thesis of this chapter: Black male sexism and racial contradictions symbolically sever[8] the collusive bond with Black women, particularly those women whose inner strength or relational ties with other Blacks provide them an inadequate rationale for remaining loyal in the face of male abandonment. Rhoda's narrative describes some of the events that militate against felt loss and eventual disaffection toward Black men. Andria's narrative describes how the sense of isolation prepared her for disidentifying with the group of origin.

Blacks, Personal Choice, Postmodernism

This chapter has examined the racial-abandonment accusation directed toward Black men as a prelude to a consideration of Black female recovery discourse. The perceived Black male abandonment came to be characterized as a rhetoric of "personal choice," a most unwise and problematic choice of *topos,* regardless of its perceived validity. When some Black men chose this theme to dramatize their contradictions in interracial intimacy, they undermined the ideology of Black liberation and its "Black is beautiful" rhetoric.

The greater misfortune, however, was that the recovery project of the larger society, the white man's recovery of his cultural and national myths, converged with a racial recovery project — the Black rejection of white definitions of "Blackness" in aesthetic, social, economic, and political terms. As white expectations and demands of Blacks came under attack, Blacks began to challenge the expectations they had made of their own members, especially those constraints that discouraged them from pursuing white mates and middle-class materialism.[9] The rhetoric of personal choice arose out of the desire to be free both within and without. It was the rhetorical expression of a recovery motive.

This rhetoric of personal choice, bear in mind, came more from the events of the period than from any secret desire "to preach Black and sleep white." The wish to be free to choose one's mate related more to this cultural ethos than to a desire for such forbidden fruits as "humanness," "whiteness," and "white woman."[10] Nonetheless, Black use of a personal-choice rhetoric led to a violation of essentialist ideologies promoting racial identity and collusion. It also helped this theme become the rationale of choice among many Black women seeking to exercise a wider range of personal choices. Choices sustain life, and having made them, a chooser resists further change. Yet change is also essential to life. Choice, therefore, creates a necessary tension — between continuity and change — for people as creators, as builders of reality. When society faces pervasive unrest and disenchantment with the old choices that confront new, unfamiliar choices, it experiences a "crisis in identity," which continues until circumstances force change. A major product of this fomentation has been the spirit of postmodernism.

The personal choice of the Black male belongs to this landscape of change. Perspectives like Julius Lester's — identifying Black sanctions as politically equivalent to white racism — also belong to this landscape. But problems arise when such a stance carries beyond literature to personal life and becomes a necessary course for the new "middle passage." Yet Lester's stance is valid; it is, moreover, to his credit that he identifies the significant "ports of call" and "shoals to avoid" on the new voyage: self-love versus self-hatred; Black self versus Blackness.

The rhetorical choices Lester and others identify and prefer as sensitive to the dangers and demands of the new journey are, however, problematic precisely because the right to live life as a personal matter has been existentially and ethically defined within the postmodernist world vision that has characterized much of the social and cultural thought of the past two decades. This convergence means, in part, that the pursuit of self-interest encourages a neglect of a historically real collective oppression in the racial, economic, and political spheres.

The Black seduction into a "new invisibility" through the inviting gate of postmodernism is easy to understand: the rise of postmodernism converged with the rise of Pan-Africanist thought, both rejections of the traditional Euro-American vision and domination of the world of ideas. Identifying the ideological roots of postmodernist African-American writers (such as Margaret Abigail Walker, Ernest J. Gaines, Clarence Major, and Ishmael Reed), Bernard W. Bell wrote:

> If Euro-American modernism challenges or violates traditional assumptions about what is real, true, and therefore meaningful by separating literary text from the external world and defining it as an autonomous, self-sufficient world, then postmodernism compels us to consider that literature has no meaning, that its meaning is to be found in the indeterminacy of its language. Postmodernism moves beyond modernism of the 1950s in an effort to expand the possibilities of the novel and to reconstruct the liberated lives of the generation of the 1960s. (B. Bell 1988, 283–84)

In short, postmodernist thinking became a "natural" outlet for much of the imaginative impetus of the Black liberation movements of the 1960s and 1970s. But we have already seen a tension between Black and white liberation agendas and visions, and the collision between the Black male and the white female illustrates this tension. Postmodernism itself presents merely another occasion for such tension. Returning to Bell, we gain a partial sense of the tension's source:

> Black modernists and postmodernists...are definitely influenced by the traditions of Western literature and committed to the freedom of hybrid narrative forms. But because the legacy of institutional racism and

sexism that shaped and continues to shape their consciousness fosters ambivalence about their culture, and because the struggle for social justice
continues, most modern and postmodern Afro-American novelists, like
their nineteenth-century predecessors, are not inclined to neglect moral and
social issues in their narratives. (B. Bell 1988, 284)

The persistence of racism explains the continuity of racial concern in the
African-American novelist. Yet addressing social and moral issues may
or may not be the same as retaining a collective vision of racial identity. The very ambivalence Bell mentions encourages a postmodernist
stance among whites that recovers hegemony rather than championing
social justice. Moreover, this ambivalence among Blacks allows many
to disidentify with Black liberation agendas as they establish new relationships and make choices that enable them to experience "human
liberation."

This peculiar brand of "social consciousness" and "justice-seeking"
occurs because the abandonment of "history" as a vessel of the "truth"
means that contemporary whites and Blacks may also abandon the guilt
and responsibility for past and present injustices.

If all meaning resides in the individual, yet life proceeds as a collective enterprise, then moral responsibility is either largely alleviated or
becomes negotiable according to situational power. This, then, is the gift
of postmodernism to the historically and currently oppressed: you may
reject past definitions ("You are a nigger and unworthy"); but you now
have no moral base from which to argue or persuade. Today we see this
slipping of the moral anchor when, accused of racist acts, whites claim
that Blacks are themselves racist or otherwise are wrong to utter the
word "racist" in accusation.

When the individual replaces the Other as center, we stand to grow,
but all growth becomes both defined and compromised by context. As
one seeks to find viable and available Others for co-creation and collusion, one may well choose to tell a story, and what significantly shapes
much of contemporary Black female storytelling is an understanding
that the gifts of postmodernist thought must be tempered with the recollection of a cultural identity (Gilkes 1979) that helps one avoid the
loneliness of autonomy in an oppressive world. The importance of Black
feminist ideology inheres partly in its function as a stabilizing and unifying matrix for individual experiences and feelings. To be a part of an
ideological system is to belong, to have a source of validation for the
solitude and sadness that may dominate one's life in a fractured and
fragmented society.

The Black female recovery discourse to follow places the Black woman and her survival as primary, at the center of the racial motive and narrative. This discourse is the ideological context that has helped the individual Black woman, privileged to participate in its discursive community, with some of the rhetorical stabilizers found in the Black female narrative.

3

Black Women's Recovery Narratives:
Character as Communicative Choice

❖

Michele Wallace's own journey and becoming are not private mat-
ters. They reflect the experience of any activist woman (or man)
who has witnessed the tremendous waste of resources each time
"strong woman" or "manhood" is used to beat back activist
women. It echoes the warning of anyone who's witnessed the
sacrifice of potentially viable organizations on the altar of the
male ego.

—Toni Cade Bambara (1979)

Michele Wallace's 1978 book, *Black Macho and the Myth of Super-*
woman, told a personal story and projected a private vision. But private
visions are not the province of the oppressed. Oppression denies people
the right to step back from the Other (parent, sibling, racial group,
country), contemplate the nature of the bond, see what tensions it entails, judge how it meets or fails to meet the needs of those involved,
and determine how it might be changed for the better. But times like
bonds change; and some times, like the present, lead to the rejection of
oppression from both within and without the group. Recovery is a central concern for anyone challenged by forces from within and without
to grow.

Toni Cade Bambara's review of Michele Wallace's book suggests the
collective resonance of Wallace's voice and vision (Bambara 1979). Bambara acknowledged an audience for the narrative and the recuperative
powers of this discursive form. She sensed that when many individuals
express personal experiences of oppression, that can allow some persons eventually to identify with others and thereby to politicize those
personal experiences. While many tried to negate Wallace's *Black Ma-*

cho because of its contradictions, confusion, and threat to traditional racial ideology, her voice was not silenced.

Wallace's book stands as an illustration of both recovery discourse (talk about the recovery project) and recovery rhetoric (an act of persuasion by offering one's own journey as an inducement to particular others). Like Julius Lester's narratives, Wallace's work entered the new space for multiple and competing "Black selves." But important differences exist between Black male and Black female recovery action and discourse.

The Black female concern for self, according to rhetors like Michele Wallace and Alice Walker, is neither narcissistic nor a threat to the traditional Black family. Whether or not they are right, it is true that Black female recovery rhetoric does present a concern for the race, and its vulnerability to privatization is due largely to the loss of the former comrade, the Black man. The narratives presented in part III, below, reveal women grappling with these issues in real-life situations. But to understand the ways in which these women adopt the language of recovery, we should first place Black female recovery discourse in its historical and psychological context. We must also understand how and why Black women sought their own recovery even as they decried Black male recovery; we must find a collective communicational context for such iconoclasms as this one by Mary Helen Washington:

> We need stories, poems, novels, and biographies about Black women who have nervous breakdowns, not just the ones who endure courageously; stories about women who are overwhelmed by sex; wives who are not faithful; women experiencing the pain and humiliation of divorce; single women over thirty or forty, trying to make sense out of life and perhaps not being able to; and what about Black women who abuse and neglect their children, or those women whose apparently promiscuous behavior has caused them to be labeled "easy," or those Black women in interracial relationships? Until the sacred cow is killed, these stories cannot and will not get told. And I long to read these stories. I need the insight they can give me about real Black women. (Washington 1975, xxxi–xxxii)

This chapter explains how women like Washington helped "kill the sacred cow," the mythic-traditional Black woman, through recovery discourse and rhetoric. But we shall be most concerned to see how this "killing," thought by some to be a blow to the sacredness and survival of the race, has been rhetorically managed. Such an examination provides clues to the nature and structure of recovery rhetoric.

Black Women's Recovery:
An Emergent Discourse

The female "surrender" to males is a complex and infrequently discussed feature of oppression. Because its discussion so seldom reaches the public in these terms, radical feminists like Andrea Dworkin, who recently declared before a Penn State University audience that intercourse per se is violence against women, often scandalize their audiences. But the idea of surrender, sexual and otherwise, is not all that far removed from violence, and a little thought tells us that female surrender means, in part, a willingness or necessity to place one's self and interests second to a larger, collective interest and that this larger, collective interest is often the functional equivalent to the "male ego" (Miller 1973; Gilligan 1982).

For Black women, surrender during the movement era amounted to allowing the Black male to exercise hegemony on behalf of the race (Marable 1980). From this view, surrender entails a sacrifice and implies an expectation of unconditional Black male care. By 1970, the Black male violation of this bond had already become a major theme (Bambara 1970; Hare and Hare 1970). The violation of this collusive bond and the expectation of male care, in fact, gave rise to recovery rhetoric among Black women. As Michele Wallace wrote:

> If Malcolm X had lived, if white America had been able to calm its racist paranoia, . . . if the groundwork for a profoundly deep hatred of himself and his woman had not been so well laid in the Black man's soul by four hundred years of relentless conditioning, the years that followed 1965 might have been very different and perhaps more constructive. (Wallace 1978, 38)

But Malcolm X did die, and as part of his legacy, he left a narrative that invited enlargement (Benson 1974) and, through it, recovery. Thus, such Black women as Lorde, Walker, and Wallace saw that taking care of Black men through self-sacrifice was a no-win situation. The discourse created to address this plight is what I call *the discourse of self-recovery*. This discourse shares qualities with others, such as Black male recovery discourse. But important differences are grounded in the perception of Black male self-recovery efforts as self-hating narcissism. This apparent self-hatred aided the necessary growth of Blacks beyond the historical perceptions of racial identity, and it helped Black women reexamine and modify aspects of their psychological development.

To follow the reasoning of these Black women writers and to understand their rhetorical appeal, however, one should realize that comparatively few Black men actually gave themselves over to rampant narcissistic self-indulgence or relentlessly pursued "the white goddess." Some, of course, did, and in so doing, they revealed a potentiality, exposed a crack in the collusive bond, and fulfilled a pivotal racial myth: integration would lead, inevitably, to Black-instigated miscegenation.

Additionally, those Black males challenging this personal-choice movement fought with traditional political discourse; they lacked the persuasive metaphors needed to convince a "me-first" generation of Americans to yield to a collective myth of oneness. Thus, individualistic Black male writers like Julius Lester were able either to soothe or to shock the imagination of the country. Black men like Molefi Asante, Nathan Hare, Harold Cruse, and Langston Hughes went largely ignored in the wake and backwash of those men who violated Black women with their narcissistic self-indulgence in matters both collective and individual.

The intent here is not to make invidious distinctions or to suggest one group of men were or are preferable to another. Rather, I suggest only that the various individualistic and collectivistic Black male visions posed difficulties for many critical Black female writers. Because the Black male visions did not — indeed, could not — adequately represent Black women, the women had to tell their own stories. Moreover, this storytelling became an act of self-love because of the perceived failure of Black male love for the Black woman.

Inevitably, therefore, Wallace, Shange, Lorde, and Walker, among others, would come forth and demand the return of their goodwill, love, and self-esteem. The rhetorical communication of this emphasis on a recovery of self-surrender reached its peak in the 1970s choreopoem, *For Colored Girls Who Have Considered Suicide When the Rainbow Was Enuf,* by Ntozake Shange. In this work many of the poems tell stories that justify Black women's self-interest and self-love. Two important rhetorical developments emerged from this perception of failed love and collusion defiled: storytelling as self-love and storytelling as heroic recovery. The first of these developments was a logical extension of the reaction to Black male recovery efforts. The second was a natural extension of the former but also separate because of its being the site of the rhetorical aspect of Black women's recovery. I will consider the first development, then, a part of the personal-choice movement and take up the second development later as a part of the rhetorical structure of Black female narrative.

Narrative as Self-Love

Black women have often felt themselves misrepresented in both literature and reality. Black men, moreover, sometimes cause this mis-
representation. Thus, Black female storytelling has largely evolved out
of a need to forge an alternative story. Black women's stories about
themselves, therefore, often say a lot about male-female collusion and
separation. But they say more, as Mary Helen Washington suggested in
her assessment of the emergent Black female voice in literature:

> When I think how essentially alone Black women have been — alone be-
> cause of our bodies, over which we have had so little control; alone
> because the damage done to our men has prevented their closeness and
> protection; and alone because we have had no one to tell us stories about
> ourselves — I realize that Black women writers are an important and com-
> forting presence in my life. Only they know my story. It is absolutely
> necessary that they be permitted to discover and interpret the entire range
> and spectrum of the experiences of Black women and not be stymied by
> preconceived conclusions. Because of these writers, there are more models
> of how it is possible for us to live, there are more choices for Black women
> to make, and there is a larger space in the universe for us. (Washington
> 1975, xxii)

Washington's words illustrate the connection of recovery discourse to
a particular rhetorical activity: *storytelling*. As she indicates, this form of
discourse allows Black women as speakers to focus on the dual concerns
of differentiation of self and an enlarged range of relational options.
The first of these relates to the need to distinguish self from both Black
males and white women. This particular concern found expression in
the title of an early black feminist anthology, *All the Women Are White,
All the Blacks Are Men, but Some of Us Are Brave* (Hull, Scott, and
Smith 1982).

The second concern, an enlarged range of relational options, means
that Black women also seek to escape the burden of being defined in
terms of their roles. This need appears in an essay by Rhetaugh Thomas
Dumas:

> I have felt the pangs of guilt evoked by those who would lead me to believe
> that to protect myself and promote my general welfare is to let my people
> down. I am now beginning to see how it is possible to let my people down
> by *failing* to protect myself and my interests and to seek fulfillment of my
> own needs. Indeed in modern organizations, racism and sexism dictate that
> *I am my people. I am BLACK. I am WOMAN.* (Dumas 1980, 214)

Dumas wrote these remarks at the conclusion of a study of Black
women's role in corporate America and, in particular, the multiple de-

mands Black women encounter from both white male bosses and Black group members. Passionate and powerful, her words also carry a certain mystical or esoteric quality I attribute to the need for female storytellers. This quality appears to be a consequence of breaking with the traditional expectations and initiating a new definition of the situation, of the self, and of one's relationship to the Other. This "mystical" quality signals the forging of a new collusive bond, a new myth by which to explain connection.

This storytelling is an act of self-love because it starts, as Audre Lorde understands, with a need to love oneself as one has loved others. Recall the biblical exhortation to love one's neighbor *as oneself*. This exhortation also implies the *transcendental* mandate upon which the rhetorical motive underlying all recovery rhetoric is based: to rebond with the Other. What sets much of Black women's recovery discourse apart from most Black male recovery discourse is this self-conscious struggle with the tension and terror of this dual task of recovery.

The felt difference between the Black male and Black female recovery motive explains Audre Lorde's observation that Black male recovery is "narcissism" and "self-hate" and that Black female recovery behavior is "self-love." The Black male has broken the collusive bond by acts of omission and commission. He has, therefore, freed the Black woman to act accordingly. Her recovery acts become survivalist and self-loving. We must understand that this reasoning is the logic underpinning racial recovery; this is the reasoning of Kenneth Burke's "Negro": I can be free as a "human" only if I am free as a "Negro," but I may have to abandon aspects of my "Negroness" in order to become "human."[1]

The rhetorical dimension of recovery discourse, then, is that conversation aimed at convincing self and others that connection and continuity of care persist despite the obvious break with those signs and qualities historically defined as connecting and caring. The rhetorical aspect of racial recovery shares this concern with continuity of care vis-à-vis abandonment. This concern, according to the argument, is why Julius Lester denied that he was self-hating and countered by defining traditional racial expectations — choosing Black over white — as "narcissistic."

An intrarace clash of visions of caring becomes evident when we recall that Lorde called Black men "narcissistic," in part, because they chose white over Black; and that Lester views as "narcissistic" the expectation (implied in Lorde's indictment of Black men's "personal choices") that one would permit "racial self-love" to dictate individual choices about how to live one's life. This clash of racial visions is precisely what

I call *Black apocalypse*: it is the split and privatized understanding of self and Other as a racial entity, as a historically and contemporarily oppressed racial group.

Molefi Asante understood this tension and tried to resolve it by the call to return to things "Afrocentric." Afrocentricity asks a person to deny self and select the group, an immense request for the Black American drawn to postmodernist sentiments. Afrocentricity as an ideal may or may not result in the kinds of relationships and connections the individual needs for support in today's world. For example, consider this Afrocentric request of the Black homosexual:

> White racism, with fangs, claws at the soul of Black manhood, which results in an alteration of Black womanhood as well. Afrocentric relationships are based upon sensitive sharing in the context of what is best for the collective imperative of the people. All brothers who are homosexuals should know that they too can become committed to the collective. It means the submergence of their own will into the collective will of our people. An ideology of Afrocentricity is derived from our history and provides all the guidelines for action. The homosexual shall find the redemptive power of Afrocentricity to be the magnet which pulls him back to his center. (Asante 1988b, 57–58)

This call denies the passion embedded in the recovery project of African-Americans as humans and Black postmodernists. Afrocentricity thereby contributes to the racial apocalypse by intensifying the privatized experience of African-Americans. (Some, of course, would dismiss Afrocentricity merely by labeling it by the code word "essentialist.") For this reason, Asante's position becomes as problematic as Lester's although one sees clear differences in motives, morality, and possible outcomes.

Rhetorically, the Afrocentric position is an exigency; it constitutes a part of that great external pressure an individual apprehends as oppression to be resisted. Kenneth Burke summed up the rhetorical possibility of all external voices that would persuade in the fashion of Afrocentric ideology: "Only those voices from without are effective which can speak in the language of the voice within" (Burke 1968, 563). I emphasize Asante's Afrocentrism because it implies a mindfulness of the racial past and present: he is all too aware of the immense need for racial loyalty and collective action in contemporary American society.

Because most African-Americans still subscribe to some form of collective control over the individual even as they pursue the pleasures of postmodernist materialism, they do not so much reject an Afrocentric perspective as receive it selectively. The result, nonetheless, finds this pro-African stance significantly nonrhetorical for most except the long-persuaded. Afrocentricity is, in this sense, apocalyptic.

Still, in Black women's writings and lives we see the struggle to transform this apocalypse into a new, shared vision. Although I consider the work as incomplete, it is nevertheless instructive and is most apparent in the narratives. But to observe the effect of the effort in the narratives, we must first consider the persuasive motive and method narrative sets up for the storyteller in search of reconnection.

Narrative as Heroic

One of the more gifted theorists in the sociology of race relations, Cheryl Townsend Gilkes, addressed the difference between Black male and Black female recovery in her seminal research on Black female commitment. Reflecting on her study of Black female community leaders in a southern community, she wrote:

> [T]he process of becoming committed involves a process of negotiation between the self and sets of others. A person must organize her social relations in such a way that some speech communities become sovereign in her personal organization and become the primary sets of others entitled to accounts and for whom she shapes her words or deeds. In order to manage the establishment of her commitments, she places certain sidebets or takes risks that create options and place limits on her behavior. These options and limits open pathways to certain behaviors and close pathways to others. (Gilkes 1979, 239)

In Gilkes's view, Black women have traditionally held the race together by integrating, or counterbalancing, conflictive and contradictory sources within the Black community. Her prototypical Black female traditionalist has found a way to satisfy her own personal needs within this contradictory world. She is a heroine in the tradition of Ernest Becker: managing the generic contradictions of life without resorting to escapism. She understands and accepts certain behavioral constraints as being necessary. But the women Gilkes studied belonged to the racial past, to a time long before the collusive break. To be sure, many Black women remain committed to a unified and undefiled vision of the racial bond. But the many who do not must also grapple with the connection mandate. In their struggle we confront another aspect, if not form, of the Black heroine, and in the narrative that heroism receives its rhetorical construction. Consider this passage from the narrative of Eartha, presented more fully later:

> I think what is most important to her [Eartha's cousin] right now is that she thinks of herself as a "Black woman," and she believes in the Black

movement and stuff, but she can't deal with it. She can't deal with the Black man, so how can she possibly believe in something a part of which she won't accept? You have to accept people and stop balking at this person's color because you had an experience with one kind of person. And a lot of it has to do with sexuality: because you had a bad experience with the opposite sex, you want to turn to the same sex because you don't want to challenge any more of that experience within yourself. [My cousin] has this idea, "I am a strong Black woman and white men love strong Black women," and she said, "If I were to die and come back again, I would want to come back as a Black woman" because she thinks Black women have the best deal.

Eartha described here a cousin who dates only white men and is soon to marry a white man. Eartha introduced this cousin to indicate that she is unlike the cousin even though she, too, currently dates mainly white and non-Black men. Eartha believed her behavior to be qualitatively different from her cousin's because she does not define herself as a "Black woman" but as a person (or, as we shall see in her narrative, as an "earthling"). Eartha is, in fact, one expression of the new Black heroine.

Moreover, both Eartha and her cousin illustrate Gilkes's observation regarding commitment: each has identified a speech community and others who validate her self-definition. But Eartha makes an important point: her cousin takes an ideological stance that conflicts with her personal choice. It is difficult to "sleep white" and "preach Black."

This behavior revolves increasingly around the issue of personal choice as character. Consider the literature on "double-consciousness." Mary Helen Washington observed, for instance, that "the theme of double-consciousness is found in most literature by Blacks. The theme of the divided self, woman split in two, [is found in the writing of women, both Black and white]" (Washington 1980, 208–9). In her anthology of women's literature, Teresa de Lauretis saw the emergence in feminist writings of

the concept of a multiple, shifting, and often self-contradictory identity, a subject that is not divided in, but rather at odds with, language; an identity made up of heterogeneous and heteronomous representations of gender, race, and class, and often indeed across languages and cultures; an identity that one decides to reclaim from a history of multiple assimilations, and that one insists on as a strategy. (de Lauretis 1987, 9)

More and more Black women have begun to forge their character in terms of this paradoxical stance toward self and Other, and telling or reading stories is central to this process.[2] Narrative has correctly been identified as a historically important and existentially relevant vehicle for this self-recovery task. Narrative's role as a recovery vehicle is its power as a heroic story.

Alice Walker, a Pulitzer Prize–winning author, seems in her short story "A Letter of the Times" to share this view of narrative, heroism, and recovery:

> [A]s I read the narratives of Black people who were captured and set to slaving away their lives in America, I saw that this inner spirit, this inner capacity for self-comforting, this ability to locate God within that they expressed, demonstrated something about human beings. It was as if these women found a twin self who saved them from their abused consciousness and chronic physical loneliness; and that twin self is in all of us, waiting only to be summoned. (cited in Conklin, McCallum, and Wade 1983, 80)

Walker's passage includes two astute observations. First, narrative provides an ideal vehicle for the attainment of self-recovery. Second, within the narrative mode, Walker "discovered"[3] a "twin self" to facilitate a woman's capacity for *self-soothing*.[4]

This perspective on narrative resembles that offered by both Ernest Becker and John Hanna: it is the person herself who must accept the challenge to change the reality *that is* into *that which might be*. Thus, the individual effectively critiques the Other: mother, father, family, and social group. This critique of the Other becomes an act of self-love. Some have even declared it to be an act of racial love. Michele Wallace, a protagonist in the 1979 Black sexism debate discussed earlier, observed on one occasion: "I just want to get us talking. Criticism is an act of love" (cited in Klemesrud 1979).

Narrative becomes an act of self-love for the woman of color because she has been betrayed and because she has been traditionally predisposed to love everyone but herself. Then having learned self-love, she proceeds to self-care, the next passage in the litany of love. Here, in fact, we have the message of Audre Lorde: "And this call for self-value, self-love, is quite different from narcissism." But Lorde continued her thought this way: "The Black man's well-documented narcissism comes, not out of self-love, but out of self-hatred" (Lorde 1979, 18).

I introduced Lorde's observation earlier as an example of recovery discourse. Let me now reintroduce it as illustrative of the paradox, depicted in the excerpt from Eartha's narrative, that inheres in the suggestion that Black female personal choices are heroic rather than cowardly and that Black women who choose become heroines because their choices are survivalist reactions rather than "motivated abandonment" of the race. From this viewpoint, we cannot regard the presence of contradiction within Black female behavior solely in terms of a mathematical logic; rather, we must see it in terms of its narrative logic.

From the perspective of narrative logic, Black women achieve heroism because their behavior emanates from their powerlessness and vulnerability with their choices predetermined before they act. This notion of the heroine differs from the classical one presented in texts centered on privileged white males. Yet, not surprisingly, this alternative notion of heroism is the archetype we find in narratives of women and powerless men: heroism is achieved in understanding and accepting limits and one's humanity (Pearson and Pope 1981). The hero who does not happen to be male, white, and "chosen" inspires and instructs through her vulnerability and her transformation of weakness and degradation into personal strength and nobility. This imagery is, of course, not limited to the woman or person of color. It is the genius of the modern playwright, novelist, and poet to see Everyman as precisely this form of hero, from Fyodor Dostoyevsky's Raskolnikov to Langston Hughes's Simple.

Yet the Black woman has evolved as the prototypic hero of the twenty-first century: the rebuilder of sacred and collective meaning. Nor have Black women been unaware of this special place in contemporary history. In their discourse about their mission we can often find the incipient structure of the logic of narrative recovery as heroic.

The Recovery Structure of Heroic Narrative

Ebele O. Eko introduced her study of Paule Marshall's *Praisesong for the Widow* this way:

> [This book] is not only a chronological continuum of her exploration of growth and maturity processes.... The author [also] advocates that the Black writers' burden should be one of recreating Black history in heroic terms with the abundance of folk tradition around them.... The double reaction which this novel elicits, is deliberately anticipated. (Eko 1986, 143)

Barbara Christian, exploring "the interdependency of character and culture in the novels of Paule Marshall," enlarges the heroic theme introduced in Eko's passage:

> Paule Marshall's works, as psychopolitical images, elucidate the people who affect their culture and are affected in turn by their creation. Because of this thrust, her works remind us that all of us compose our own experiences in our minds and that our individual shapes are kinetically poised in

a unified sculpture called the universe; that we all are continuity and process, shape and space, and that our sculpted creations are ourselves; that
we change our world by changing our shapes, yet our world will change
whether or not we want it to. Marshall's novels manifest history as a creative and moral process, for she graphically describes how we compose our
own experiences in our minds as well as in the objective world; how we as
individuals and whole cultures decide upon the moral nature of an act, a
series of acts, a history. (Christian 1980, 135–36)

For both Christian and Eko, Paule Marshall's creative work recapitulates a normative style and struggle: to fuse character and culture
in an ever-changing, open-ended dialectic. At the heart of this "psychopolitical" task, so central to the work of Paule Marshall, is a (re)negoti-
ation of the meaning of oneself vis-à-vis the Other. This task, moreover,
is dependent upon the author/actor's composition of personal experiences into a morally compelling creation — a creation that is nonetheless
mediated by the given or inherited possibilities of the culture.

Metaphoric invention is critical to this creative work. Within Black
women's writings and oral statements, metaphoric invention focuses, as
for Paule Marshall, on self–Other metaphors. For the past two decades,
especially, Black women have been creating and interpreting this creative work. From the earliest postrevolutionary writings of Toni Cade
Bambara, Angela Davis, Alice Walker, and LaFrances Rodgers-Rose, to
the unabashedly feminist and radical work of Audre Lorde, Barbara
Christian, Barbara Smith, and Mary Helen Washington, there has been
a consistent message: Black women are heroes; and this heroism consists
precisely in the apprehension and actualization of the mission of "marginal" perspective and representation. Thus, it is often in the metaphors
they use to speak of themselves in relation to Others that we can see
metaphoric invention tracing out the structure of racial recovery.

Self–Other Metaphors

Metaphoric invention, the creating of new metaphors, is a renegotiation
process. Gates (1988) identified "naming" or "revising" as a parallel
to this renegotiation process. Earlier, Colin Turbayne (1970) called this
process "inventing a new metaphor" and observed that when metaphors
wear out or no longer convey the desired irony and enlargement, one
should change them.

The logical vehicles for conveying the limits of old connections and
relationships, new metaphors are generic to the recovery project. For
example, Audre Lorde called the Black male the "ex-comrade." What
a powerful way of saying that Black men were once related to Black

women by a shared racial oppression, but that this relatedness is a thing of the past!

Robert Ivie noted that "metaphor is at the base of rhetorical invention" (Ivie 1987, 165). Taking this view of metaphor's relationship to rhetorical invention, one can argue that the pivotal goal of metaphor in racial recovery rhetoric is to induce the listener or reader to share a view of the loss and to appreciate the courage and care implicit in the proposed recovery. Thus, racial metaphors serve as tools for inventing a new connection.

Rhetorical invention among Black women "in recovery"[5] has thus far featured two uses of metaphors: to soothe and console the self in one's pain and privatization and to legitimate the break by serving as a mirror to the Other. In the narrative, these two forms of persuasion assume a characteristic configuration. Before we examine this configuration, however, here is how I define the two forms of metaphor and their relation to other figures of speech:

1. *Self-Metaphors.* These focus on the self-soothing aspect of rhetorical narrative. For Audre Lorde, "Black woman as sacrificial lamb" is a self-soothing metaphor. The idea of "Black woman in search of new comrades" seems an implied metaphor, when paired with the "Black man as ex-comrade" concept.

2. *Other-Metaphors.* These serve a relational (disassociative or connective) function and emphasize how the Other is related to the self. As an "Other-metaphor," Lorde posits several ideas regarding Black men: "Black man as ex-comrade"; "Black man as self-hater"; and "Black man as narcissist."

These two forms of metaphor are central to any recovery process seen as heroic, but other heroic figures of speech become involved in this overall recovery process. Some of the texts and narratives discussed here provide interesting uses of the major tropes (Burke 1968; Gates 1988), and the combining of the self–Other metaphoric forms with these additional figures results in the rich rhetorical inventions found in Black female recovery discourse. The following examples represent instances where the classical tropes are employed as devices for recovery.

Other Major Tropes of Black Female Recovery

Metonymy. Black woman equals oppression, and the Black woman equals liberation motives. These metonymies reflect the idea that Black women — characterized by the "multiple jeopardies" of racism, poverty, and sexism — are the same as "oppression" writ large. This idea has been the basis for a particular marketing strategy — using Alice Walker or Maya Angelou as the symbolic keynote speaker — employed by predominantly white professional associations; examples of this occurred at recent national conferences on domestic violence and on family therapy for a diverse society. In the first instance, audiences concerned with domestic violence were invited to connect that problem to the plight of "Black women as oppression." In the second instance, Black women were employed to connect family therapists to liberation.

Molefi Asante enlarges upon this sense of metonymy in Black discourse:

> [W]e are a people in tune with our God-force whether in a night club or a church. The feeling is the same; it comes from the same place. Quite early in our American sojourn we adapted the internal strivings of our souls, the religious needs and desires, to the western religious experience making a combination with African essence and Christian form. In the centuries since our forefathers and foremothers effected this change we have forgotten why it was done. Nevertheless, most of us retain the urge to shout whether we are Baptist or not. (Asante 1988b, 74–75)

Here, Asante brings a listener, particularly an Afrocentric African-American, to the threshold of *his* recovery vision: something was lost, but the possibility of recovery remains. As with other recent narrators on ancestral Black genius (Gates 1988), the essence is "buried in the past" and must be "dug up" or permitted to "spring forth."

Synecdoche. Taking a part for the whole is a convenient way of conceptualizing the recovery challenge: if I must act for myself on my own behalf yet remain connected to a collective and historical liberation agenda, then I must somehow visualize the mirroring of self and Other. In the narratives, several striking figures emerge. For example, Eartha speaks of herself as *earthling.* I define this as her self-metaphor; but it is also an instance of taking a part for the whole: Eartha as earthling equals Black woman as earthling.

This understanding of recovery discourse, moreover, helps show how Rhetaugh Dumas (1980) could declare: "*I am my people. I am BLACK. I am WOMAN.*" In short, Dumas is both race and gender. Returning for a moment to metonymy, we see this configuration is possible because the parts, race and female gender, can be viewed as the whole, oppression. Thus, Dumas is race and gender writ large because of her experience of oppression in the workplace. This formulation of self, moreover, is precisely what various Black feminist theorists (V. Smith 1989; Henderson 1989) describe as "simultaneity" in Black female fiction. But we can see it in choices and character as well. Herein, we also encounter irony.

Irony. In 1979, Audre Lorde declared that Black women needed to learn commitment to themselves and such commitment would be only fair given Black male narcissism:

> In this country Black women traditionally have had compassion for everybody except ourselves. We cared for whites because we had to for pay for survival; we cared for our children and our fathers and our brothers and our lovers. We need also to learn to care for ourselves. (Lorde 1979, 18)

She went on to point out that the idea of personal choice, which many Black males invoke to legitimize their various transracial commitments, applied equally for Black women:

> In the light of what Black women sacrifice for their children and their men, this [call for self-compassion and self-love] is ... much needed. ... And this call for self-value, self-love, is quite different from narcissism. ... The Black man's well-documented narcissism comes, not out of self-love, but out of self-hatred. Black women also cannot be denied our personal choices, and those choices are increasingly self-assertive ones, and female-oriented. "Personal choice" and "ontological" reasoning are knives that cut both ways. (Lorde 1979, 18)

Audre Lorde's famous comment — that the Black male is narcissistic — is ironic. But the fullness of this irony in her allusion to Black racial self-hate appears in her further comment: " 'Personal choice' and 'ontological' reasoning" are knives that can "cut both ways." The irony here is that Robert Staples (1973), the scholar closely associated with the personal-choice rationale, had previously observed that Black women were not becoming "male-hating" radical lesbians like white women. Then in 1979, he seemed to contradict himself, leading Audre Lorde, a self-avowed Black lesbian feminist, to remind him of his earlier appraisal.

The frequent use Black women make of these figures indicates their sense of the paradox of racial recovery in a race-dominated environment as they attempt both to move toward larger personal options and to remain faithful to the racial bonds necessary for group protection. This is a difficult task for two reasons. First, the group itself must resist efforts to change its cultural identity. Second, the absence of a collective vision — a viable shared meaning for group identity and collective experience — promotes privatization.

These two barriers operate in recovery discourse so as to fragment the Black liberation discourse into several competing discursive communities. Recovery thus occurs primarily within a privatized and personally compelling space. The collective persuasion mandate remains under-addressed; and racial rapprochement goes unachieved. Within recent years, nonetheless, some Black writers have struggled with this problem in a way that one may call developmental. That is, they have replaced the formative images of exclusion with those of inclusion; images of self-encapsulation have changed to those of self-enlargement. For these formative images to be effective, however, Black writers and activists must confront and resolve the impasse implicit in the rhetoric of personal choice.

The Limits of Personal Choice as Recovery

Personal choice is a key idea in this impasse because it facilitates a break with prior commitment or collusion and the claim that betrayal has recurred. Here we have an ironic use of personal choice because it encourages an individual to rename, revise, and choose. Richard Brown has called this process "dialectical irony," observing that it

> leads us towards reflexivity, both as social scientists and as citizens. Dialectical irony involves making a statement that is open to ambivalent interpretations, that is, interpretations of opposite weights and meanings. The ironist must thus be an explicitly social actor in that to practice her irony she requires a public that is (willing to be) enlightened. In order to be ironic, the ironist must impel her publics to make choices. By her ironic method of derealizing reified meanings, she challenges her publics to create meanings for themselves. (R. Brown 1987, 179)

Irony, however, carries the danger of detachment, springing as it does from the personal empowerment that accompanies a sense of "standing outside of history." This is the danger of Black postmodernism lived at the extreme. Black recovery efforts must confront this danger.

In real life and in fiction, the danger, when confronted, may lead one to experience either greater closeness to the group or greater estrangement from it. It may be instructive that we find so much fiction concerned with seeking after wholeness and connection with an estranged Other. Barbara Johnson, for instance, concluded her essay on Black literature with these thoughts: "The search for wholeness, oneness, universality and totalization can never be put to rest. However rich, healthy or lucid fragmentation and division may be, narrative seems to have trouble resting content with it." Here is Johnson regarding metaphor and metonymy in *Their Eyes Were Watching God* by Zora Neale Hurston:

> Far from being an expression of Janie's new wholeness or identity as character, Janie's increasing ability to speak grows out of her ability not to

mix inside with outside, not to pretend that there is no difference, but to assume and articulate the incompatible forces involved in her own division. The sign of authentic voice is thus not self-identity but self-difference. (Johnson 1984, 212)

This is a provocative place for the oppressed person to discover herself or himself: surely related to, but from different from, the Other. This is where many Blacks have consciously arrived. This is the contemporary racial expression of the "birthright" crisis depicted in postmodernism.

Thus, the rhetoric of self-recovery signifies a break from a historic *and* collusive bond. It is a betrayal. It is also a kind of "coming of age." It is a response to both the shame of oppression and the shamelessness of a rhetoric that would seek to confine (Black women's) choices in a transitional world. It encourages recovery of the power to redefine (racial and gender) identification in terms that allow for the integration of contradictory values and conflictive reference groups. But this type of discourse clashes with the conservatism of liberation groups — that is, their need to forge a collective and maintain interest groups. The oppressed person's coming of age as an "American on the move" clashes with his or her ascribed reference groups: Blacks, women, gays, the aged, the poor.

Indeed much of the dialogue taking place between Black female and male intellectuals today breaks down because of this conservatism. We see this failure even in some Black female writers who, like Staples, want both Black females and males to project a public discourse that emphasizes holism, tradition, conciliation, and the past (the traditional myths and values). For example, commenting on Michele Wallace's book *Black Macho and the Myth of Superwoman* and Ntozake Shange's choreopoem, *For Colored Girls Who Have Considered Suicide When the Rainbow Was Enuf* (which had sparked the Black sexism debate published in *The Black Scholar*), Sherley Williams said, "These works, whether one thinks them valid or not, have in common limitations based on the fact that they are portraits rather than group scenes, monologues rather than conversation. But our sense of ourselves as a people cannot be developed from isolated snapshots or monologues" (Williams 1979, 51). Williams is correct. In this regard, moreover, she anticipates Celeste Condit's argument presented in chapter 1. But this argument neglects a psychopolitical reality: soliloquy may be a needed step in the groundwork for dialogue, conversation, and group scenes. It is precisely the failure to understand the space that must exist between self and Other — the differentiation of self — that explains so much of the pathology and pain of overinvolved families and ethnic groups. From a rhetorical stance, I have elsewhere argued that

> to neglect the monologues and soliloquies of the violated is to neglect the fact that none of us is free of such self-oriented conversations. Indeed, it is exactly in the messages of Shange and Wallace — and of Freud before them — that this sociopolitical requirement of togetherness often conceals a narcissistic impulse which repeatedly rears its head, making a public mockery of both the rhetoric and reality of shared fate, collective plight, and the collective struggle for liberation. In short, it is that very necessity to ignore "isolated snapshots and monologues" which lays the psychomoral groundwork for most betrayal phenomena. (Gresson 1982, 80)

Like Hugh Duncan (1962), I see soliloquy as an effort to resolve contradictions between self and Other, as the verbal stance that allows one to articulate personal voice in the semipublic spaces of our world and thereby to renegotiate the ground of relatedness and care. But we must still consider this conservatism in terms of its own recovery motive.

In the narrative writ large we can see evolving this search for new ways to connectedness. I believe that the psychology of narrative and dialogic inquiry are ideally suited to encouraging this evolution. Through their assistance we may ultimately find more ways of transforming the plight of those persons who find their only means of resolving untenable collective contradictions in a privatization of "public troubles" into personally valid stories.

Molefi Asante argues that one needs an Afrocentric rhetorical stance to appreciate fully African-American discourse; furthermore, he says,

> In an Afrocentric conception of literature and orature, the critical method would be employed to determine to what degree the writer or speaker contributed to the unity of the symbols, the elimination of chaos, the making of peace among disparate views, and the creation of an opportunity for harmony and hence balance. (Asante 1988a, 177–78)

From this viewpoint, narratives as soliloquy present an opportunity for revealing and resolving certain collective contradictions. But some important aspects of African-American history present in such narrative encounters cannot be readily understood by Eurocentric modes of explication. In this regard, Molefi Asante says, "Orature is the total body of oral discourse, styles, and traditions of African people. It is the metaphoric discourse of reintegration" (Asante 1988a, 177–78). He goes on to clarify the relationship of orature to rhetoric: "Thus, rhetoric is a transforming power, a mythic discourse in the midst of a plethora of symbols."[6] Audre Lorde illustrates this type of rhetoric when she said this to Adrienne Rich:

> When a people share a common oppression, certain kinds of skills and joint defenses are developed. And if you survive you survive because those skills and defenses have worked. When you come into conflict over other existing differences, there already is an additional vulnerability to each other which is desperate and very deep. *And that is, for example, what happens between Black men and women, because we have certain weapons we have perfected together that white women and men have not shared. I said this to someone, and she said, very rightly, the same thing exists within the Jewish community between Jewish men and Jewish women. I think the oppression is different, therefore the need for connection is on a different level, but the same mechanism of vulnerability exists.* When you share a common oppression, you have certain additional weapons against each other, because you've forged them in secret together against a common enemy. It's a fear that I'm still not free of and that I remember all the time when I deal with other Black women: the fear of the ex-comrade. (Lorde 1981, 734–35; emphasis added)

Within the condition Lorde describes there resides the very possibility of "freedom" that oppressed people require. But this condition means that each encounter may, in a more or less decisive way, intrude upon the collective psyche. Here we have the key to understanding the relationship between storyteller and audience. Alice Walker describes the African-American's development of self as a dialectical process this way:

> [B]ut crucial to our development too, it seems to me, is an acceptance of our actual as opposed to our mythical self. We are the mestizos of North America. We are Black, yes, but we are white, too, and we are red. To attempt to function as only one, when you are really two or three, leads I believe to physical illness: White people have shown the madness of that. ... [R]egardless of who will or will not accept us, we must be completely (to the extent it is possible) who we are. We are the African and the traitor. We are the Indian and the settler. We are the slaver and enslaved. We are oppressor and oppressed. Freedom should force us to stop relating as owner and owned. (A. Walker 1988, 82, 89)[7]

Walker explodes here the idea of "the race": we are not Black. We are much, much more. This has been true for much of the "Black diaspora." Still, we must see this stance as something significantly different from the sentiment encoded in the legends of the "middle passage." In chapter 9, I will introduce the African trickster god, Esu-Elegbara, whose essence is his multivoiced multiplicity of selves. As we shall see, Esu is the symbolic equivalent of Walker's postmodern Black: one who must acknowledge but transcend Blackness by embracing the white Other within the Black self.

Other Black women writing within a woman-centered vision (Hogue 1986) do not necessarily share Walker's perspective. But it represents a powerful rhetorical space for Black women precisely for its iconoclastic rejection and dereification of traditional Black visions. In the narratives to come, the position arrived at by the postmodern Black is profound and problematic: it asserts Blacks' basic humanity (as if it were ever truly in doubt rather than denied by racist ideology) but does so by blaming Blacks rather than whites for the forced oneness and racial mythologizing that have characterized much of the past four hundred years of the African diaspora in America. This position sees the real racial advances of the past three decades as forcing the race to abandon much of its racial mythology. The irony, of course, is that to achieve and sustain this freedom as a "human Black," one must deny the persistence — indeed, in some venues, the resurgence — of white racism; and when the rationales for breaking with traditional expectations compromise the need to remain wedded to the race around precisely the collective values that have been rejected, one comes face-to-face with the very paradigm of a paradoxical predicament.

Conclusion

Three points made thus far in this chapter require some reemphasis. First, for women like Audre Lorde, Michele Wallace, and Alice Walker, Black male recovery activity was "narcissistic"; although many Black women did not share this view of Black men, they did collectively react with loss and a recovery agenda parallel to the Black male's personal-choice *topos*.

Second, their reaction made "self-love" a counter-*topos*. For these women, and many more, Black female recovery behavior — including behavior traditionally not identified with Black woman — was "self-love." Audre Lorde's reference to Black male and female intimacy as a special "collusive bond" underlies this perceived difference and serves as an expression of the logic of Black female recovery rhetoric.

Third, the limits of this reactionary rationale for rhetorical persuasion have introduced a "transcendental theme" in Black women's recovery discourse. But the rhetoric of self-recovery fails to convey fully the persuasive dimensions of this transcendental theme. Indeed, the failure so far to persuasively set forth this transcendental theme plagues Black female rhetoric of recovery, leaving it vulnerable to criticism as monologic and selfish. Nevertheless, the transcendental theme remains within the rhetoric of self-recovery, revealed in terms of both its rhetorical and transcendental concerns only in certain circumstances. One such circumstance is narrative discourse, and the narratives in Part III help illuminate the rhetorical tension of Black women's concern for self and Other. A fuller appreciation of these narratives and their contribution to understanding the implicit theory of recovery rhetoric will follow a brief consideration of the form and function of Black recovery narratives.

Rhetorical Narratives and Implicit Recovery *Topoi*

For the Black woman (or for that matter, anyone breaking with an established tradition or bond), the recovery task is to convince the Other that one has not broken faith when one's situation or circumstances say otherwise; to convince the Other that she or he is mistaken to think that one no longer shares the historical narrative that was a bond, a collusion, a oneness. But a monumental difficulty exists here for the rhetor: the collusive bond more or less shared by Blacks through several hundred years suffered severe damage during the narcissistic periods including and following the 1960s.[8] Thus, the Other must be both renegotiated and reeducated to the rhetor's understanding or knowledge even as she claims to know the Other as fellow traveler and sociocultural ally.

This rhetorical requirement is the wellspring for racial rhetorical narratives aimed at recovery, and these narratives seem to possess a characteristic form or structure. For example, consider the following case. The speaker is a prominent educator whose marriage to a Jewish man had occasioned some controversy upon her elevation to the presidency of a Black community college:

> In some ways being married to a white man has made me more sensitive to being Black. He and I have developed a relationship that respects our own backgrounds. It was us against the world. (*Boston Globe*, January 29, 1983)

This statement appears to serve as an *ex post facto* rationale and validation for miscegenation, but Blacks are not necessarily of one spirit, kind, or goal, as a subsequent observation shows:

> There is a schizophrenia that wants the group to get ahead but does not want individuals to go out front and does not want to accept leadership. I know what it is to be poor. I know what it is to use education for a vehicle. I know their concerns. I have worked with students over a very long time. I have been very active with Black women for policy action. I was one of the founders of the New England minority administrators.

These subsequent remarks represent an attempt to sustain the shared racial narrative of "Blacks together." The speaker begins her own "recovery project" by inferring a story with which the students are presumed to identify. This story has three features: (1) recollection of suffering and struggle to get beyond the pain of an undeserved plight (in this case poverty); (2) discovery of a vehicle (education) that enabled the narrator to overcome the externally imposed barriers to full growth and fulfillment; and (3) successful reintegration with the group achieved through discovering the folly of remaining loyal to a past racial ideology rather than one based on character and choice.

In this illustration, the rhetor renegotiates the meaning of the students' concern by first exposing their flawed racial ideology, then recasting their concerns in terms of educational and class advancement. She thus seeks to induce them to identify their own concerns not as a continuity of racial traditions against miscegenation but rather in terms of the traditional emphasis on education and class advancement. In a sense, she says to her readers or listeners, "Successes are yours as they have become mine, but you must first disidentify with the flawed racial ideology that insists we all act in concert. Moreover, if you do this, you may even discover, as I did, that you will learn to care even more for your race than you might otherwise."

This rhetor also cited a paradox characterizing the rhetorical narrative: her husband has been less threatening and more helpful to her racial self-development than Blacks. For her, marriage across racial lines helped her to become "more sensitive"[9] to her race.

The implicit theory of persuasion in the rhetorical narrative is that the listener *knows and can be influenced by* a narrative that includes these facts:

(1) the in-group is not a monolithic whole and has competing, often contradictory loyalties;

(2) all group members have experienced these contradictions at one time or another as a violation of personal racial commitment; and

(3) experiences with non-Blacks, notably whites, are often more liberating (enabling recovery of freedom as a "human" rather than as a "Negro") than remaining loyal to previous racial mandates, whether imposed from within or externally.

This implicit theory of recovery rhetoric implies that the listener also "wishes to be free" of the constraints of race and can see himself or herself mirrored in the rhetor. Yet it relies on a structure that is both privatized and heroic. This important paradox explains the need for persuasion and the danger of rhetorical failure. The rhetor must both insult and induce the Other by pinpointing a shared flaw (as Blacks) that may help free the rhetor or expose her or him as selfish and opportunistic. This paradox emerged in the previous example where the rhetor said that the race wants to keep the individual from moving ahead. To be successful, this rhetor must quicken recognition in the audience around Black intragroup weaknesses, particularly the tendency to be ambivalent about individual success that takes the individual away from traditional forms of racial loyalty. But it is precisely because mainstream Blacks must generally succeed on terms defined by whites that the racial group fears individual success and defines it, at times unfairly, as "Black opportunism."

Thus, the rhetorical narrative may fail because Blacks who break with the tradition do so under conditions defined largely by whites; therefore, their actions become problematic, and their recovery rhetoric — stories of victory over oppression — is weakened. What the rhetor ignored as she sought to redefine the meaning of the students' attitudes is this: the group's behavior springs from the ever-present fact that "Black opportunism" is often required for "Black success" within a white-dominated society. Thus, her allusion to education and miscegenation as nonracial and nonrelevant factors was problematic. At some level, she knew that separating from the group and joining (colluding) with the white man, "the Oppressor" of Blacks, compromise the historical myths Blacks forged as a reaction to a racism and oppression that change over time but remain far from diminished or defeated. In fact, the need to deny or downplay this persistent fact makes the narrative "rhetorical" and creates the possibility of rhetorical failure, the possibility that the action and stance will not be believable. It is, after all, difficult for Blacks who have experienced racism to believe there are Blacks who have not had this experience.

Nowhere has this possibility of rhetorical failure been more evident recently than in the debate that surrounded Clarence Thomas, President George Bush's nominee to the Supreme Court. Blacks divided over Thomas's nomination according to whether or not they identified with his recovery narrative: a strong Catholic upbringing and a supportive family committed to the "American work ethic" were all he needed to attain the American dream. Those who could not identify with this story were likely to be those focused on an alternative (and implied) narrative: Thomas is an opportunist.[10] They read betrayal in his decision to become a Black conservative and serve a president and party that have reversed previous governmental policies enacted on the behalf of minorities, notably Blacks.

Privatization and Heroism in the Recovery Narrative

Racism persists, opportunism remains an ever-present issue, and the recovery narrative must transcend these facts. This is where heroism occurs in two ways. First, the African-American hero is oppositional. Sherley Williams, in *Give Birth to Brightness,* says: "Heroism for Black Americans has always meant some measure of revolt against social structures, for these were the instruments of their oppression rather than their protection" (Williams 1972, 57–58).[11]

Second, the hero forges a bridge between the immutable contradictions of life, creating a passage for those to follow. We would do well to understand this heroism. It is a dramatic rather than a static force. It has no existence until the rhetor is challenged enough to narrate and explain a persuasive vision of herself or himself. Thus, heroism represents an effort to make the privatized vision, the lived experience of recovery, meaningful to the Other. To describe this process and the relationship between privatization and heroism in the recovery narrative, I turn at this point to the three narratives presented in part III, elaborating on these themes of privatization and heroism and indicating how they both contribute to and compromise rhetorical success and failure.

PART III

Narrative as Recovery: Three Cases

❖

The formation of an oppositional world view is necessary for feminist struggle. This means that the world we have most intimately known, the world in which we feel "safe" (even if such feelings are based on illusions) must be radically changed. Perhaps it is the knowledge that everyone must change, not just those we label enemies or oppressors, that has so far served to check our revolutionary impulses. Those revolutionary impulses must freely inform our theory and practice if feminist movement to end existing oppression is to progress, if we are to transform our present reality.

—bell hooks, *Feminist Theory: From Margin to Center*

Preface to Part III

The case material used in part III is taken from a psychological study
of racial commitment attitudes and actions among a sample of Black
women (Gresson 1985b). In so-called empirical research it is custom-
ary to describe one's sample or collaborators in great detail, indicating
who they are and in what ways they resemble the persons who might
read their stories or the more general population. While I do not intend for these case materials to be read as empirical evidence or proof, it
may nonetheless be helpful to describe briefly how I gathered these case
materials and precisely how I have used them here.

In the earlier study I set out to find a diverse range of women with
respect to age, education, career, politics, and sexuality. They came from
diverse backgrounds and experiences. The selection of my collaborators
was based on the following two general rationales:

Heterogeneity. Blacks are a diverse population despite the politics
and racist history that force them into a single cohort. Increasingly,
Black social scientists demand that research reflect this diversity as a
means of both differentiating among Blacks and moving toward greater
representativeness of the samples used for inquiries (Engram 1982). In
short, we know that Blacks hold a wide range of views, values, and attitudes about themselves and their relationships with the rest of humanity
(Jackson, McCullough, and Gurin 1981; R. S. Jones 1980; 1983). My
study included participants presumed to hold different views regarding
commitment in several domains: self, sexuality, family, parenting, and
career. Educationally, they ranged from high school graduates to holders
of terminal academic and professional degrees. Economically, they came
from diverse backgrounds and maintained widely differing lifestyles,
financially speaking. Some of the women were single and had never married; others were divorced; some had children and some had none; some
were religious and some were not. Some had Black mates; others had
white mates. Sexual preferences also varied across the collaborators. The
ages ranged from nineteen to sixty.

Work Type. The scholarly and popular literatures have proved conflictive and contradictory regarding the influence of class and color
complexion on Black self–Other differentiation and racial identity commitment (Staples 1973; Wilson 1978). Gilkes (1982) did find class-
related variables — family background, education, and income — to
be significant with respect to when particular Black women entered
community work. Thus, class as a work type (Eisenstein 1979) was
a selection criterion. Specifically, the participants were selected from

five diverse work-related populations in deference to Zillah Eisenstein, who argued that "a feminist class analysis must begin with distinctions drawn among women in terms of the work they do within the political economy as a whole" (p. 14). The following is a breakdown of the collaborators according to work type: (1) *Welfare* is considered a work category in the radical feminist literature; this category included women who were employed at home and received general relief as the sole means of support for themselves and their children. (2) *Manual laborers,* blue-collar workers, and general laborers were included in the same category. (3) *Students* pertained to full-time undergraduates and graduate students. (4) *Self-made professional* referred to women with no college or special training who held semiprofessional or professional positions as a result of working themselves up the career ladder. This category included office managers, research associates, personnel managers, and sales managers. (5) *Professionals* referred to women with a college degree or specialty certificate prior to full-time employment.

The Interviews

I interviewed more than fifty women; most were interviewed between June 1982 and July 1984. Some were referred to me by friends and families, and others were self-selected because of an interest in the study or because they wanted an opportunity to share their thoughts. Three additional women were interviewed in 1989. Two of them were reinterviewees. All but three were living in the New England region. These three lived in the Midwest. Conversations with fifteen additional women about various parts of the study enriched and broadened my understanding of the initial interviews.

I selected these collaborators after initiating contact with female psychologists, community and organizational leaders, and friends. Using this reputational approach, I informed potential participants of the purpose of the study and invited them to participate. Several persons were recruited by collaborators who, after being interviewed, felt that a particular person would provide an "interesting" interview. This recruitment process illustrates the collaborative aspect; it also indicates how many of the women provided behavioral clues to their own issues around and perceptions of commitment. For example, a fifty-five-year-old mother suggested I interview her youngest daughter, a twenty-six-year-old, indicating that she did not understand why her daughter dated so many non-Black males. The mother, just interviewed, reported that she had once dated a white man but found that she did not like white men as intimates. The daughter, in turn, suggested that

I interview her cousin, whom she considered particularly interesting: the cousin did not date Black men at all; she was engaged to a white male (she later married him). Interestingly, each of these collaborators revealed her sense of propriety and the boundaries of enlargement: the mother could deal intimately only with Black men; the daughter could date white men (she later had her first child by a white and then married a Black) but would not abandon intimacy with Black men; the cousin would not deal at all with Black men and chose a white mate.

As indicated earlier under "work type," class was the only control feature I used to categorize the participants. I based this sampling decision on Gilkes (1982), who found in her qualitative study of twenty-five Black women that the most salient variable differentiating her sample of popularly recognized community leaders appeared to be class origin. That is, family background, income, and education differentiated between those women whose community-oriented commitments followed a "focused education" period and those whose commitments seemed to be linked more to their roles as mothers. Gilkes designated these the "rebellious professionals" and "mobile mothers," respectively (p. 292). Similarly, my study sampled welfare mothers as a work category because of evidence that bore on commitment orientations: Marlene Chrissinger's (1980) study of welfare mothers who worked and those who did not led her to argue that a "culture of mobility" rather than a "culture of poverty" was operative; that is, women seemed disposed to work when they felt that to do so would significantly alter their situations or the opportunities for their families (p. 44).

In conclusion, I used the sampling procedures discussed here to expedite the theoretical work and to join the growing number of respected researchers who challenge the adequacy of classical research techniques for answering certain types of questions, particularly with minority populations or individuals (Engram 1982).

The Three Cases

In the present instance, I have chosen parts of three women's interviews to illustrate ideas developed in part II. One characteristic of qualitative research is its *inductiveness* — it encourages the formulation of hypotheses and generalizations from an examination of the data (Merriam 1988). In this instance, the three women help illustrate the nature of recovery, particularly its specific relevance to the complex loyalties racism generates for African-Americans. These cases present specific, particular perspectives on racial matters and reflect individual solutions and strategies for survival. The case material also helps identify clues to the dynamics and experiences relevant to the formulation of a formal recovery theory, which I present in chapter 7. The thoughts and insights of these women are used as the basis for the dimensions and dynamics depicted in the theory of recovery discourse.

The women are presented in the specific contexts that seem most relevant to their lives and interpretations of their experiences. The social environment — family, work, school, friends — is used as the basis for analysis of the cases. But I do not confine my discussion to their social and cultural settings; I try to relate these to the broad recovery agenda described in parts I and II. In this way I seek to contextualize the theory itself.

I have chosen two women who had children by white males and one woman who, at the time, was reassessing her relationships with both Black males and females. I do not intend for these cases to be representative of all Black women or even all Black women in similar situations. Not all Black women interpret their bad experiences with other Blacks as conditions for interracial mating or disenchantment with the race. The ways in which Blacks or any category of people respond to seemingly similar events and experiences will vary greatly; even the same individual may act differently in a certain situation at different times in her or his life. I chose these cases and have emphasized certain parts of the interviews because they best dramatize the complex issues associated with "racial collusion" — a theme introduced earlier in a statement I cited from Audre Lorde's interview with Adrienne Rich in 1981 (see p. 67, above).

These cases, by highlighting the presence and complexity of Black vulnerability, provide clues to the discursive tasks characterizing loss and recovery in racial discourse. And since it is with regard to miscegenation that the most painful inter- and intraracial "narcissistic wounds" are inflicted, I have focused on cases that expose the raw emotions of guilt and shame.

One final note: each of the three cases begins with a description placing the individual within the sociocultural context relevant to the emphases I forefront in her story. I then present selected segments of each woman's thoughts and experiences, categorized according to the three themes shaping the recovery discourse. My analysis is embedded in both my questions and the commentary I present after the narrative proper. Thus, the case material is both unavoidably and intentionally "contaminated" by my presence and motives.

4

Monique:
The Self-Metaphor in Narrative Discourse

❖

As a Black woman who has a choice between Black and white men, I prefer to date white men, and I do not have any misgivings about my decision. Why should I or any other woman who chooses to date men of the "opposite race" be ostracized or scorned? I have been accused of turning my back on the Black race a number of times. . . . Many Black men . . . exaggerate their oppression in order to gain a woman's sympathy and exploit her emotions, transforming her into a passive shadow that ultimately is left alone to struggle, suffer, and weep. I and many other Black women cannot and will not get involved in these games. Why should we be condemned? To whom are we doing harm?
— Linda White (1977)

Background of the Narrative

The Inheritance

In *Afrocentricity,* Molefi Asante (1988) invokes memory of the traditional love of Afrocentric woman and man. He speaks of the "collective consciousness" they share, steeped in history and African culture, a sharing that sustains and permeates their mutual care and deeply spiritual intimacy. His vision is hardly all myth, as many, many couples know. But one can hear discordant voices.

Linda White uttered the unutterable truth of the schism (see the epigraph, above). As an individual, White has made a choice, a choice that feels right for her, a choice that allows her room to grow, expand, survive. And yet her "choice" is not entirely a private matter. So often we conceal the fact, but on occasion our choices as private matters are ex-

78

posed in all of their collective and historical wretchedness. This is the point where the casting off of the yoke of traditional racial identification signals a break in the collusive bond. Linda White understands this tradition.

Linda White inherited a particular kind of legacy as a Black woman. To suggest this is not to indulge essentialist (Black patriarchal) fantasy or to invoke a totalizing gendered mandate of racial uplift. I mean only to rehearse Audre Lorde's insight into the collusive nature of the racial bond once accepted — nay, created — by a "critical mass" of Black women and men. It is this tradition that Linda White has inherited and that compels her to speak through the pages of *Essence* magazine.

To choose white men as cherished intimates is a decision some Black women may have made from the first instance they saw a "white" man; the choice is a decisive break with the bond and bondage of Black womanhood. It cannot be ignored. It must be addressed. How it is addressed becomes the rhetorical situation.

Linda White may — and must — exercise choice as a free Black woman and a free human being. The rhetoric of personal choice, however, provides an inadequate explanation for the miscegenation she exercises, just as it is an inadequate explanation for the Black men who exercise it. White knew she had to find some other means of persuading both herself and those others who have held her accountable for her choice of white.

Linda White's statement offers an incipient narrative. She begins to identify herself as violated and betrayed. Her questions, while essentially rhetorical, are unpersuasive. She has disavowed the need to suffer as a Black woman, as a committed member of an oppressed race. She "jumps ship." Hers is no doubt a true story, but it is not a good story. It fails to persuade us that the choice, the decision, came as an act of racial love. It lacks the essential redemptive feature. To see her choice as justified from a racial perspective, we must "feel with her" that any other choice but the one she made would have violated the collective spirit. She must make us feel her need to move beyond the tradition. Her failure, however, may reflect the limitations of nonnarrative exposition. A full narrative account might be more persuasive.

Indeed, in narratives of recovery one can often plot the passage from violation and betrayal to recovery through discovery. This is the part of the story that carries the persuasive power. In the previous chapter, I identified the "self-metaphor" as the rhetorical strategy normally used in this task of recovery. In her narrative, Monique demonstrates the role of the self-metaphor in the recovery project.

The Rhetorical Situation

I met Monique in 1988. She is a beautiful woman and a stylish dresser with a magnetic personality. She comes from a rural region with a relatively large Black population whose history goes back to the Underground Railroad and the Civil War. Monique is the youngest girl in a family with seven children, four females and three males. She was thirty-three at the time of our interview, older and more mature than most of the students in her teacher-education program. Nonetheless, she related with them well. Monique was also a leader in her home community, teaching Sunday school and serving as a spokesperson for her co-residents in the public housing complex where she resided with her son while attending school full-time.

While I knew that Monique had a seven-year-old son, she only later revealed that his father is a white male. Initially, in fact, she had indicated him to be a mulatto. Monique's rhetorical plight was complex and difficult, though far from atypical: she was trying to legitimize returning to the Black community with a biracial child whom she wanted to celebrate as biracial. Such a desire implies a powerful rhetorical reversal: the son was both Black and non-Black, both a "little boy" and a "special breed."

This is hardly a new plight for Blacks, but Monique did enlarge the familiar circumstance. She wanted her child, who once would have been considered simply Black, to be considered biracial. Before the resurgence of miscegenation during the radical 1960s and 1970s, biracial children were celebrated, if at all, as Black. But Monique placed value on "whiteness," or at least on one white male; and she had a large part of her own selfhood invested in the racial designation of both the father and son. I attributed Monique's urgency in this matter to the fact that she would no longer date white males and had found few Black males who, in her opinion, wanted to establish a permanent bond with her given her "biracial" rather than "Black" son.[1]

The Rhetorical Issues

This narrative addresses two rhetorical issues: at the personal and existential level, Monique's task was to persuade me, first, that her choices were both natural and hard-won and, second, that her contradictions were no greater than my own and those of other Black men who once dated white women. Her rhetorical task was to render null and void the differential implications of relationships between Black males and white females and between white males and Black females, even though the Black female, in this instance, was the one who bore a "man-child" whom she prefers to see as biracial rather than Black. At the collective and public level, Monique had to address her desire to emphasize her son's biracial parentage in an essentially Black community. She had to induce me, a representative of the race, to believe that her son is a special person, the "Black person of the future," and that her celebration of him was not attributable to a biological linkage to his white father but to an incipient "new world order."

From the recovery perspective of rhetorical success, she had to tell a sensible story, one in which a listener could share her knowledge of violation and betrayal, her journey through accumulating pain, and her arrival at an ultimate commitment to help others with her knowledge and experience.

The Narrative as Recovery Discourse

Loss, Violation, and Withdrawal

Monique felt dual violations at the hands of men, and she felt, as well, two distinct losses. First, shamed by the rejection of a Black man and feeling like an "unattractive failure" as a result, she "fell in love with a white male" after the undisclosed betrayal by the Black boyfriend. The second violation and loss involved the white male lover. In narratives involving betrayal dynamics, the precipitating events often emerge only later in the discourse (Gresson 1982). This was the case with Monique.

> I was in love with him and unfortunately he was white. I don't want it said that my preference was not for a Black man. I fell in love with someone. It was assumed I would have one [a Black male]. I think that it was a rebound situation. I can't explain it—it happened. I was seventeen, and he was sixteen...very young....He was my first everything....How could I find this blue-eyed thing? [Laugh] Gosh! [Pause] What happened is that it was a church affair, and he was with a group, and me being in church always, and it went on from there: his college days, my working days, and eventually to our son, the engagement, and the unfortunate incident on his part. My family and friends were accepting of him....This was not uncommon in the community. Well, yes,...some Black families saw that as the ultimate taboo, especially when there were so many available Black males. So many Black men you could be with, how could you?

Monique presented her first loss as the one that led toward "this blue-eyed thing." Thus, her white lover was a means, in part, of recovering from the loss of a Black male; she simultaneously saw, however, a chance to escape the Black man in general. But she conveyed this choice

only under pressure when she conceded that her behavior was unac-
ceptable in the Black community, especially when there were so many
available Black males.

Telling her story to a Black male (like living in a Black world) somewhat qualified Monique's discussion of Black men, but her feelings seem
clear enough. Her sense of Black male failure appeared in her narrative
of Black male behavior toward white females (with whom, ironically,
she did identify):

> Less than forty hours ago I observed a situation in a bar. And the Black
> guy to me he had no respect for her whatsoever. When they came in the
> door, there was only one bar stool available, and he took it and she had to
> stand.

Her withdrawal from Black males appeared in the same portrayal when
she contrasted the white male–Black female couples with the Black
male–white female couples:

> I have known some [white men] who treat them [Black women] as their
> partner, their equal. They show them the utmost respect. Uh, she is not
> docile, she is not a servant. She is someone who he truly cares about in
> his way. But on the other side of the coin where Black men are concerned,
> maybe that is his way. Maybe that is his way of treating the white woman
> as his partner, his equal. Maybe I am wrong to judge him, but I personally
> look at it from the viewpoint that I don't want to be treated like that. If
> she [the white woman] looks at it as acceptable, it's okay. I have seen them
> whip them, and nine out of ten times we are talking about whipping her
> in the bar, then going home to her home.

Monique here identified the basis for her racial withdrawal and disidentification. Her self-love and survival instincts told her that she did
not wish to be mistreated. So, although she "fell in love," she did too
"fall away" from the Black male as love object. Her stance is like Linda
White's quoted at the start of this chapter. In this logic of self-love and
survival, moreover, we see the road to Monique's share in the self-love
and recovery project called for by Audre Lorde. She thereby converges
with other Black women and emerges as Black Woman where Black
Woman equals heroine. Black Woman is heroine, and Monique is Black
Woman.

Earlier we saw that this use of the heroine notion appears commonly
in Black female recovery discourse, and here it is in Monique's narrative.
Later, we shall see that this notion of self, linked to the idea of education
as a path to recovery (recall the Black woman administrator introduced
in the last chapter), enabled Monique rhetorically to convince herself

and attempt to persuade me that she is a heroine. For now, however, the important point is that Monique transcended her privatized experience and perspective because she identified a common foe: the Black man — a man who treats both Black and white women badly, a man who does not deserve a Black woman, a man who just might (recall J. A. Gardner's words in chapter 1) be a "sexist bastard or worse." But Monique's rhetorical identification with Black Woman as heroine is more complex than merely defining the Black male as villain.

Black Woman — and Monique — is characterized by a self-survival vision and is thus different from the white female who has stood for what Black Woman — Monique — would suffer from neither a white male whom she loved (and whose son she bore) nor some Black male whom her family and race expected her to choose. Her story also presents her as different from the white male, who remains ensnared in the Black Woman *mystique,* and the Black male, who is liable to treat women, Black and white, as less than human.

Monique wants to see herself, as Black Woman, untainted by a desire for the white man as "white." In this self-view, she differs from the white man and woman who remain trapped in stereotypic and depraved associations with Blacks: the white man sees the Black woman as mystique; the white woman permits herself to be misused by the Black man; and the Black man mistreats both Black and white women.

Monique also differentiates herself from her Black girlfriend who chooses a white male and consciously employs "the mystique." Monique, as Black Woman, is "the cream of the crop":

> In that particular instance, . . . she is not "the cream of the crop" of Black women. To me, she is the type of woman who fills the stereotypical belief of white men about Black women, a myth: that we are quick to go.

The Monique of this narrative is a proud Black woman. She has strong and positive feelings for Black women: her mother, her sisters, the women in the church. She conveys a conviction that Black women who choose white men have a right to do so, but they must not violate the ideal that permits them to break with tradition: their humanness, their right to be respected, and their right to be treated like ladies. Monique's friend failed by her willingness to let a white man mistreat her, to permit his white wife and her therapist to humiliate her.

Earlier I introduced Eartha and her cousin, two other women who chose white males. Eartha also told a story in which she defined herself as Black Woman by disidentifying with certain other miscegenational Black women. In both Monique's and Eartha's cases, this violation allowed the narrators to tell stories of both racial differentiation and continuity of racial identity and pride. In her report of her refusal to be mistreated by a white man, Monique tried to persuade the listener that she was still a "good Black woman" and, therefore, still worthy of connection to the race. (Eartha tried to convey a similar continuity and connection by suggesting that her willingness to forgive Black men their transgressions — even though she was choosing white — was qualitatively different from her cousin's stance. Neither woman was totally persuasive, as we shall see in the next chapter.) The problem is a contradiction all Blacks influenced by white aesthetics share: the desire for some part of "whiteness." Monique revealed a collective racial tension. *The Pan-African legacy in the diaspora makes all Blacks vulnerable to this tension regardless of their personal preferences, shade of skin color, or texture of hair.*

As this tension pertains to Monique, I recall that Frantz Fanon said the woman of color must have felt something special the day a white man chose her for his mate. Yet Monique's mate's behavior undermined her rhetorical stance of transracialism; he unintentionally brought her to the truth of her own imagination and shame. She had sought to escape her "Blackness" even as she used it as Black Woman. But the protest that race has become irrelevant remains too great a lie, too great a jump. Monique wants to be Black and human, but what did she find? Her lover, too, was enthralled by *Blackness*. The evidence is so clear that even Monique must confess, "Even now his preference is a Black woman." He is entranced by Black Woman.

Although Black Woman is as much a myth as "the Man," Miss Anne, and Uncle Tom, myths motivate and move humans. Monique is a Black woman, but only one among many that her lover as white man can have. Perhaps in this realization hides the unconscious meaning of "mystique." Monique's mate objectified her; she was not subject. Thus, she felt thrust back into Blackness. She knows that all white men are not like this man, but this knowledge did her no good, for her true pursuit has been forever deflected: she is Black, and, integration notwithstanding, she fears forever being thrust into her Blackness by a white male.

As I said above, Monique's plight is hardly unusual. Many white men abuse their women, including their Black women. But the hopeful rhetoric in miscegenation is that the new comrade, the new intimate Other, is a "human" and "the one." Monique, however, could not apply this rhetoric to her miscegenation. Her mate's "failure" closed a door. She must return, according to her personal values, to the Black community.

She cannot say, like the college administrator in the previous chapter, that a mixed marriage helped make her more caring for Blacks. Rather, she must say that the betrayal has rendered her vulnerable to the original source of her loss and violation. Still, she knows how to achieve a kind of recovery.

Recovery through Discovery

Monique is a remarkably traditional Black female. She values religion, family, and education highly, along with the continuity of "racial up-lift" through one's personal achievements and service to the community. Monique's recovery from experimentation with "the forbidden fruit" is intricately linked to her traditionalism. Indeed, her story of "the fall," to extend her imagery, is steeped in such traditionalism: she met her first lover and "fell in love" in church, where she spent much time. Her recovery must return her to the traditional, yet as with her loss, it must address both Black and white males as failures.

First, she must recover her loss of face occasioned by her white fiancé choosing another Black female. Second, but relatedly, she must recover her place within the Black community. Thus, her recovery pertains to a twofold experience: the loss of Black women as cherished "girlfriends" and the discovery of education as a means to stay free of the Black man. She achieved the first of these recoveries through her *discovery that her lover saw her as mystique.* She achieved the second through an *enlargement of her self-definition of Black Woman in terms of the traditional role of savior.* In fact, this latter achievement contextualized her recovery. Because she returned to the Black community with a biracial baby and could not find a "suitable" Black male who wanted to be a "biracial father," she stood apart from other Black and white women who must deal with the "local brothers." Indeed, she observed that

> these white women are without education, and I...have sympathy for them. I feel that they have an anchor around their neck, and I have an interest in women like them because I feel that there is something out there for you — you do not have to feel trapped.

Ironically, Monique rediscovered the traditional Black way of avoiding the wretchedness of being trapped: education. Yet she seemed neither to make nor to feel a connection between her strong empathy for white women and their plight and her own heroism — her own self-metaphor as savior (and survivor). More exactly, she did not attribute her self-perceived heroism to the fact that she — unlike them — crossed the "color line"; gained the prize of the journey, a "special breed" of child;

and returned home to find Black men who do not routinely mistreat her. Her failure to understand her own enmeshment in their pain is, interestingly, conveyed in her lament that the Black men who have gone across the color line and returned do not want her because, unlike her, they have not brought back a biracial child, at once a prize and burden:

> I have encountered Black males who cannot deal with the fact that I have a biracial child. The ones I have dealt with have had relationships with Black and white women, but they have not had a child through the relationship, so they can't deal with it. They find it hard to be a father to a child by a white man because of the identity problem: "What color is this kid?" And it bothers me because I feel that they can't look beyond the fact [and see] that he is a little boy — that she is a little girl — even if her father was white.

Moreover, because she still emotionally and symbolically operates within the "white world," though she lives in a Black neighborhood, her recovery remains in flux: she is caught between the Black male who mistreats his (white and Black) women and the white male who prefers Black Woman and perceives her as a *mystique* and is therefore unable to be faithful only to her. So Monique's recovery is truncated, as we can see in her self-metaphors that, however, yield an ironic twist.

Rhetorical Analysis

The Self

Monique employed two self-metaphors to soothe and reintegrate herself into the Black community:

1. *Black Woman as Mystique.* The logic underlying Monique's openness to "falling in love" with a white man is that "racial integration" equals a destruction of racial myths and motives. Monique, like many Americans, chose to emphasize the obvious racial advances of the past two decades while underestimating the strong continuity in attitudes and actions along racial lines. This type of denial enabled her to rationalize her behavior as "just" falling in love since this type of response presumably goes beyond the control of the individual. After all, he was in her church, and she went all the time, and thus she was vulnerable to what her church, historically Black, has welcomed through its open doors. But she did not see her fiancé's behavior as a personal — that is, a nonracial — misfortune. She was unable to go on with her life and find another white male despite her obvious attraction to white men and their interest in her. For her, all white male interest became a response

to *mystique.* Thus, she said: "Perhaps it is unfairness on my part, [but] I think a lot of it is because I have been hurt by a white guy."

Monique experienced pain and had to make sense of her choice in terms of that pain. Additionally, she had to validate her refusal to pursue other white male mates (since, in most respects, she clearly prefers them), and she had to offer some viable reason for turning toward Black males, about whom she had few positive things to say. (I must note here that Monique is certainly able and willing to acknowledge the admirable qualities of individual Black males; it is only the Black Male as category that she denigrates.) She attempted to undertake these tasks by focusing on the plight of the white female. In this presentation, Monique herself evolved as both equivalent and superior to the white female. She is a Black Woman; she is also a savior.

2. *Black Woman as Savior.* Monique's initial burden was Black men; it then became white men. Men, in general, have violated her and taken from her. Black men, collectively, could not provide her the same social status as a (Black) woman as white men can offer (white) women. But white men, collectively, cannot deliver her equity with the white woman, blinded as (Monique believes) they are by the myth of the Black Woman as *mystique.* Consequently, she had to recover from the white man part of what she gave him after her failure with the Black male: self-respect.

Who, then, is Monique's audience? White females. Notice her apparently incongruous pronouncement: "These white women are without education, and I . . . have sympathy for them. I feel that they have an anchor around their neck, and I have an interest in women like them because I feel that there is something out there for you — you do not have to feel trapped."

Monique both identified with certain white women and saw herself as their "role model" in the struggle to conquer the difficulties inherent in a single-parent, biracial family. Her fascination with white women, particularly those who have suffered at the hands of Black men, is apparent. Her connection with them comes through her shared experience at the hands of both Black and white men, and her personal discovery and recovery are her "gifts" to them: "*Education,* the point system, self-sufficiency — it's a way out of the abuse and neglect. *The answer is not a man.*"

Monique seldom applied her disgust with Black males directly to herself; she continued to castigate them solely in terms of their abuse of white women — women whom she can feel superior to because she, despite her skin color, "chocolate," is not "door mattable":

I am just saying that they seem door mattable to me as if all they have ever known is this — and including the white men they were with before they came to Black men. It is a cycle. "Well," they say, "this is what I deserve," and once they get it from a white man and they encounter a Black relationship and it is the same thing over again, they begin to believe that "this is what is due me," and I don't believe that.

Here Monique described her own story of recovery.[2] It seems, though, she had first to tell it through a focus on white women. Monique validated her break with traditional intraracial mating behavior and her subsequent rejection of white males by identifying herself as white women's "heroine." Ironically, she redefined the notion of mystique to mean not "sexual mystery" but "survival mystery." Hence, we see her true recovery is from the Black man. Her perceived heroism thus becomes more sharply focused as a model of how a "biracial mother" (a condition she shares with white women) avoids Black male abuse.

In a subsequent discussion, Monique reported that she felt "funny" around the women in her community because they considered her different. I asked who these women were. She said, "Mostly the white women who are single parents like me. They see me going to school and doing well. They think that I am someone special, not human like them."[3] But what of the Black women in Monique's life? How do they figure as the Other?

The Other

Monique mentioned two Black women in her narrative: two friends who behaved as "stereotyped" Black women. Each gave herself to a white man — but under conditions that Monique sees as "stereotypical." Monique has a complex, if not a confused, understanding of Black women as they affect her life. They are betrayers of Black Woman. Monique distinguishes herself from other Black women who love white men by her insistence upon respect: Black Woman equals self-respect.

These two friends' apparent lack of self-respect reinforced Monique's sense of both mistrust and superiority. Still, Monique, too, expressed, under some encouragement, her own fascination with the white body and a belief in the *white mystique*. She even confessed that she could identify with those Black women who gave themselves to white men sexually: "My lover was extremely wonderful. . . . He was incredible. I am not going to take anything from him. . . . He was incredible."

Yet Monique also feels competitive with Black women for Black men. She is friendly with the Black women in her community, but they are not her close friends. Indeed, she believes they experience her as a competitor because she is beautiful, better educated than most of these Black women, and working to get beyond the downward pull of a depressed environment.

What makes Monique's relationship with Black women interesting is that she views them very much as she views white women who mate with Black men: as victims. This is true for her sisters — except one, whose Black mate she considers a special Black man — as well as other women. Thus, while she deals with Black women, cares for them, and senses their sisterhood, so to speak, she remains removed or isolated from them.[4]

Their victimization notwithstanding, Monique does not see herself as a savior of adult Black women. She did not speak of influencing them to change, even though she faithfully defends and speaks for specific Black women in her community. She does not have a child by a Black man like the other Black women. Her son is "biracial" like the white women who choose Black men. One can infer her disidentification with the Black women in her community from passing references to "the cream of the crop" and to the Black community's ambivalent reactions to her son. But something important lies just beneath the surface here: her son is her link to the larger world. She alludes to her son as a "special breed." But she is the primary member of the "special breed," the trailblazer. Hence, it is not precisely "whiteness" she seeks, but that place beyond color domination. In this, moreover, she is like many who are seeking to get beyond essentialism.

For young Black females, moreover, she considers herself a role model and works hard to maintain this image, especially in her church and community. Perhaps this behavior reflects the fact that they could easily become women who would be trailblazers like her. Young, developing, heirs to a changing world, and blessedly free of the baggage of Black men, they best stand a chance of going beyond the traditional borders of Black womanhood. To feel this way about and hope this way for the young Black female suggests that Monique has little use for Black men.

The Black male, however, remains a complex Other for Monique. Black men, her several brothers included, are fascinating and attractive to her, especially those men who have successfully entered the American mainstream. But they frighten her because their adaptation, including a perceived preference for white women, to a white, male-dominated society leaves her little hope of finding a mutually respectful and loving mate. She sees Black men, in general, mistreating Black women.[5] Yet Monique's father and her brothers are all loving, strong men who provide for their families and are respected in the community. And she loves them even though she fears their power over Black women.

Like Eartha's and Andria's, Monique's narrative is closely linked to her contradictory experiences with Black men. Thus, she wants to find a Black man who is powerful yet malleable. She wants a Black man who will resolve the contradiction in her return to the Black community. Ironically, she wants a traditional Black man who accepts her as a nontraditional Black woman with a nontraditional child. She expresses her major sympathy for Black women in this context:

> I feel very strongly for Black women who have crossed that line because you know that it is not just you yourself anymore. You are talking about a child who is between two cultures. And I feel personally that coming home, so to speak, to my race again... is very important. I don't feel that there is anything wrong by a Black woman who chooses to have children by a white father.

This is a complex statement. It points to a critically important idea: *even those Blacks who disidentify with racial history and continuity of commitment may contradict themselves in a crisis situation and seek precisely the support they have denied relevant to their lives.* This behavior is generally associated with adolescence: the young adult-to-be wants to be independent of the parents yet retain their commitment and support.

Monique shares aspects of this tendency, as do most Blacks who disidentify with the racial past within a still-racist society. In Monique's case, this tendency expresses itself in a paradoxical fashion: she wants her child to be more than Black yet Black, too. She wants to be free of the Black man yet depend upon him to rescue her from the white male. Although Monique has rejected one type of Black male — those who mistreat their women — she seeks another from her cultural past: the Black father who historically acknowledged all degrees of Blackness as Black for the sake of the race. Indeed, it is her father who serves as the father to her son: her father is the Black man in her son's life.

This is an immense irony. But this is not an unusual event: many biracial children are being raised by grandparents or parent surrogates with contrasting racial identities and heritages. In the commitment study, several Black women similarly relied on their fathers: their fathers served as surrogate fathers for their biracial sons in the absence of the white fathers. In these cases, the white male had been chosen but ultimately failed to provide the Black woman an alternative culture and community; and these women returned to the Black community that had been left behind. But Monique's allusion to her son's being caught between two cultures must be recognized as referring less to his reality than to the one that she has imagined for him by insisting that he is not Black even though his world is Black. It is this understanding of the Other as son that allows us to make fuller sense of her comment: "I feel very strongly for Black women who have crossed that line because you know that it is not just you yourself anymore. You are talking about a child who is between two cultures."[6]

The notion of her son as a "special breed" becomes the Other-metaphor that allows her to reconcile him — Black and white — with his rejected ancestry. When I pressed her regarding the possibility that her son — as a "biracial white" — might in the future prefer Black women because of their "mystique," she replied that she was not sure how she would react to this, adding that she hoped she would be able to accept whatever decisions he made regarding Black or white mates. The point is not that Monique differs from other mothers in her ambivalence regarding her son's possible future sex-related values and choices. Rather, the issue is that her self-metaphor has a parallel with respect to her son. Moreover, this Other-metaphor renders him as much a "mystique" as she perceives herself as Black Woman to be. Finally, her desire to have him share in his father's heritage as white man (he belongs to both cultures and may choose the white one despite her alleged preference for the Black culture) opens him for adopting an alleged white male stereotype of Black women.

In both herself and son as Other-metaphors, Monique weaves a poetic and dialectical narrative of heroism. Her tribulations, her discoveries, and her contributions to others all tell a story of a human being doing heroic things. But the hero's task, managing collective and personal contradictions, provides the test for gauging rhetorical success.

Monique's Rhetorical Success and Failure

Monique chose to mate with a white man, to have his child, and to bring that child into the Black community in which she grew up, among her family and friends. She exemplifies Joseph Campbell's individual who has become the source of meaning over against group tradition. For despite her initial claim that the Black community supported her choice, she later acknowledged the negative reaction and even claimed that she would not choose to make these same choices if she had to do it over. At one level, Monique tells a powerful and compelling story by presenting incidents with which one may identify and find it difficult to take issue.

Yet Monique's rhetorical challenge transcends the simple choice to mate with a white man and have his child.

The larger rhetorical issue is to justify her return home and reintegration into a family and community she had in a significant way rejected. Her tasks were to say why her son should be treated merely as a little boy when she wants him (and herself) to be seen as a "special breed." In short, her task entails explaining away the guilt of her apparent abandonment and persisting ambivalence.

Monique fails at this task. Indeed, she must fail because the answer is too painful and too ugly for a private resolution: she wants to get beyond Black. Such a story requires an Other who likewise "forgets" and co-creates a world where skin color is meaningless. In the previous chapter, the college administrator observed that the group resists a member who goes "out in front." I suggested there that this is partly so because the Black group must suffer for this vanguard action just as all group members suffer for their leaders' growth and power and status.[7] This administrator, in fact, could say what she says only from a position of power because, unlike Monique, she had become one of the "lucky ones" who forged a new collusive bond. Recall her words: "It was us against the world." But Monique has "bad luck" linked rhetorically to the very metaphor she employs to define herself in relation the Other as white man: *mystique.*

This self-designation exposes her personal failure and its collective message: "You are truly a Black woman, a Negress; you are what we [white men] have made you and continue to perceive you to be even as we pursue, woo, seduce, and love you." This fact, reinforced by the betrayals of both her man and her Black female friend, hurls her back into Blackness, and it is within this world of contradiction that she must recover a place. Her recovery story, then, is about why she ought to be able to return home as victor.

This narrative must unfold for Monique differently than it would for a woman who has succeeded in establishing a racially mixed family, complete with loyal and loving spouse. Monique enjoys some rhetorical success with her "Black Woman as savior" metaphor. She is, after all, a traditional Black woman, and she is inclined to love and take care of family, friends, and community members. Her only "sin" was to choose the "wrong" family, friends, and community.

But her failure also relates to her narcissistic wound at the hands of her white lover: she was unable to gain the white male exclusively, and she knows she is not special to him. She is thus wounded. But she has his child, a "special breed." This is why she must keep him beyond "Blackness." He — and, therefore, she — is greater than just Black.

But ultimately she must do precisely what the earlier Blacks did: divine and devise a collusive bond of Blackness. This is the rhetorical meaning of the notion of *mystique*. Monique sought to induce the reader to join with her choice; she simultaneously celebrated and rejected her lover's bondage to the myth of the Black Woman as Sapphire or Jezebel. Thus, she actually sought connection with me, her interviewer, because of her mate's quasi-racist weakness and his infidelity: although she personally rejected him for his infidelity, she rejects other white men ostensibly because they share, as white men, this misperception of Black women. Ironically, however, she also seeks validation of her choice of mate because, she says, he was still better than the Black men she knew: he treated her like a lady; was an accomplished lover; and, even in his weakness, preferred Black women.

Self-Metaphors and the Management of Folly

Monique tells an interesting and valuable story, one in which a listener grows to appreciate her knowledge of violation and betrayal, journey through instructive pain, and arrival at an ultimate commitment to help others with her knowledge and experience. The interview gave Monique a chance to verbalize thoughts not yet fully developed and integrated in her mind. This is why she occasionally preferred to reflect on a particular question. She was aware of her feelings and beliefs, but the interview revealed their problematic features.

Nonetheless, it provided an opportunity for her to express certain opinions. First, she considers Black men "bad actors" in the game of intimacy. She prefers white men but fears their ability to wound her narcissism. Moreover, Black males are insensitive to the need for a biracial child to go in any cultural direction he or she prefers. This latter point is especially ironic because Monique wants something for her son that conflicts with her own experience and racial history.

My own collusion with Monique, an important point to recall with respect to the conditions that make recovery persuasive to the Other, is that she knows I had been married to a white woman and that I introduce the possible emergence of a community sympathetic to her stance. That, given her stance, Monique can also play to a listener is evident in this declaration: "And on a personal note, if I had to sit down and weigh it all out and if someone said, 'Would you do it again?' This is my own personal feeling interjected here. I would have to say, 'No, I would not!' "

One might consider Monique's apparent preference for a "biracial" rather than "Black" designation for her child as the logical outcome of a postmodern view. Traditionally, one would associate her value with self-hatred, but this is clearly not the only or necessarily the preferred perspective. In the postmodern worldview, the need to project a collusive racial identity undergoes close scrutiny while discussions abound regarding the question, Who is Black? Monique's attitude appears to be an example of this postmodernist style.

As a listener, I gave Monique less validation than she desired. I realized that her choice, whether she wanted to see it this way or not, was hardly private. She did not just "fall in love with a guy who happened to be white." Rather, she chose not to fall in love with a Black man, even though her community expected that choice since "there were so many available." As a Black male interviewer, I confronted her with her choice and its failure. One who seeks to understand recovery should know that "success" must become "truth." From this viewpoint, the narrative is "exploratory logic" in search of a "believer." But the narrative must be believable both to the narrator and to the listener. Monique's narrative, though not her life, is less than believable; her recovery through discovery is truncated; and her reintegration is less than complete.

Monique's narrative falters, despite its logical consistency, because of the difficulty in biculturality. She wants to break away from the group, to rush into the promised land—a place beyond race. But to do this, she must deny the very facts that propel her forth. Here Monique's behavior presaged that of Clarence Thomas during his confirmation hearings. This parallelism, moreover, is critical to the thesis of this study: the persistence of racism and the accompanying Black vulnerability render the postmodern Black a perennial candidate for contradictory behavior and attitudes. Monique and Clarence Thomas both reflect this vulnerability, and it makes their narratives problematic. Each seems to have embraced the postmodernist spirit; and each has been forced to step back from it, if only for a moment.

Postmodernism challenges the misuse of the individual. The hold the group had on the individual occasioned much destruction and damage to creativity, choice, and life. It seems fair, therefore, to permit an individual like Monique to experience and express enlarged possibilities for herself and the world community. It seems increasingly possible, moreover, to enlarge one's world vision before "social conditions" warrant it, like Black Americans trying to abandon the invisibility of exclusion for the welcome of inclusion. Recall again the behavior of Clarence Thomas. On the day following his "betrayal" by his former aide and protégée, Professor Anita Hill, he declared before the Senate Judiciary Committee, "This circus is a high-tech lynching for uppity Blacks who dare to think for themselves."

This expression of vulnerability to betrayal from both within the race and the mainstream white leadership he embraced conveys the paradoxical, if not contradictory, dimensions of a postmodern vision of racism and racial loyalty. With his words to a committee of influential white men, Thomas was, whether he understood it or not, reconnecting to the very collusive racial bond that he had sought to transcend: the bond, flawed and chauvinistic though it is, that accounts for Black survival. Even the Black postmodernist, rejecting the so-called metanarrative or superstory of racial oppressiveness and Black vulnerability, must eventually return to some version of that narrative.[8]

Thomas's effort to return failed; it lacked believability. Although many considered his references to lynchings effective, many more sensed duplicitous behavior. I consider here merely the probable outcome of an example of postmodern Black life, and Thomas's narrative failed even though his audience accepted his charge of racism. This fact is illustrated very graphically in a *USA Today* (October 14, 1991) poll, mentioned earlier, that found that more men and women believed Thomas than Hill, that more supported him than her, and that 62 percent (versus 24 percent) accepted his claim that racism was implicit in the handling of his confirmation: a success on one front, a failure on another. Recall the position of one of the Black women polled, Shawn Kennon, a thirty-two-year-old Black lawyer referred to earlier. Kennon initially supported Anita Hill and was prepared to hate Judge Thomas. Although she changed her opinion, she said: "I'm appalled at his emotionalism in trying to diffuse the issue by talking about lynch mobs" (*USA Today,* October 14, 1991, p. 2A).

Thomas's "return to Black ideology" to contextualize the events taking place at the hearings parallels Monique's return to the Black community she had essentially abandoned. Her narrative, like Thomas's, includes a certain offensiveness because her rationale for discontinuing her intimacy with white men requires her to "return to Black ideology," an ideology her choice of a white male sought to explode.

With the increasing mingling of races, it may soon be feasible to deny that "whiteness" stands apart: immensely powerful; determined to remain on top; dominating aesthetically, technologically, and politically the various races of colored people. But for the present, one cannot assume a new colored racial identity and lineage and move on with one's life unencumbered by past and present contradictions. Monique's narrative reveals the need for a believable personal sense of inherent worthiness on the part of the person of color to achieve this parity of paramours. Yet such parity generally comes through the celebration of the "reference" group, the racial group. It is difficult to move from the racial group to the dominant group on equal terms if the groups have yet to reach collective parity.

An enlarged racial identity in a racist society is difficult to achieve, as Monique graphically illustrates. She tried to go beyond the constraints of traditional African-American unity by becoming intimate with a white man, but she continued to need the support of traditional African-American unity. Thus, for the time being, she still tries to find a safe place somewhere between the "Black abuser" and the "white betrayer."

But Monique shows us something important about recovery and the implicit rhetorical theory employed in its behalf. Recovery is, ultimately, a private matter. If one can generate believable metaphors of the self and Other that soothe one and enable one to experience the self as hero — as transcender of contradictions — then one can recover something of the loss of self-respect and self-esteem.

A beautiful, courageous, and generous woman, Monique faces her weaknesses and her contradictions with determination, faith, and humor. Although some of her notions do not yet make "collective sense," they do point in a promising direction: a convergence of racial and human freedom and dignity. Ultimately, Monique's persuasive narrative powers awaken in a listener the realization that we all desire to be free, to be among the first, and to be loved.

The self–Other metaphor is the rhetorical vehicle that makes sense of the recovery posture. But the quality of this metaphoric creativity varies; and in this variance we find a clue to the persisting question of narrative evaluation: What makes a narrative persuasive? I contend here that the believability of the metaphor and its potential for enlargement are aspects of narrative persuasiveness. In the next chapter, Eartha's narrative provides a story of self-deception and privatization, two barriers to the attainment of a self-metaphor with which the Other may connect and through which the narrator may convey her heroic struggle against internal and external contradiction.

5

Eartha:

Privatization in the Narrative Experience

❖

I'm also angry that the Black man has been unwilling to admit the legitimacy of my experience as a Black woman, that he dismisses it as light stuff compared to his.

— Michele Wallace (1979)

Background of the Narrative

The Inheritance

Robert Staples (1973) implied that the forced intimacy between white slave masters and Black women, the white man's statement of total mastery, wounded Black manhood. Although many Black men found this view of intimacy between Black females and white males painful, they also, ironically, saw it as consoling — *the forced possession* of the Black man's "woman" being more endurable than her willing choice of the victorious male.

But the 1970s saw the destruction of this source of consolation. Audre Lorde's identification of the Black man as "the ex-comrade" (Lorde 1981) proposed a radically alternative story, and the primary intimacy some Black women willingly bestowed upon white men and women confounded the traditional racial myths and intrarace conjugal chauvinism.[1] Lorde understood this choice could be a "weapon" in the hands of white men and women, and she feared this vulnerability of the race to the break between Black women and men. And in the stories of Black women who have used this "weapon," we often find this fear. Such women frequently work hard to repair the damage inflicted upon the race by their miscegenational choice. If they are successful, they find acknowledgment of their efforts in conciliation and a more or less comfortable *modus vivendi*. Nonetheless, this path to rapprochement

97

is hazardous; many traps await, and obstacles may forestall the integration of the "biracial Black person" into the Black community. One danger is privatization, which is also a central rhetorical issue within the narrative.

The Rhetorical Issue

Literary scholars like Mary Helen Washington (1975) have expressed a concern for Black women's need and right to tell their own stories, whether true or fantasized. Students of rhetoric (White and Dobras 1990) have expressed a parallel concern and identify the narrative as a vehicle for empowerment. Observing the narrative's prominence, rhetoricians began to ask, "How do we determine the rhetorical legitimacy of the narrative?" (Farrell 1985).

As recovery rhetoric, the narrative poses yet another, though related, question: Does the road to recovery aid rapprochement, thereby earning its moral force? This question raises the problem of *privatization*. Privatization occurs because Blacks increasingly know both whites and Blacks as individuals. They tend less and less to see whites as "them" and Blacks as "us." Black persons isolated from the racial group have a double vulnerability: an inaccurate understanding of the subtle power of ethnicity in daily life and an ignorance of their own cultural history. They are vulnerable to establishing a privatized self-understanding, one that cannot benefit from mutual sharing and nurturance of the racial history. In short, they are vulnerable to a peculiar form of self-deception, one in which members of the race are experienced as more "racist" than members of the dominant group. Such persons then adopt the view that it is possible to juxtapose white and Black oppositionists as equal in either their oppressiveness or their power (Gresson 1992).

The rhetoric of self-recovery for persons who resort to privatization stands a good chance of a failure attributable to the fact that the narrative form adopted invites identification, if not action, beyond the narrative itself. For success, the rhetoric of recovery must be heroic, and heroism demands open and honest confrontation with the internal and external contradictions of daily life. If a narrative of recovery is to be instructive, we need to see the ways in which privatization undermines this honesty and heroic transformation. Privatization is the focus of this chapter. A young woman I call Eartha is the storyteller.

The Rhetorical Situation

I met Eartha through her mother, also named Eartha, with whom I had worked earlier. A mother of six, four daughters and two sons, the older Eartha was a vibrant, active matriarch of fifty-five. She had struggled to raise her children alone after her estranged husband, an artist, had moved to the Midwest. A high school graduate, she worked herself up into a social service, para-professional position. She was well liked and well connected in her community. A native of western Massachusetts, she reflected many of the values — including a regard for conventional success, hard work, and integration — found among many other African-Americans in New England. Eartha's mother had once dated a white male but felt uncomfortable in interracially intimate situations. She asked me to interview her daughter and said, "She is a very interesting girl [of twenty-six], very talented, but lately I've been worried about her. She is dating only white and Puerto Rican men. Her cousin, Margie, is also dating a white man. They plan to marry after graduation from Boston University. I'd be interested in what you think of Eartha."

Eartha expressed enthusiasm about the interviews and my work. She also said she thought I should interview her cousin, Margie, "who has a real problem; she only dates white guys." (Subsequently, I did talk with Margie and even counseled her white fiancé, whose mother was upset with the impending marriage.) I interviewed Eartha first in May 1982, and we had several other sessions over the next three years.

The Narrative as Recovery Discourse

Violation, Loss, and Withdrawal

Eartha was unaware of racial loss as such in her life. Yet her personal loss is indeed racial. This loss, which is both apparent and multileveled, pertains to the sacrifices her mother made to a Black man who abandoned his family; to a dead sister whose Black husband killed her with a knife with the children in the house; and to a Black boyfriend who introduced her to drugs and threatened to beat her with a belt shortly after her sister was slain. I received my first glimpse of this loss and the subsequent withdrawal from Black men — and, in a way, Black women who suffer their brutality — in the discussion with her.

Even before, however, a hint of the withdrawal came from the mother who named Eartha and had also once tried to date white men. The two Earthas form a paradoxical twist of the mother-daughter archetype described by Mary Helen Washington (1980). Washington noted that novels depicting Black mothers and daughters have the daughters seeking liberation and the mothers attempting to hold them to traditional ways. In the case of Eartha and her mother, the evidence suggests that Eartha is effecting the break with Black men her mother could not achieve for herself. It is, accordingly, ironic that her mother asked me to interview Eartha — to offer her daughter an explanation for the behavior she had partially inspired. The sisters too participated in this drama, though they disclaimed any responsibility. The sisters' anger that Eartha had returned from the Midwest pregnant to a non-relational white male, the mother's initial confidence, and Eartha's own description of her place within the family — all have a collective force-fulness. This energy seems to direct attention to the abandonment by the husband and father for the Midwest, where he could more conveniently mate with white women.

Eartha herself addressed this theme, and her vacillation between the two places, the East and the Midwest, is both symbolic and substantive.[2] Washington (1975) observed that Black women have been alone partly because racism destroyed their men's capacity for tenderness and intimacy. She saw this and related effects as the explanation for Black women choosing to be alone in the future. There are alternative scripts, however, as she well knows. Single parenthood is one such option. Miscegenation is another. Lacking the traditionalism of Washington, Eartha uttered the unutterable: the Black female's choice of the white man. The white man, and subsequently, a biracial baby, validate Eartha's status as "human," and this "tops" the father and brother who date only white women. They have not yet "created" an "earthling."

From this viewpoint, Eartha's recovery is related to Black men. Like the women described earlier, Eartha has seen Black men make "personal choices," and she must do it too. But her choice is no more conflict-free than her father's and brother's choices. The pressure Eartha experiences from her family, friends, and Black male strangers requires her to explain and legitimize her choice. This need to explain herself is the basis for her recovery story.

Recovery through Discovery

Peace of mind is to realize I am a good person, that I have a lot to give. It is the realization of myself as a good person. Okay, I'll tell you. When I was twenty-one, I had a nervous breakdown, and it was because of a lot of shit. I was angry with the world, with myself, and I went through this whole self-destructive, hate trip. And I think that a lot of that developed from when I was sixteen: I lost my virginity, and I got pregnant the very first time. My sister was murdered the same year I started to get involved with the drugs and that was awful; it was like a foundation for self-hatred. And then when I was nineteen, twenty, twenty-one, I was very self-destructive. I was very unhappy taking drugs, and I wanted to die, to commit suicide. I *was* committing suicide in a way. Then I went through therapy for a year. I brought myself to a psychiatrist. They had told me there is nothing wrong with my mind. I was telling them that I wanted to be spiritually involved, I wanted to die and go to another world. I wanted to go to the spiritual world and all that stuff.

What Eartha recounted here is the archetypal journey.[3] Her desire to transcend the world even as its transitional objects — sex, drugs, money — consumed her (Gresson 1987) hints of the "other-worldliness," the narcissistic sense of self as the core of action:

> I was into that crazy head trip, and I can remember the psychiatrist — a Puerto Rican male psychiatrist that deals in spirituality and all that stuff at the health center — when I told him I wanted to die. He said, "My, you have high standards." At the time it didn't mean anything. I was baffled. I was just, like, wow! Then later, I thought about it and I was like laughing because he was telling me that I had a nerve wanting to die so soon, to end all of this shit, to not want to deal with reality and life. He was telling me that my standards were high.

Eartha's recovery occurred, then, through discovering that she is "human," not called to sacrifice herself through drugs and the life of the inner-city she associated with the Black male who introduced her to this life (that is, the same type of male who violated her cousin and her Puerto Rican friend). Recall that Monique also related her growth to "discovering her humanity." In Eartha's case, though, she did not immediately profit from this encounter with her "humanity." She must return to the Midwest and her father and brother: those who hate Black women. She learned that she was pregnant a second time, presumably by the Black male she was dating in Boston. She returned home later,

> still whacked out of my emotions. I was working at the welfare department in Medicaid as an investigator. And I was *on* Medicaid, which meant I did use my card. And I was on Social Security at the same time and had put out a lot of lies to get on it. And I had a job at the same time. So I was making about one thousand dollars a month. [Laughs]. My attitude slowly started changing. I was still taking drugs a bit and was involved with this man — I don't know if I should call him a man because he wasn't at the time. I was involved with this male; he was immature. That was really a weird, fucked-up relationship. I don't regret going through the relationship because it has helped me see myself as a different person today. It has helped me become a stronger person today. I mean, I learned how to think for myself.

She recovered as she learned to throw off the influence of this Black male from Boston. Note that her final pregnancy occurred in the Midwest, where she was free to date white men. Her father and brother, of course, would condone this behavior since it helped legitimize their own preferences and choices. Only in Boston do the mother, sisters, and other friends try to control her, as does the Black males she dates.

Rhetorical Analysis

The Self

The essential task of the recovery narrative is self–Other creation: through my narrative structure I tell you who I am, how I came to be me, and why I see you, the listener, as a mirror of me.

The analytical task is to illuminate why the speaker or storyteller remains connected to the Other despite the changes — including breaks with tradition — described in the story. Metaphor as self-soother and self-enlarger is central to this process of relating and persuading. Eartha stated: "I am the only daughter that really expresses anything to my mother. I can talk about sex, I can talk about drugs, I can talk about anything, where my other sisters would be a little more frightened to talk about themselves. See, I express myself right down to details sometimes, where they would probably generalize."

We can easily read "generalize" as "stereotype." Eartha's self-metaphor, "earthling," is grounded in her particularizing everyone by using synecdoche. In this way, she escapes categorizing and race, with all of its limitations. She said, "No, I encouraged her to accept me. . . . I am so much different than my sisters. I am not a conventional person at all."

Eartha also conveys this self-view in her story of a young woman who, from childhood, was a universalist, someone who prayed at night for world peace and understanding:

> What is Black, what is white? What does that mean? It don't mean anything to me. See, from the time I was a little girl I can remember praying, "I want world peace and people to be happy with each other." I wasn't looking at different colors, and a child is so innocent anyway. You don't separate colors unless that has been taught to you.

Moreover, Eartha naturally attracts and responds to all kinds of people:

> I have gone out with every nationality there is. That's me, I guess. I'm a universal person I guess. I attract a lot of foreigners. I attract all kinds of colors. I think that [Blacks' resistance to marrying outside of the race] is their own security [issue] and something that they have to deal with . . . cause we are all earthlings. Goddamn it, we are all on the same goddamn planet. Why can't we live on this planet?

She also indicated that her stance is grounded in her discovery of the routine positive responsiveness of non-Blacks, on the one hand, and the duplicity, self-stereotyping, and insecurity of Blacks, on the other. This discovery is the basis for her conclusion: we are all human and this is the beginning and the end of the matter.

The Other

Eartha addresses two types of Others: those who try to suppress her living her mission and those whom she wants to help become more like her (individuals whose self-discoveries, rejections of Black men and urban pathology and suicide, and acceptance of themselves as they are lead to the flowering of their missions). We see all of these components together in her encounter with a Black male in a club:

> I went to this club in Newport, Rhode Island. . . . I mean it was an all-white club, and this Black guy came up to me and said: "You've got a nerve being here." . . . Yeah, he came up to me in that club and told me that I have a nerve to be at that club. He said, "The white men were just looking at you like you were a piece of meat." This is what he told me. That they just want to pick up a piece of ass or something. So I said, "Number one, I am not here for display or business, you know; number two, I don't look at people that way, so therefore I don't expect to be looked at in that way, and if I am, that is their problem." I didn't have to explain myself to him, but I felt it was necessary to give him some information, to share some information. I felt he needed to learn a little.

Eartha was vulnerable to this Black man because racism persists and she cannot merely wish it away. This is really why she responded to him, notwithstanding her trite, "I felt he needed to learn a little." But she was angry at his personal duplicity: he was with white women not Black women. Was he also "meat" for them? His dishonesty had strong symbolic meaning for Eartha as a Black woman because he, like her father, wanted to do his own thing without being held accountable. Yet he expected the rest of the "racial family" — symbolized by Eartha, whom he had the audacity to criticize — to continue loving and respecting him as the self-sacrificing protector of family and race. His reference to Eartha as "meat" reflected this misplaced continuity of racial care and concern. This behavior, of course, pictures precisely the "postmodernist confusion" of Black men that helped break the collusive racial bond. Given this perspective, Eartha should have been angry.

Still, Eartha denied that her anger was related to the failure of this misplaced concern about her personal honor and Black womanhood. She said, "I didn't have to explain myself to him." In truth, emotion-

ally, she did have to explain. Also emotionally, and in the symbolic
retribution of the Black woman betrayed by the Black man, she must
choose white mates. She must go where her mother, tied to loyalties
and habits, could not travel. Admitting this, however, means acknowledging the race's collective shame: whites defined a standard of female
beauty and excluded Black women; and each Black male, despite his personal rationale, who chooses a white mate implicitly affirms this white
standard.

However, Eartha's choice of self-metaphor proved too broad for her
own rhetorical effectiveness. *Earthling*. Yes, we are all earthlings. And
the notion does convey the folly of racism and all other invidious cat-
egorizations. But it does not allow Eartha to tell a story with which I
can connect. Her models are largely her father and brother, who are
in the Midwest. They cannot deal with Black women; therefore, they
are, to recall Jean-Paul Sartre, "inauthentic" — that is, they deny reality in order to assert the possible. In this denial of the real, they isolate
themselves from aspects of themselves. They choose to be other people.
Eartha, ironically, does likewise. But not, as she claims, because she is
an earthling. She acts as she does because she must as a Black woman.

Eartha is "Black." She cannot change this fact, but she tried. She
even tried to distort racist incidents. As we shall see in chapter 8, this
is the same behavior whites adopt when they want to deny their racist
behavior or seek other words to describe it. Eartha illustrates the convergence of fantasies and fears of both Blacks and whites who, under the
guise of "the new world order," seek to escape the continuity of racism
in America.

But Eartha's problem, in the immediate context, is that she lacks
Others with whom she may weave this alternate picture of reality. In
particular, the interview forced her out of her "hole" of privatization.
Here we might recall the passage from Lewis Carroll's *The Annotated
Alice* where Alice laments the loss of her ability to remember and recite
poetry. Like Alice, Eartha is afraid she will be stigmatized if she leaves
"the hole."

In cases like this, the listener plays an ironic role in the recovery of
voice: the listener both validates the story in the immediate present — the
occasion of its narration — and in its projected retelling. The interviewer
as listener also plays this ironic role, especially during a study with multiple relationships between collaborator and researcher. In this case, as
interviewer, I was perceived as a partner, a validator of the storyteller. I
both asked questions according to a predetermined interview plan and
invited and allowed the speaker to pursue the self-validational motive.

With Eartha, I found this collaboration evident in her implicit comparison of me with other Black men. I was clearly sympathetic regarding the encounter with the Black man in Newport, and I suggested that he must have been enjoying himself. Eartha answered:

> Yeah, he seemed to be enjoying himself just fine. He must have been there for that reason. [Laughs]. I was there to have fun, not to be picked up for a piece of meat. He was stereotyping me as a Black woman. He was not going up to any white women saying, "You are here as a piece of meat," you know. It was so strange to me. And he was from D.C.! The majority of the people there are Black, and he was at this white bar in Newport, and I couldn't understand it.

Eartha was being "rhetorical": she was reverting to an intragroup racial stereotype of Black men. She intended her choice of phrasing, I believe, for both herself and me: we shared an understanding about his presence at the club. When I asked, "Why do you think he was there?" she replied, "I don't know, maybe to rip off some women or something with that attitude. You know, it didn't seem like a really honest attitude."

She also defined herself over against her cousin. In suggesting that I ought to interview her cousin, she was selling herself as genuine and telling me what I ought to see as suspect:

> I don't have an identity crisis. I know I am a person, and that is the most important thing to me. I think what is most important to her right now is that she thinks of herself as a Black woman, and she believes in the Black movement and stuff, but she can't deal with it. She can't deal with the Black man, so how can she possibly believe in something a part of which she won't accept? You have to accept people and stop [balking] at this person's color because you had an experience with one kind of person. And a lot of it has to do with sexuality. Because you had a bad experience with the opposite sex, you want to turn to the same sex because you don't want to challenge any more of that experience within yourself. . . . [My cousin] has this idea, "I am a strong Black woman, and white men love strong Black women," and she said, "If I were to die and come back again, I would want to come back as a Black woman" because she thinks Black women have the best deal.

Hence, Eartha's cousin, Black men, her mother, and her girlfriend all need to hear her story. Indeed, all other Black people need to encounter her and hear her story. How does she tell it? She is a "reader," a fortune-teller: "All of the Black people came to me." This is where her self–Other mission emerged. But her growing recovery of self seems to revolve around her sister's death and the betrayal by the Black men she has seen in her life.

Most men, thank goodness, are not the evil abusers stereotyped in the literature and the media. Yet much of this abuse exists. My personal and clinical experience with abuse led me to hear Eartha's story of a potential beating with a belt in a private way. An occasion for her recovery had presented itself to me in the immediate situation. I invited recovery by associating with this part of her story: I saw myself in the story; I felt for her plight; and her choice became acceptable for reasons I understood and appreciated. Although I remain ambivalent about miscegenation, I expressed a shared disenchantment and, symbolically, condoned the break with "the ex-comrade." And Eartha accepted my connection:

> And I thought, I said — God, I was seventeen at the time — I said, "Is this how it is supposed to be? Is this how the relationship is supposed to be?" I was stereotyping myself!

Here a suppressed and disenfranchised voice addressed this distortion with a plea for an alternative vision. Eartha wants to be "an earthling." On the one hand, her vision is suppressed by a reality: racism. On the other hand, her vision becomes its own oppressor: she denies aspects of reality to find some degree of closure, however tentative and temporary. She told me she would like to be on another planet. She subsequently followed through and conceived a baby by a white male despite her family's and friend's protestations. But she returned to Boston to have the baby in the home of her mother and in the presence of the Black women she loves and needs.

Eartha, in short, revealed deep and powerful contradictions. She denied any racist experience in her work life, but the denial collapsed when she related an encounter with a white woman she worked with in a bookstore:

> Let me tell you what this white woman said to me. She is supposed to be a regressor; she is supposed to regress people to their past lives — which I believe is full of shit — and while she is running it, she is just making money. She was working in the same bookstore that I was working in. I asked her if she would regress me. She goes through this whole trip: she tells you where you came from in your past life. And she tried to tell me, because I was trying to check out what she was all about, "You want to be white." She said that I was a white woman in my past life, and I want to be a white woman today in this life. And that right there showed me where she was coming from. She did not know how to relate to me as a Black person, so she had to put a label on me to say that I wanted to be white.

She had been ready to tell me how Black people stereotype and oppress her, but she actually described an experience with a white woman, thereby revealing precisely what she had denied: her vulnerability to white people's acceptance or rejection. I, her foil, a practiced observer of others, had obviously seen aspects of Eartha's behavior as a desire to be white. Her mother and girlfriend, as well, had seen her compulsion and anticipated her subsequent pregnancy to an itinerant white musician. Still, she went on:

> To me I wasn't a stereotyped Black person but I was to her [the white woman]. And I said to her, "I don't want to be any color. I want to be me." I am me. I am a female. I realize I have brown skin. I enjoy having brown skin. I am thankful to have this color when we talk about visual effects.

Eartha's "entrapment" by her racial history drove her to deal with race in a distorted way: as a matter of aesthetics. She wanted to be "brown" not "Black." She wanted to be "artistically" colored. But she is African-American, a fact driven home by a white female — a white female, moreover, who practiced mystic crafts (card readings and fortune-telling) like Eartha herself. She called this woman a charlatan. She also called the Black male dishonest. Is everyone dishonest who criticizes Eartha? Perhaps. She had so privatized her struggle for a viable racial identity and for a connection to whites that she denied the problems of a race-conscious society:

> I don't want to put labels on anything. I don't want to be labeled as a female, as a Black person. I want to be labeled as an earthling. Maybe I want to go to another planet. [Laughs]. I've had it with this planet, I mean it! It's just plain and so immature to me. You get into all these categories, and everyone keeps banging their heads against each other and for what? Why? So much wasted energy!

Eartha's Rhetorical Failure: The Rejection of Contradiction

Eartha's rhetorical approach assumes a sympathetic and inducible listener. She predicates the sympathy on an identification with the contradictions, the failure of Black men, and the paranoia of the race. She predicated the inducibility on a listener's admiration of the growth portrayed in her narrative (see the quote on pp. 100–101, above).

Thomas Benson (1974) saw the Malcolm X autobiography as inducement because of its "drama of enlargement" and the growing self-understanding Malcolm conveyed. Although Eartha also showed growth, her story lacks self-understanding because she negated the very contradiction that should have been her strength; thus, she glossed over her mother's plight (contradiction); nor could she integrate the white woman's story into the conflict of racism. In fact, Benson, in a text cited earlier, observed that precisely this contradiction of racism vitalizes Malcolm's narrative and permits the integration of others into his story: "What makes Malcolm's life a drama — an enactment of conflict — rather than mere growth is the presence of racism, the agency of constriction, domination, and injustice" (Benson 1974, 9).

In her denial of racism, Eartha hardly resembles Malcolm. She does not want to deal with its sacrificial demands. She does not want to be bound by its unfair expectations of those who just happen to have "Black skin." Like many others in current society, she wants to have everything her way but not give up anything. This is why she is ultimately unpersuasive and is partly why she eventually denied an understanding of race, asking me to explain it. In this, she seeks also to gain a collusive bond of shared definition around a concept whose postmodernist meaning must be negotiated with an Other.

By denying a knowledge of "race," Eartha can travel back to the past to visit her innocence and her cultural history. For her, however, the trip produces universal rather than racial uplift and accounts for her self-metaphor, "the earthling," which for her validates personal choice. But some metaphors are more persuasive than others, and the problem with this one is that it is too inclusive for meaningful identification (Gresson 1978). It may soothe Eartha, but it does not join her to the real world. Thus, when she ventures beyond the borders of her metaphor, she falls into contradiction and confusion. Even my acceptance of her choice (for my personal reasons) becomes problematic. Ultimately I must disidentify with her (and her choice), for I see and struggle with racism daily. I could find no consolation as "an earthling."

Eartha's rhetorical failure, for me, relates to a larger issue: the limits of identity enlargement. Erik Erikson discussed these limits:

> What historical actuality can the Negro American count on and what wider identity will permit him to be self-certain as a Negro (or a descendant of Negroes) *and* integrated as an American? ... What wider identities, then, are competing for the Negro American's commitments? Some, it seems, are too wide to be "actual," some too narrow. I would characterize as too wide the identity of a "human being" bestowed, according to the strange habit of latter-day humanist narcissisms, by humans on humans, patients, women, Negroes, and so on. While this strange phraseology of being "human beings" may at times represent a genuine transcendence of

the pseudospecies mentality, it often also implies that the speaker, having undergone some revelatory hardships, is in a position to grant membership in humanity to others. I would not be surprised to find that our Negro colleagues and friends often sense such a residue of intellectual colonialism in the "best" of us. For even within a wider identity man meets man always in categories, ... and "human" interrelations can truly be only *the expression of divided function and the concrete overcoming of the specific ambivalence inherent in them:* that is why I came to reformulate the Golden Rule as one that commands us always to act in such a way that the identities of both the actor and the one acted upon is enhanced. (Erikson 1968, 314–16)

Erikson cites the limitations of certain formative ideas ("human beings") for the development of a wider, transcendent identity. Eartha chooses precisely this type of self-metaphor, and that, consequently, accounts for her rhetorical failure. Eartha's pursuit of a wider identity lacks an established collective basis despite the familiar rhetoric of diversity and global oneness. She neglects to confine her interactions to the communes or closed systems that share her stance. She tries to be something of a "secular" mystic or communalist. But mystics and communalists typically "leave the world" in order to validate their identity shifts, while Eartha tries to remain within the Black world and redefine it to meet her "mystical" vision. Subconsciously, Eartha does indeed want to leave the world; subconsciously, she wants to have the "freedom of choice" granted by the world without accepting the definitions and constraints imposed by the realities of the white or Black world. Thus, Eartha does not make connections, see contradictions, or acknowledge the historical and contemporary basis for other people's views of her behavior and stance. We finally recognize her need for a privatized reality in her effort to deal with race as a matter of aesthetics. She wants to be "artistically" colored, which leads her into a pathetic position:

I like my color, you know. I am proud of it. Artistically speaking, if I had a choice, I would keep this color cause I think it is much more attractive. But that doesn't have anything to do with race. I'm proud.... I don't know how to explain it because I don't put things in a category. I can confuse myself when I try to understand it, ... how I look at it. What does Black mean? That is what I want to know? I've had people look at me and go — because I recall this friend of mine who was real uptight because I was going out with white guys, and I told her, "You have got to stop thinking that way if you want to be my friend." I said, "Color doesn't mean anything. It is spirit. And that is how I am attracted to people. Chemistry. I am not attracted to a person because of color. Thwang! It's more than color, and I am an earthling. I am someone in this universe that wants to be able to follow my intuition, to follow what is real inside of me. Why shouldn't I go with what is real inside of me?"

But she could not escape race, so she wanted me to "study" others:

I think it would interesting for you to interview my brother in Minneapolis who dates only white women. He's having a hard time being Black — I don't have a hard time being Black — because I noticed things when we're with all Black people, and he has a hard time being comfortable, where I am comfortable with people.

Nor could she escape her womanhood and her "matriarchal heritage." I asked if she thought being a Black woman had been helpful to her, knowing she had earlier disclaimed the meaningfulness of the label. She replied:

Yes, it has. It's helped me because Black females don't have that many, . . . people don't have too many expectations of where they are coming from or how they are. A Black female is real hard for people to put in a . . . to define. There is an expectation but there really isn't. People don't really know what that expectation is.

Once again I saw an invitation to identify with Eartha's confusion: "I see what you are saying. On the one hand, there are a lot of expectations and stereotypes of the Black woman. But, on the other hand, we really know her so little." She replied:

Yeah, we don't know what to expect. I myself don't know what to expect from some Black women! . . . I just don't know what to expect of people because I look at people. I don't know what to expect from a Black man, I don't know what to expect from a white man, I don't have that all laid out. I don't write scripts before I meet people to play through or run successfully. And I think a lot of the problems that we put ourselves in is that we write scripts even before we meet somebody. A lot of this is us, it's us. We are writing our own scripts — we are fantasizing — what we expect or how we expect one to respond to us. And the only way you can expect one to respond to you is to truly know how you are projecting yourself. To truly know yourself is to have an idea of what to expect, and it goes across the line with anyone. And a lot of people don't understand the chemistry we give off to a lot of people.

Asante (1988b) correctly saw racism as a core contradiction in American society that influences a good deal of Black identity development. Caught within her own contradictions, which are inextricably tied to the larger societal contradiction, Eartha grappled with her mother's fears and her friend's caution regarding intimacy with a white male. Here it may be worthwhile to present a quote already given above:

I don't want to be any color. I want to be me. I am me. I am a female. I realize I have brown skin. I enjoy having brown skin. I am thankful to have this color when we talk about visual effects. I like my color, you know. I am proud of it. Artistically speaking, if I had a choice, I would keep this color cause I think it is much more attractive. But that doesn't have anything to do with race.

Freed of collective context and support, such words become problematic and belie a struggle for self-definition.

Many Blacks struggle to renegotiate their space in a white- and male-focused world. How they go about this negotiation is not always easy to understand. In Eartha's case, the contradiction, her own sense of confusion (she can acknowledge it but can find no source for it), is balanced and sustained by the ideology of the Black male's fear of Black women. She defines herself in terms of this image of a strong but ambiguous Black Woman. She disavows the force of race except as an aesthetic quality.

Rhetoric and the Attainment of Reintegration

Throughout the course of our association, Eartha took what she had to have: "whiteness." Thus, she saw the Black man as the source of racism. This is the postmodernist outcome of the deconstruction of oppression: the victim becomes the villain because of an adherence to a dated code or racial expectations. Because she is alienated from this tradition, Eartha's connecting sentiments are significantly detached:

You can help by starting with children, working with Black boys and influencing them to be individuals, humans. I think that humans are number one on the list. You have to be a humane person to be a real person; then you can deal with your Blackness or your own material things. But I think one has to find [herself] to prove that [she is] a person to [herself]. You won't find yourself to prove that you are a Black person, because that is irrelevant.

This is important advice; it is also correct in a number of respects. Eartha may even assume a role in hastening this change. But it is not her current focus. Locked into a neurotic conflict with Black men, she returned from the Midwest with the biracial baby and married the very man about whom she said:

I think the guy is really sick. But he still calls, he still tracks me down. He says, "I don't care if you are married, have kids. I'm still in love with you, I still want you." I said, "You don't even know what kind of person I am." But he is — he's been — married, and he's going through a divorce now and this whole trip. He says, "I'm legally separated now," and I'm supposed to run and get in his life.

In some ways, Eartha's narrative resembles Monique's. Monique also chose a mixed racial relationship and had a child whom she preferred to see as "just a human" — but also as Black *and* white. Both returned alone to Black communities to live with their biracial children. Eartha's story suggests a collective plight: the possibility of losing oneself even as one hastens to find or create a new self. It is both necessary and desirable to destroy racism and the other forms of oppression that limit both individual freedom and expressions of group identity. The best of worlds would allow people to mate without consideration of their racial groups. Likewise, it should be possible for such individuals to speak of race as only one aspect of their total identities. But a world still dominated by race-conscious power groups keeps this move toward an enlarged racial identity from becoming a simple act of will.

As an "earthling," Eartha is both freed and trapped by the imagery of her self-metaphor. It allows her to meet a class of people likely to validate her struggle to become something other than what the world has planned for her, and her narrative says something about the struggle within us as a species to grow beyond categories even as we use them to thrust ourselves forward:

> Some Black women are real uncomfortable because they are attracted to white men, or cause they might be attracted to a white person. But if everyone was blind, the world would probably get along a lot better. The fact that we have vision causes so much tension. There was this story: Harry Belafonte gave this show for blind children, and he picked up this little blind child and he told her he was Black, and she said, "What does that mean?" What does Black mean to a blind person? . . . There are prejudiced blind people, but you know, he was choked up. He didn't know how to answer that question. What does it [Blackness] mean?

A champion of human rights, a successful Black entertainer, and a father of a biracial daughter (who herself has reached success and fame as a beautiful and talented woman), Harry Belafonte is Eartha's model of reintegration. Like him, she is stunned by the absurdity of race consciousness, and like him, she aims to transcend it. One might expect someone who sees the world this way to crave a separation from the race in at least some ways, and Eartha does:

> I happen to be a part of it, and I understand it, and I love learning about it. But I don't feel committed. . . . I know I am a part of it in the cultural sense. . . . [But] I have an obligation to people. My obligation is to share

love as much as I possibly can. And if I am in a position to help people, ...nobody comes first on the list because of color. I think that it is an important attitude and most people should have this attitude because we complain — different races complain — about race all the time and then it's so hypocritical to me for people to want world peace, love, and happiness. I think everyone wants the same thing basically — I'm not sure a devil worshiper would — but all people want something good, want the same thing. But I think that color causes a barrier with people who want the same thing. For example, religions all want the same thing, but they are always fighting each other, which is hypocritical: love thy brother and thy neighbor but hate each other because of the way they do their ritual and their ceremonies, the way they talk to God, or try to understand him, or whatever.

With these thoughts Eartha brings us to the threshold of the privatized Black person's enlarged vision: race is dead. It should have never been. Blacks must free themselves of the reality they acquired during the "middle passage." They can now encounter white persons as persons, and they should. To do otherwise would only perpetuate a wretched stereotype with the villainous perpetrator of the stereotype being, this time, the Black man himself.

The "data," as they say, do not sustain such a vision of postmodern Black reality. But data need interpretation, and interpretation here is private, personal, individual. This is the essence of the apocalyptic tension: the individual versus the group, the Black individual versus the Black group, the white and Black individual versus the Black and white groups.

Some recognize this tension as the danger it is and try to find alternatives that will acknowledge the possibilities and constraints of racism in the twenty-first century. The narrative we examine next illustrates this sense of danger. In Akia's narrative, we see how the rhetorical challenge of postmodernist relatedness — "I find my friends and family where I can and *my* truth equals the Truth" — is enunciated by someone who refuses to privatize racism as a means of constructing a rationale for enlarging her relationships and commitments to include previously excluded Others.

6

Akia:

Narrative Construction as Heroic Recovery

❖

We stand together holding up the collapsing roof, and this is the most awesome knowledge confronting us. We handle this awesome knowledge by maturing a collective sense. This is the secret of African American spirituality; that is, while we recognize the individuality of the responsibility, we know that cannot be carried out without others. We can reach our own transcendence, but never without the help of others. If I run to the sea alone, my solitude finds me searching for new ways to come together with others.
— Molefi Asante (1988a)

Background of the Narrative

The Inheritance

The iconoclasms of the 1960s and 1970s revealed lies, exposed collusions, and created new illusions by which to live. Most adult Americans shared in this iconoclastic purge of society's duplicities around matters of race, gender, class, intergenerationalism, and sexuality. Black women shared in this breaking down of cherished myths and collusive bonds, and Monique's and Eartha's contradictions and confusion largely result from their ancestors' activism: they reflect remembrances of past racial values and pursuits. They even share some aspects of past racial visions of survival and liberation. But the glass through which Monique and Eartha see the world of racial relatedness and collective efforts has been shattered, and the result for these two women is a complex, confused, and incomplete rendering of their lives as race-conscious persons.[1] Moreover, they suffer immense pain as a part of their racial and gender identifications.

114

An iconoclastic inheritance has led few Black women to the extreme tensions revealed in the narrative of Eartha in particular. They know the confusion and contradiction inherent in racial matters, and they know pain as well. But they continue to promote racial liberation and to bond with the Black male. Or, in the language of Audre Lorde (1981), they actively pursue and create a collusive racial bond, the bond of the oppressed, and a conscious core around which racial values and styles of life form, build, and are celebrated.

But intragroup contradictions do not disappear merely by fiat or the refusal to abandon the "collapsing roof." These Black women must also find the rhetorical means to keep themselves from getting out from under and finding their way alone in a race-conscious and race-cruel world. These women, too, need recovery as humans and as Blacks.

This chapter shows how the pain associated with Black men as mates and racial leaders, and a growing ambivalence among Black women regarding the efficacy of the traditional female commitment to the racial survival mission, affect recovery. Denying the source of their pain paralyzed Monique and Eartha; they could neither feel nor effectively grieve their losses. Thus, their narratives reflected privatization and isolation. Akia's narrative also conveys pain and pathos. But Akia also grieves and faces, to the extent her development allows, the contradictions marking her existence.

The Rhetorical Situation

Akia had been a student of mine at a northeastern university (called Eastern in the text that follows) years before the interview presented here. Born in the South, she was one of several children. A child of the post–Black Power era, she and her peers, particularly the females, had participated in the neo–Black Culturalist movement of the late 1970s. Her narrative reveals varying degrees of self-interest, racial self-consciousness, self-proclaimed commitment, and a pain-ridden personal history. It also reveals a remarkable awareness of the plight of the young Black female and her place within the contemporary racial drama. Akia and I had several discussions over some two years, and the four sessions I taped covered some ten hours. The interview occurred in a two-day period at the end of Akia's first year in graduate school.

In this narrative, Akia tried to persuade me that she remained faithful and steadfast to the racial dream and bond despite the absence of support from her "Black sisters" in graduate school. Her decision to attend an elite, predominantly white university removed her from among the relatively large number of supportive, like-thinking Black women she had known in undergraduate school. She had moved into a highly competitive, often unkind professional market. Individualism, not racial love and loyalty, typically reigns in such environments, and race-conscious Black women find difficulty there. Akia's narrative revolves around her losses and the recovery she desired.

This narrative, then, is the story of the break between her remembrance of a vital and effective collective past and the disillusionment of the present. Because Akia was a strong advocate for and collaborator in the study of Black female commitments, her narrative is often self-conscious and self-reflective. For Akia, I am both researcher and confidant and play an important — though silent — role in her narrative. Symbolically, I am Black Man. Thus, this story is Akia's recapitulation of the Black female disillusionment discussed earlier. But, in another sense, it is something more: Akia's narrative places us squarely before the dialectical nature of cultural identities. Stuart Hall, writing on contemporary Black cultural identities, states this dialectic succinctly:

> Cultural identities come from somewhere, have histories. But, like everything which is historical, they undergo constant transformation. Far from being eternally fixed in some essentialist past, they are subject to the continuous "play" of history, culture, and power. Far from being grounded in mere "recovery" of the past, which is waiting to be found and which, when found, will secure our sense of ourselves into eternity, identities are the names we give to the different ways we are positioned by, and position ourselves within, the narratives of the past. (S. Hall 1990, 225)

Akia's narrative is a story of recovery in two respects: (1) at the existential level, finding an alternative father-mate figure to me; and finding an alternative support group to the "Black sisters"; and (2) at the collective level, finding a way of avoiding the potential rage, confusion, and duplicity of the older Black and white women to whom she looks as models.

Akia's task at the collective level is to avoid the personal and political dangers of Blacks and white women. The recovery solution is her self-metaphor: *The Extrapolator* — one who expands into an unknown area in order to arrive at a unique place; the steadfast Black woman without mate or sister; or the Black woman who creates a racial vision without the benefit of adequate guidance and support from the previous generation; one who draws forth understanding and courage from history writ large.

The Rhetorical Issues

Collusion, of course, requires two or more participants. A lone colluder finds confusion, depression, anger, and, possibly, a need to change friends and reference group. This fact also has a rhetorical significance. As Thomas Benson observed:

> Taken by itself, any one of the rhetorical modes of action is incomplete. Knowledge alone becomes decadent and effete, existence alone becomes narcissistic and self-destructive, and power alone become dehumanized technological manipulation. Perhaps only when rhetorical knowing, being, and doing are present together can rhetorical action truly be said to take place. (Benson 1989, 1)

One aspect of Benson's argument pertains to existence. He implies that one needs significant Others to provide a supportive and constrictive context for one's knowledge and agency. Without an anchor in knowledge and power, existence becomes narcissistic and self-destructive. But in a world plagued by racial iconoclasm, it is difficult to combine rhetorical knowing, being, and doing. The needs are difficult to keep separated in neat categories; boundaries, too, become vague and abstract. How, then, does one recover holism? How does one try to retain or recover the old ways? How does one, knowing that the old ways are gone and empowered to act on behalf of one's own interests, induce another to share the chosen or inherited existence? These are the rhetorical issues raised by Akia's narrative and its analysis.

The Narrative as Recovery Discourse

Violation, Loss, and Withdrawal

In a Langston Hughes poem, "The Negro Mother," an aged Black mother recounts her life, from the precolonial bliss of Africa through enslavement and acceptance of the burden of "racial uplift." Though a fictional character, Hughes's Negro Mother knew who she was and what she must do for the race. She had a "cultural identity." Cultural identity refers to a memory of relationship around which to mobilize care and concern. Akia also has a cultural identity:

> My neighborhood was Pan-African.... My neighborhood was... what Harlem was to New York in those days, and I couldn't get involved in all of that stuff, and all through high school and stuff, I kept wishing I was six years older. And I think that part of my depression at this stage in life is coming to grips with I'm twenty-three and I'm not six years older and know how to experience that stuff. I have a different mission in life. I don't know what it is.

But the 1960s and since have changed so much for women like Akia that she does not know what her mission is, what is expected of her. Nor can she find fulfillment in the old ways.

This separation from the past is essential for understanding Akia's narrative and those of many other young Black women. It is the collective and constant message of Black female literature. Because of this disjunction, Mary Helen Washington wanted Black female storytellers whose rhetorical solutions might persuade and console young Black women like Akia. But Akia can find escape in the rhetorical solutions of these fictional works no easier than she can find it in the rhetoric of miscegenation. She finds few models for her mission. Indeed, Akia later reveals her dissociation with the movement in her description of these older women as confused, bitter, and betrayed. Akia senses that the cultural context is contradictory: it was exciting and inspiring and nurturing for a time, yielding the fruit that was the "revolutionary babies." But the experience of nurturance is now the *memory of betrayal*. Akia now expresses her generation's awareness that having babies will not deliver the race.

With betrayal, bitterness, and the loss of an ideology to sustain commitment as cultural identity, Akia and her peers experience the confusion and depression of their role models. The absence of a movement to inspire and contextualize commitment and identity arouses in her an intensified need for the women of her own generation, and in these terms we can understand her observations about the lost movement, the absence of support from the Black women in her graduate program, and the younger generation's understandable but misguided belief that it can forget about things "Black" because money will buy them acceptance in the larger society.

Akia has a strong emotional memory of or connection between her racial identity commitment and her relationship to Black women. She is "womanist" in orientation, despite a need for and vulnerability to Black men.[2] When the Black women in her graduate program do not respond to her as she expects and wants them to, she experiences a violation, which reminds her she has lost the support of the women from her undergraduate days at Eastern. This loss sets up the first part of her recovery story as a *logical and necessary* survivalist drama. Who can deny the powerful aloneness she now feels without models? To be "heroic" under such terms is not to be sacrificial, as has occurred in the past; rather, it is to be willing to strike out alone along a previously alien and antagonistic path: the world of white people. The Black male,

Juan, replaces me as father-mate. He also leads her along this path of recovery she has chosen.

Juan's presence in Akia's narrative is both substantive and symbolic, as is my absence from the story she tells. After all, I had a share in the narrative and know where the absence of my name (like the silences in a conversation) is itself a comment and communication. Thus, Juan miraculously appears in the story: an attractive, sensitive professional (a practicing dentist who is near my age and studying for a public health degree). Initially, he takes Akia as a platonic roommate and consoles her (like the white women in her program) by telling her she is too good for both me and the Black women who have betrayed her love and commitment.

Two central betrayals bedevil Akia here: one by a traditional (older) Black man (that is, me); another by nontraditional (opportunistic) Black female graduate students. Juan counsels her to reject both these women and, as she revealed in another conversation, me. The rejection also proceeds in two ways. First, she rejects the Black women by becoming open to white people's writings and kindness, and then revealing Black unkindness and betrayal. She also refuses to relate to these Black women. Second, although only marginally involved at this point with me, Akia symbolically rejects me by rejecting what I presumably represent, Blackness, by becoming Juan's roommate rather than taking responsibility for her own life (that is, getting an apartment and finding work).

Akia reveals the symbolic nature of her rejection of me by permitting herself to be economically and emotionally supported by a man with no acknowledged sexual interest in her. This is a journey into recovery, but it is a constructed journey. Recall that Akia had refused to take responsibility for her adjustment at the university, saying that she knew how to take care of herself but wanted to be pampered as she had pampered others. Those others (namely, myself and the Black students), however, neglected to provide the pampering, the violation that enabled her to recover from any overinvestment in Pan-Africanism she may have made. In short, the slights were real, but Akia constructed their scope and significance.

The decision not to speak about me directly in the narrative, even though she felt loss and pain around that curtailed intimacy, makes her story an allegory: I stand for the Black women and the Black movement; Juan stands for the white women and feminist movement. My relationship with Akia carries the pain and disillusionment she feels for the Black women and the Black movement. Juan's relationship carries the unexpected, almost magical, deliverance Akia finds from the white women and feminist theory. Ultimately, she must extrapolate from both Black and white traditions and relationships, since we all carry some degree of disappointment for her: (1) I did not pursue the relationship when Akia left the East; (2) the Black women played the competitive game of white academia; (3) Juan celebrates his "skin color" and wants to marry a dark-skinned woman and have "brown people"; and (4) white feminists want to be identified with the oppressed but enjoy the gains of the white man. The discovery of her need to extrapolate is the story of her relative recovery from these betrayals.

Recovery through Discovery

Philip Rieff once wrote that "our cultural revolution does not aim, like its predecessors, at victory for one rival commitment, but rather at a way of using all commitments, which amounts to loyalty to none" (Rieff 1968, 21). Rieff went on to talk about "the coming of Psychological Man," that personality type whose intellect and victory over superstition and community left few deities to worship. In a world where so many losses and disillusionments occur, it is easy to understand, in part, the scenario Rieff and others foretold. It occurs, moreover, in such a world, where out of their human birthright and certainly in imitation of men in a brutal world, women find it possible to be grand-scale takers. If this taking has begun, we may well believe the trauma Akia felt when she

> realized that these women do not know what a collective experience is about; they do not know what it is. And that was painful to me, you know. I kept saying, "It's not important, goddamnit, I don't care if you get out first and I get out third. I don't care. What is important to me is that we learn this stuff and all three of us get out because they need Black health administrators out there."

"Saving the race" was a traditional Black value. Not all Blacks shared it, but most had to share it because few could have survived solely as individuals, even those Blacks who ultimately acted as individuals. Thus, "saving the race" once nearly equated to self-survival. Today many Blacks disdain the notion of "racial survival." The ideology that the Constitution and the national conscience are "color-blind" masks for many African-Americans the reality of racism and white race-preferences.

Among her Black classmates in graduate school, Akia found the basis for her racial commitment compromised. Granted, individuals ought to be sufficiently inner-directed that they will not readily abandon commitment to others when others fail them. But survival in a society lacking a unified and persuasive value system requires an alertness to changing times and conditions. Moreover, as Akia said, "I was hurting and everyone could see that!"

This is her tour de force: even white folk and a non–race-committed Black man could see her in pain. Why couldn't these women? (Why couldn't I?)

Akia's sentiment is rhetorical: she knows that these women are even more pained and frightened than she is. She says, in fact, one woman was fat and unattractive, unlike herself, and therefore more vulnerable to white inducements.[3] The rhetorical significance of the sentiment is that it enables her to disconnect, and appropriately so, from both the women and I.

Akia describes her recovery as a twin discovery: the unavailability of traditional allies and the availability of historical enemies. Unavailable are the Blacks (including me) and women: Black men had failed her as father and mate, Black women had failed her as Black and female, and white women had failed her as female. Indeed, whites as male and female and Blacks as non–race-committed are now the "new comrades." This is her recovery story.

Because Akia told this story largely to convey her sadness at the losses of her old classmates and intimate friend, one cannot guess how much Akia changed herself by telling the story. Presumably, it enabled her to enter a satisfying relationship with her new mate and mentor and to establish successful relationships with whites toward whom she may have once felt some ideological antagonism. We can at least analyze her narrative in terms of these twin accomplishments.

Rhetorical Analysis

The Self

> What is painful for me is that group of women [the Eastern class of 1981], we will never be together. And, Lord, do I need them, wherever I am. I guess what will happen for us — I know we will rise again. Maya Angelou [laughs]: we will rise, fill our eyes [laughs]. Anyway, I know we will rise again, and what is important for us is that we keep writing, we keep calling every now and then, so that we can say to each other that we will rise again, okay?

Here we find a powerful point: Akia has connected with the Black female writer Maya Angelou. Here her thoughts and associations seem to transcend the narrative: the narrative becomes a vocal expression of grief around the loss of the group, those women with whom Akia studied at Eastern. They are, after all, the ones whom Angelou seeks to speak for in her own writing and witnessing as a Black woman.

Beyond Akia's discourse of grief, we also find a discourse of self-persuasion. This concern with her own image appeared early in the narrative when Akia declared that she was tired but that her desire to "escape for a year" was an unsatisfactory solution. The problems would still be waiting for her. This important point is the logic underpinning her narrative and her choice of an ultimate social vision. She knows that the vulnerability of the race cannot be wished away: those Black, middle-class youths entering predominantly white schools and the white work world soon learn the reality. The presence of Black success stories on television and in other media cannot eradicate the race-related pain of Black Americans. So Akia's choice, unlike Monique's or Eartha's, cannot easily be to deny the persistence and prominence of racism in the daily lives of Black people. Even though she seems unlikely to abandon Blacks in a comprehensive or dramatic way, she seems to believe she has cause to do so. Her story presents a rationale for a break with tradition, and if Akia should "slip" into another bond, one outside of the traditional mandate, we would see her struggle as real and lengthy and identifiable. But Akia seems unlikely to break any major bonds. She has told Juan about her suffering with me; she has told the white women about her pain at the selfishness of the Black students. But this is the extent of her retaliation. She remains concerned with the Other in a collective way in her narrative. This distinguishes it from Eartha's and, to a lesser degree, Monique's.

The Other

Although Akia grieves losses, she is consoled by her sense of her racial self; and this racial self relates to how she managed the contradictions of the Others in her life. Those Others, therefore, figured to a great extent in her recovery and the way she sought to persuade me that she was still faithful to me and to Black women despite our apparent failings. In fact, she seeks to demonstrate some of the very superwomanly heroics and sacrifices she consciously rejects. In this manner, she does receive the strokes she said she wanted: "I knew where to go; I wanted someone to pamper me," and in the same vein, "Juan was saying to me, 'Leave the niggers alone, Akia!' "

But neither the Black students nor I console her. Where, then, is her recovery? What is her heroism? Akia is an *extrapolator*. This is her self-metaphor. This is who she has become through her journey of recovery through discovery. Akia *is* her ability to *extrapolate* from the feminist literature and theory. This character trait enables her to conjoin her story to the weight of millions of other storytellers; and we see, in effect, not one but many Akias. The very quantity of this suffering moves us to declare: Do what you must! After all, she has framed her journey in terms of a pursuit of "truth":

> This is where I'm changing: anything that white people wrote [about Black people] I discredited, you know. So now I'm in a space where I am reading it and...I'm really looking for both the truth and the fallacies. You understand what I'm saying?[4]

Akia offers a view of one person's understanding of the shifting contexts that promote differentiation of self from collective racial identity. Unforced commitment—in fact, contra-indicated commitment—brings us to the "loss of memory" and the pursuit of immediate satisfactions. We see this when Akia remembers the past but must juxtapose it with an uncomfortable present and doubtful expectations for the future:

> Who were the leaders and who were the Black community at Eastern? The Black women. We did everything. And for the first time in my life, probably since my parents separated and stuff, I was dependent upon a Black man ...and [laughter] some white people.

Akia has many ideas of the Other: Blacks, whites, males, females. These begin to take on some vital roles in her search for an understanding of the world to be. Thus, one Other is the Black woman who has chosen the white man. Ironically, while Akia remains steadfast in her commitment to Black men and the movement and disidentifies with Black women who marry white, one wonders whether she is so far from seeing such women as positive role models after all. How much more felt violation and failure at integrating some generic contradictions can she sustain? Is the Black woman who marries a gentle, loving, prosperous white male worse off than the poor, destitute Black woman who even now has to sell her body to men — white and Black — or who gets battered and raped by Black men?

Of course, Akia's early attempts at escape are a part of a comprehensive contradiction matrix. As such, her actions and attitudes will continue to be conflictive and unresolved until time and circumstance (a new cultural context) prove more favorable. Thus, we see the vacillation. Weinstein and Platt (1969; 1973) pointed out how the experience of violation stimulates the emotional capacity to let one's intellect work on one's behalf. This experience of violation, however, is a part of a complex process of suffering, pain, and gradual dwelling with the fact that one is in pain and yet strangely continues to live. Akia tells how this goes and what one might be experiencing:

> [T]hey did not support me when I was down and out, and that is something that I would not have done: I would not have let a woman like me go down. And I watched them watch me ... suffer. And so I had some feelings about filling a spot [as a leader] because they are not the type of people I would want to be associated with, or lead, or represent, or anything.

The Other as "girlfriend" (a Black female term of endearment) became problematic. Amazingly, perhaps, but certainly in keeping with the theoretical perspective, Akia connects change to pain and pain to separation:

> So I really dealt with that, you know, and at that time I really started changing. I really felt a need to start separating from organizations. I had these feelings, you know: I wanted to get away from Black people, I wanted to get away from Black organizations, and what was really scary is that my white friends came to my aid during that time.

This self-observation, however, can be deadly:

> [I]n our relationships with men, we are not feminists at all, you know? [Laughs.] And this is where depression comes in for most of us, especially for me. ... It is almost like I separate and watch this other self exist, ... and that's depressing because here I am writing about these things and reading these things and believing in these theories, and professing all this stuff in class on an intellectual level, but personally ...

Akia's Rhetorical Success and Failure

Humans are, of course, highly adaptable. Given the oppressive roots of African-American (in contra-distinction to African) identity, we might well expect that Akia's early reaction to "good white folk" amounts to fear and denial, but perhaps with some pleasure and guilt around finding that stroking she wanted. "I'm capable of being Superwoman" (read as "I'm self-denying — but I would rather not be") is what we might interpret her as saying. Even so, she seems proud of remaining loyal and, in fact, being Superwoman:

> And you know I didn't tell these white folks anything until the end of the semester because I wanted to protect these Black people who were hurting me. And then one day I said, "You know, Jane, let me tell you what has happened to me all semester." And that was a change for me because I had been into — you know — you don't tell white people this; I don't care what happens to you, you present a united front. Well, fuck it! It was obvious there was no united front and I was suffering.

Akia tells a story full of pain, loss, and courage. Her struggle with intraracial failures pushed her beyond the limits of a chauvinistic racial identification: Blacks can cause pain and destruction just as whites can; and some whites overcome their addiction to racism to co-celebrate the compassion humans are capable of generating for one another.

A key to this recovery of her humanity is Akia's ability to surrender. It also accounts, in part, for her persuasiveness as rhetor. Recall that Eartha's failure as rhetor lay in the absence of a willingness to surrender, to acknowledge the contradictions within her narrative, and to articulate a believable reconnection. Akia conveys a willingness to surrender, thereby revealing surrender to be a rhetorically significant aspect of recovery rhetoric and her rhetorical success.[5]

Akia's Rhetorical Success: Surrender as Rhetorical Act

Thomas Benson saw Malcolm X's struggle with his flaws as an aspect of his character that attracted and induced others. But what is it precisely that wins our commitment to walk the same path? Benson described Malcolm as a man "whose natural powers and sympathies undergo a gradual but powerful opening up to embrace wider scenes of action and larger groups of people" (Benson 1974, 9). This "gradual openness" is a critical notion; it describes the point of crossover from despair to hope. It signals an awareness of the universal fallibility of the species and the simultaneous compassion for self and species. It is the rhetorical act that allows one more fully to induce others to share in one's vulnerability and to know compassion for one as actor and speaker. I call this process "surrender."

To induce the Other to "surrender" is hardly a novel rhetorical act.[6] It is, in fact, the message of Christ struggling with his burden, the cross. He stumbles and falls, gets up, tries again, falls yet again, only to regain his footing and finally reach his destiny. Seen this way, is not surrender the foundation for recovery? Considerable psychological evidence suggests surrender is generic to recovery. For example, in *A Different Voice*, Carol Gilligan (1982) speaks of the experience of failure and the acknowledgment that often precedes a turning point in a young woman's life.[7] We hear Akia say:

> I just...I guess...I'm drained because, Aaron, I'm always giving. I've always given...even those who were putting me through so much last semester. I kept saying no: one is a hundred pounds overweight and I can understand where she is coming from, and the other one is very insecure. You know, here I am flunking out of school and I'm getting copies of old

exams from my white friends and xeroxing them for them. And it was painful.

This pain, this surrender to the fact of possible failure, allows Akia to offer a connecting self-metaphor. And finally, we hear her self-assessment, her narrative structure: racial heroine. This self-metaphor, as I call it, is critical to the recovery process if the contradictions are to be balanced; and it is, of course, the balancing of contradictions that the heroine must achieve and that we, as audience, expect as the terms of endearment. Akia's earlier self-metaphor, "extrapolator," merges into and completes the newer, enlarged one. Akia has been weaving, perhaps unwittingly, a story of heroism against confusion and contradiction, betrayal and abandonment, loss and isolation, weariness and despair. She becomes persuasive when she says, "I am tired; I feel like I am an old person." She is aging faster than her years because she is gathering up raw experience (untransformed and uncivilized fact), and unifying, life-energizing myth has been snatched away from her. She confronts every "truth" on its own terms: she sees this as the condition for survival in the new world of "self."

Akia's narrative helps one recall the words of Georges Bataille: "To a greater or lesser extent every man is suspended upon narratives, on novels which reveal to him the multiplicity of life. Only these narratives, often read in a trance, situate him before his fate" (Bataille, cited in Barthes 1970, 267). The power of Akia, then, lies in her construction of her lived meaning — her experiences mediated by her visions, values, and violations, inflicted and endured.

Akia and I — speaker and listener — engage each other. She ultimately induces by her clear readiness to embrace my "truth" and "experience," as if she has been saying all along, "I am looking for something, can you advise me?" The readiness to take hold of once alien and unutterable ideas touches me, and I am finally persuaded away from harshness and distance as I hear Akia describe her living out of her "extrapolator" self-metaphor. She invites me to provide her with history she may use. I am a listener-turned-collaborator. To my observation that the losses in Black women's lives influence their depression, she observes:

> That's interesting you should say because that is something that I am dealing with right now in my own therapy: loss. And I feel like the more I climb this ladder [of success], the more I move, the more I lose, the more I give up in terms of being able to relate to Black men. I really feel it and it... it's depressing for me because of something I just got into touch with this year... stuff I read about. But "nay," I say, it's not true, it's not true because I always go on maintaining this relationship with Black men

and you know, the grassroots. And I find myself really feeling separated and [with] a sense of loss... because I know I've met very few men in my program, in my age range, who can deal with me... just in terms of conversation. And then there are the older men out there who I know I can't have really because I would fall into the traditional — I would almost be forced to, I would have to give up some of the feminism.

Akia and I were student and teacher and separated by a dozen years. I served as a symbol of something good and bad: someone she could talk to, someone who read Black women's literature, which surprised and pleased her, yet a selfish person as well. I could make decisions that collided with her fantasies; I could even interview her knowing that she wanted me to "save her from growing up" and that much of the interview was subtly designed to have me follow her back to graduate school. Yet she did not really want to be drawn into my "traditional world." Her words betrayed her ambivalence: with an older man, she "would have to give up some of the feminism."

At the personal level, then, the interview served as a working-through process for both Akia and me. For Akia, it summarized her reading of my stance toward our differences; for me, it was a chance to validate her turning away from me as Black Man. In the pursuit of my personal concerns, I broke a bond, a collusive sharing, and validated Akia's recovery of her own propensity for growth. More precisely, I validated her narrative in two ways. First, I met and "recognized" her roommate as her new mentor and mate. Moreover, I acknowledged that he was a Black man, despite his apparent indifference to Afrocentric values Akia and I had once shared. During one of our later meetings, Akia confided that she had been "blown away" by the fact that Juan and I, two Black men, met and immediately began communicating and connecting around a mutual fascination with the symbolism of American and Italian westerns. I had forgotten the incident, but for Akia, it was a pivotal event: I had symbolically accepted Juan as an equal, thereby acknowledging that his concern for her was genuine and merited her care and commitment, if she chose to give it to him. I also validated her narrative by telling her ministories about Black women and men — and white scholars, as well — who discussed the situations she was experiencing. By connecting her experiences to diverse scholars from whom she could extrapolate, I also encouraged her to create her personal perspective.

Akia acknowledged this collusion several times, but two revelations are most significant: "That's interesting you should say that because that is something that I am dealing with right now in my own therapy: loss";

and "I used to not listen to anything that whites had to say." In each of these instances, Akia used my observations to say something to me directly about her own growth away from my views and toward others. She had talked about me — an Afrocentric therapist and former confidant — with a white male therapist. But in this story, I am not her hero; rather, I am the symbol if not source of her pain and plight. This symbolic sharing with a white male healer symbolized the break between Akia and me. In a sense, I became her "ex-comrade."

Lessons from the Narratives

When Christopher Lasch (1984) described these as narcissistic times, he talked about the social conditions that force us back upon ourselves for more and more nurturance, care, and protection. When Audre Lorde discovered that she had cancer, she wrote:

> It was also a question of how could I use that perception other than just in rage or destruction. And that to put myself on the line to do what had to be done at any place and time was so difficult, yet absolutely crucial, and not to do so was the most awful death. And putting yourself on the line is like killing a piece of yourself, in the sense that you have to kill, end, destroy something familiar and dependable, so that something new can come, in ourselves, in our world. (Lorde 1981, 734–35)

One looks for the Other as savior and realizes that there is no such Other. One is one's own savior and, by necessity, the Other's savior as well. The idea that women will become the saviors of the world is close to this realization; and it is easy to see Akia in Audre Lorde's vision of the "elitism of women":

> [T]he human race is evolving through women. . . . [I]t's not by accident that there are more and more women, the — this sounds crazy, doesn't it — the proportion of women being born, women surviving. . . . And we've got to take that promise of new power seriously, or we'll make the same mistakes all over again. Unless we learn the lessons of Black mothers in each of us, whether we are Black or not — I believe this exists in men also, but they choose to eschew it, not to deal with it. Which is, as I learned, their right of choice. Hopefully, this choice can be affected, but I don't know. I don't believe the shift from conquering problems to experiencing life is a one-generational shot or a single investment. I believe it's a whole signature which you try to set in motion and have some input into. But I am not saying that women don't think or analyze. Or that white does not feel. I am saying that we must amalgamate the two, never close our eyes to the terror, the chaos which is Black, which is creative, which is female, which

is dark, which is rejected, which is messy, sinister, smelly, erotic, confused, upsetting. (Lorde 1981, 729–30)

Lorde perceives and welcomes the unfolding of woman within the world community. Men remain largely insensitive to this evolution, even those of us who are sensitive to the "Black Mother" within ourselves.[8] This myopia in man appears, to some extent, in the recent books by Robert Bly, *Iron John,* and Sam Keen, *Fire in the Belly.* But what most men still misunderstand is the creative fusion of the joy of self–Other discovery, which can come in diverse places and times, with unfamiliar people to whom we attach, body, soul, and mind.

This is the fate of the heroine, the one who discloses the promised land but is damned for the infractions — the disillusionment and discovery — that occur in the process of recovery. This awareness, moreover, explains the fear in letting go of the past:

> This is something I have been thinking about lately, especially about women in my age bracket.... One of the reasons that we are not getting what we need is because we don't know how to ask for it because even though we are career-oriented, we are feminists, and all that stuff. We are still trying to debunk the myth of the Black Matriarch, so we don't want to make these demands, and it's almost as if we are scared to demand, or to just ask for, what it is that we need; and we like. Because — you know, I don't know — we recognize that these degrees we are getting will separate us from Black men, and we are all so sensitive to what that means and are so afraid of being alone and all that bullshit.

But transformation will finally have its way, and Akia's message is that one must keep struggling with the contradictions, supplanting one after the other, using the energy gained from one discovery to endure the pain of the next one:

> One of the things I recognize just over the last four or five years since I really started studying feminist thought, taking courses and just reading on my own, and I found that the more that I read and the more I internalized [sigh], the more powerless I felt. It's like you are reading all of these books that these white women have written on feminism — theories and what have you — *then as a young Black woman you try and extrapolate from those things and apply them to your life and I don't know....* I mean this is something I'm thinking now about working on because this whole thing for me has been a feeling of being powerless ... unable to ... unable to ... be self-determined, and it may be my own thing.
>
> You see, Aaron, one of the problems with the women in my generation, unlike women thirty-six and stuff, we ... The women who are thirty to forty right now are really confused. I think a lot of them have not been able to find the man in their lives.... A lot of them are women who participated

in the '60s and are really dealing with the bitterness, the disappointment of that whole experience, right? A lot of them are career women and are just very lonely and very confused because they cannot have the old — the husband, the two kids, however many — they can't have that, and they don't like being single women. And with us, because they are the confused folks right before us, we don't have any role models, other than confusion, you know. So it's like most of my friends feel it is up to us [deep sigh]. We have to come and clear up this confusion, but we don't know how. That's where the depression comes in, and it's like we have to pull not just from Black women's history, but from history almost complete.

The imagery here is powerful. Joseph Campbell suggests that heroes come to see that they are "essence," and, as such, they will make meaning. Akia, unable to rely upon the histories of either Blacks or whites, must establish her own meaning. She describes this as "extrapolation." She must search through countless books, seeking to discover one or two primal sources that will yield the "forgotten truth" that renders the reader a "Culture Hero."[9] And what does Akia pull from "history"?

I don't know. . . . You see, we are trying to struggle between commitment to Black men and commitment to the movement, right, and commitment to ourselves, . . . but for me they are connected because everything I do is circular, so everything I do is based on beliefs, values, you know. . . .

I am growing to be intolerant of the confusion, the problems that exist between Black men and Black women; and in the feminist movement between Black women and white women. It is almost as if I am old and I am tired of trying to figure out how to make it better, not for the world but for myself. I don't know how to sort through some of this stuff. I find myself losing energy to the struggle, you know, and I find [sigh] myself focusing more on the career Akia. It's important for me now because the way I looked at my life, now that's changing.

Unable to share some "secret" discovered in this "history," Akia returns to the theme of focusing her anger and pain. She returns, as well, to the convergence of survival and the need for work: it is within the job as career that the self can find a rationale for struggling for self. Most of us can, moreover, understand this response. Ironically, Akia's argument is equivalent to Julius Lester's rhetorical query: After all, it's my life, and who's living it? This is the primal logic that propels one through the world: either you live (act) or you die.

It's almost like the exact same thing that happened in the Black movement, the feminist movement. Both of them are dead now, almost, they are dead. And you can look at them and see how they failed, you know, because they really didn't deal with those issues of change and stuff.

Akia here echoes Manning Marable (see the epigraph to part II, above). Akia presents the Black female recovery argument in its best narrative form: recovery begins with the self; listens to the inner voice monitoring daily experience; tries to love self; and identifies a metaphor, a rhetorical argument, for reconnection and continuity of care and commitment.[10]

> I mean, what I am saying to my friends is that we recognize how the movement of the '60s failed, but that doesn't mean that we have to discredit the effort and that is what a lot of people are doing: "To hell with Black shit!" [Laughs.]

But this reconnection will survive only if the Other also changes, because self-change can tolerate nothing less of the Other:

> I am changing. I just feel like I need some time away, because I don't have the support base anymore. I have few people I could talk to and work some of these issues out, and they diminish over the years. . . . The energy is what makes you wake up in the morning [sigh], . . . that makes you write, that makes you go to class, makes you read — because you want to find out where the teacher is wrong in terms of relating the theories to nonwhite folks, to women. I just don't have that energy anymore.
>
> I sit in my class and I accept things — not accept things, just let them go by. I sit here and I say, "I've been this route before." . . . I just don't have the energy anymore. It's almost, I guess I see it as being the superwoman and just don't want to be that.

Once again, Akia takes us back to the traditional commitment and permits us to examine the idea of continued sacrifice. But as Gates (1988) would say, this is "repetition with a difference." The difference is the new history, the loss of collective identity as a sure and immutable matrix for self-definition. What does this mean, then, and what is the rhetorical inducement? Recall Isaac's words to Esau: "when you become restive, you shall shake his yoke from your neck" (see pp. 138–41, below). Akia says likewise: when you become restive, you shall stand away from a *spoiled sacrifice* (Gresson 1982). And in this, you will discover what has always been the truth: your life is worth much; and you have more to offer than you have realized before. You pursue a "freedom" already in your hands. When you say "no!" to the established "truths" and discover (create) your own, you will free more than yourself: you will free the Other as well.

Absent the insight Black feminism provided Akia, Monique's and Eartha's narratives render this effort problematic. Monique sees herself as a "mystique," and Eartha sees herself as an "earthling." Like Akia, both struggle to unfold in accordance with the "Black Mother" within them. Both choose believable self-metaphors, with redemptive qualities: Monique is thrust back into Blackness and tries to retain the vision of an enlarged racial identity for herself and her son; Eartha rebuilds herself from the fragmented and fractured stereotyped categories others impose upon her to utter, "I am an Earthling. I belong on this planet. And I define me."

Although both Monique and Eartha achieve a degree of heroism, in their stories, at least, it differs from the heroism born of facing the contradictions and experiencing the accompanying vulnerability. Each, finally, stands alone, for the moment. Unlike Akia, neither seems to convey a strong memory of cultural identity, a recollection of healthier times when there was faith in a movement and when "hellified Black women" organized and sustained the Black spirit on white campuses. For each, then, recovery is chaotic rather than constructive. They give us a vision of the "birthright" of antiessentialism void of a community — however defined — to help construct new values and cultural sharings. To join with them is to join with contradiction and chaos unresolved; to engage them is to invite them to change their stories. Isolated with a problematic interrogator — and no established cultural anchor — they constructed problematic rather than redemptive stories.

Akia is not "superior" to Monique or Eartha; that is not my point. But she has an evolving cultural identity with which she may struggle dialectically. Although many Blacks seem to disdain aspects of feminism, it has given women like Akia a tradition with which to address the problematics of an essentialized Black cultural tradition — one that fails of necessity to bring the cohesion, continuity, and peace of mind sought by individuals wearied by race war. (And a Black feminist tradition has even given women like Akia, Monique, and Eartha ideological perspectives from which to challenge my right to and righteousness in interrogating them. Indeed, in the commitment study there were women who refused to be interviewed by me, my good intentions notwithstanding.)

Akia's story invites us to grow beyond the group's limitations, but we must first come to terms with guilt and tolerate the vulnerability that accompanies it. This is the road to redemption. Akia presents a narrative constructed on an "extrapolation from history" that she can use to shape a mirror the Other may also examine. Like the soliloquist, her story exposes cultural impossibilities and roots the chosen actions in the need for change. She thus provides what Lloyd Bitzer has called the "exigency" characterizing the rhetorical situation. Within the Black cultural context, she reflects the insights of both Stuart Hall on cultural identity and bell hooks on "marginal feminism." Moreover, she achieves her recovery in a believable way: we see her suffer, struggle, and survive.

This, then, is the message of the narrative of recovery: it is ultimately the edifying story that persuades the Other. Rhetorical narrative achieves this only when it reveals vulnerable involvement. In the next part, I construct and illustrate a theory of rhetorical recovery that synthesizes the ideas developed in these first three parts.

PART IV

The Rhetoric
of Recovery:
Theory and Practice

❖

AMERICA'S RECOVERY TAKES THE LEAD

Although markets around the world rallied the week of February 11, 1991, the strongest movement was in the US. The Standard & Poor's 500 index hit a record high and the Dow Jones industrial average finally recouped all that it lost after the Iraqi invasion of Kuwait.

— Jonathan Fuerbringer, *New York Times*, February 17, 1991

7

The Loss of Myth as Rhetorical Challenge:
A Theory of Recovery Discourse in Postmodern Society

❖

We saw that in order to get it [the answer to the problem of education in a democracy], the nineteenth century had to find out what man was striving for, what was distinctive about his action; and it found out that man was peculiarly the animal who strived after meaning, and the creation of meaning. The problem of self-reliance, then, the problem of human liberation, was how to permit the self-creation of meaning. Then we saw that as each discipline reached maturity, it was able to deal with a dimension of the restriction of meaning. Sociology was able to study the whole social system as a dramatic social fiction; psychiatry could understand mental illness as the constriction of action and meaning; ontology allowed us to deduce a critical individual and social aesthetic which showed us that man needed integral meaning and intensity of conviction for his meanings; theology confirmed psychiatry, and showed us that man cannot stand alone with his meanings; but theology showed us something more: that the truly free man will reach for free fellow men, and ultimately for theonomy on which to base his highest strivings.

—Ernest Becker (1969)

Ernest Becker's examination of Western intellectual history led him to conclude that humankind must gradually break away from the collective myths that shaped its, and society's, childhood. This task, Becker reasoned, was integral to the nature of the human being. But Becker also found that the break from collective myths and constraints frees no one in any absolute sense; the human being must move beyond alienation from the impositions of others and find the means — and the metaphor — for reconnection. Thus, Becker felt the ultimate task of the modern person was to remain connected to the group and society but to live a personal vision of truth. This too is Joseph Campbell's vision when he says that humans are trying to find new myths to live by.

Becker's and Campbell's discussions of the lost collective myth partially explain the rise of recovery discourse in contemporary society. As we have seen, recovery discourse and the rhetorical strategies it employs ultimately address this self–Other interest. I have argued that, to the extent it is believable, this vision presents a unique rhetorical challenge. The narratives just presented illustrated aspects of this rhetorical challenge, providing dramatic descriptions of the rhetorical and discursive features of recovery discourse. They allow us, as well, to consider now a more formal statement of recovery phenomena. This chapter presents a set of theoretical premises regarding the nature, structure, and function of recovery discourse that permits an examination of two emergent areas of ideological discourse whose recovery missions have gone largely underexamined: "the white male as victim of affirmative action" and "Black postmodernism." We begin at the beginning, with one of the narratives from the Book of Genesis, showing that recovery discourse pertains to certain generic issues and relies upon a particular set of persuasive themes.

Genesis: Prologue to a Theory of Recovery

One of the earliest accounts of the discourse of recovery appears in an early Genesis story in which Esau and Jacob, who are sons of Isaac, find themselves in conflict. Esau, as the oldest son, was heir to Isaac's name, glory, and wealth. Jacob, a younger son, was favored by his mother, who missed no opportunity to intervene, even "wrongly," on his behalf. Jacob was ambitious for himself, as well; and he understood that he could not gain status and position being "second son." The laws of primogeniture gave all to the first and none to those who came after.

With his nonchalance and arrogance as first son, Esau was less than sensitive to the sibling jealousies engendered by this law of "firstness." Against this backdrop, one of the most intriguing and ironic of the Genesis stories unfolds: on a hunting trip Jacob outsmarts Esau by persuading him to surrender his birthright for a portion of game. Later, with his mother's aid, Jacob steals Esau's blessing from the aged and blind patriarch, Isaac. In Genesis 27:34–40 the betrayed father and son confront their shared folly and betrayal:

Upon hearing his Father's words, Esau uttered a very loud and bitter cry and said to him, "Father, bless me too." But he answered, "Your brother came deceitfully and received your blessing." Then he said, "Must he, true to his name, Jacob, supplant me now a second time? He took my birthright and now he has taken my blessing." He added, "Have you not a blessing for me?"

Isaac answered, "Esau, I appointed him your lord and have given him all his brothers as servants. I have enriched him with grain and wine. What then can I do for you, my son?" But Esau said to his father, "Have you only the one blessing, father, bless me also my father." And Esau wept aloud. His father, Isaac, answered him: "Without the fruitfulness of the earth shall your dwelling be, without the dew of the heavens above. By your sword shall you live. You shall serve your brother. But when you become restive, you shall shake his yoke from your neck."

These are powerful, but paradoxical and even enigmatic, images: "[W]hen you become restive, you shall shake his yoke from your neck." The vision Isaac described implies an enlargement of, if not corrective to, the notion of societal power. His vision, to be precise, demands that Esau confront two facts: (1) he must accept injustice in the world and accept the outcomes of human flaws and duplicity; and (2) he must find a way of forging a personally meaningful life for himself and his family within this admittedly flawed world.

These are hardly new tasks for the species. People have always had to help forge myths to live by. But past times were, perhaps, less cruel in one sense: one did not have to cope with several distinct and influential theories of personality (such as Freudian theory) or discourse (such as postmodernism) that held the *self-deceptive* nature of all such mythmaking as central tenets. Thus, one constructed one's personal myths within the larger mythic context of the world to which one belonged. This is no longer the central task. Now one must also (re)persuade oneself as one weaves tales supportive of one's choices, decisions, and actions.

The difficulty, one that Esau inherits, is that once we give up our "primary narcissism," as Sigmund Freud called it, we find it difficult to recover. Behavioral and social scientists offer numerous theories to explain this phenomenon, ranging from the psychology of self-deception, unconscious loyalties, and sacralized social bonds to the shame in admitting that one has been "bettered" by another (Gresson 1982). But one attitude increasingly common to these analyses is the "loss of self" through sacrifice for another, a source of great potential danger and especially the danger of *betrayal*. Richard Sennett and Jonathan Cobb ask rhetorically: "Isn't betrayal the inevitable result when you try to endow your life with a moral purpose greater than your own life?" (Sennett and Cobb 1972, 131).

Questions like this emerge from the world of Joseph Campbell and Wilson Moses, a world configured around the individual. But a connection to the world of Isaac and Esau remains: humans across time and space share contradiction as a condition of their humanity. Thomas Hanna expressed this "shared fate" in the following way:

> This contradiction [existence] is precisely the awareness, on the one hand, of being a finite creature compelled by and subject to the demands of the world and, on the other hand, of being a free, responsible being who can never be compelled or subjected to any external force. The irony is that one *is* a contradiction, that one exists dialectically. (Hanna 1962, 281–82)

Contradiction is the "tie" that binds human to human and generation to generation. But what precisely does "contradiction" mean in this sense and what is its relevance to recovery? Once again, the Old Testament illuminates this query.

When Isaac was young, God asked his father, Abraham, to sacrifice (kill) him. Abraham loved God and initiated the sacrificial rite. But God gave Abraham a reprieve: God sent an angel to stay Abraham's hand at the moment he was about to slay his son Isaac. Abraham had been prepared to sacrifice Isaac in obedience to God. God *delivered* Abraham from his bond and from bondage.

Now consider that Isaac, as patriarch and advocate of the old way, had to hold fast to the laws that bound him to his father, Abraham, and, in turn, Abraham to Yahweh (God). As Abraham had been prepared to sacrifice Isaac in obedience to God, so would Isaac bind Esau to the laws of primogeniture: "I appointed him your lord and have given him all his brothers as servants."

God gave Abraham an escape, and Isaac, likewise, finds the words to deliver Esau: "[W]hen you become restive, you shall shake his yoke from your neck."[1]

One interpretation of this narrative is that it proposes that humans must initially sacrifice some of their own needs, wishes, and preferences for a collective pursuit or value; however, having suppressed one's own preferences, one does not really remove the capacity to change one's mind and pursue a self-interested course of action. But human qualities often keep one from exercising one's personal interests unless a break occurs in the bond and the bondage. In the story of Abraham, God had to break the bond by issuing a reprieve; the message is that God as authority can make binding demands if we wish to remain connected to

God. In the story of Esau, Isaac presents a related but somewhat different perspective: an individual may be able to construct a personal story that allows him or her to renegotiate the bond as currently understood and thereby gain a measure of personal liberty while maintaining some relation to the "old ways." As the subsequent chapters of Genesis reveal, Esau does find a way of regaining his liberty while accepting his brother's liberation from primogeniture.

A message of the two visions in these stories is this: there are points in life when one has to break with previously held values, beliefs, and commitments even though one must remain connected, in some fashion, to those who retain the "old ways." In such a situation, one must construct a rhetoric of recovery. Moreover, the committed individual is posed, like Esau, to ask and answer, How can I be both for myself and the other when we no longer share a common myth?

Joseph Campbell's and Wilson Moses's visions of the individual without a guiding collective myth implies this double-bind burden of primacy. Tod Sloan puts the situation like this in his psychological study of decision making: "Whatever the causes, there is now a population of individuals who have actually *seen* hundreds of ways of living and who must, in turn, make choices for themselves, and generally without much feeling of groundedness in their values" (Sloan 1987, 3). We have already seen how several people have answered this burden of choice. Many have misunderstood one or more aspects of this burden, but some have begun to understand its larger meaning (Lasch 1984; Rubin 1975; Gregg 1989; Boszormenyi-Nagy and Spark 1973) and would probably agree with Becker's conclusion:

> [T]he contradictions of man's earthly situation cannot be resolved by easy belief or by reflexively relaying the meaning of it to God. Genuine heroism for man is still the power to support contradictions, no matter how glaring or hopeless they may seem. The ideal critique of a faith must always be whether it embodies within itself the fundamental contradictions of the human paradox and yet is able to support them without fanaticism, sadism, and narcissism, but with openness and trust. (E. Becker 1971, 198)

Becker's notion of heroism is a central concept here. The hero is one who seeks *to balance the contradictions of life in word and deed*. But this discussion employs another meaning of the concept, the notion of hero generic to *myth,* the notion of hero or heroine as one whose mission is recovery for self and Other. Joseph Campbell helps us appreciate this definition of the hero in his description of the hero's quest during the "archetypal journey":

> If only a portion of that lost totality [the World Navel] could be dredged up into the light of day, we should experience a marvelous expansion of our powers, a vivid renewal of life. We should tower in stature. Moreover, if we could dredge up something forgotten not only by ourselves but by our whole generation or our entire civilization, we should become indeed the boon-bringer, the culture hero of the day — a personage of not only local but world historical moment. The archetypes to be discovered and assimilated are precisely those that have inspired, throughout the annals of human culture, the basic images of ritual, mythology, and vision. (J. Campbell 1968, 17, 18)

Here Campbell provides the essence of the hero's quest: to find one's own way in an indeterminate and confused world; and in this journey to recover through discovery — through experience, through the facts, follies, and fulfillments of life — and to return to the group with this rediscovered Truth. From this view of heroism, we see that Isaac was telling Esau that his *prior and primary* birthright is not something given by another man; rather, it is the inherent drive to create meaning, to discover a viable way for self and, if one is fortunate, for others as well.[2]

For Campbell, the hero is the one who recovers these lost myths in a way that is compelling for the group. Shortly before his death, however, Campbell observed that the achievement of this recovery is not something one can orchestrate: it is largely an unconscious and developmental process of recovery that humankind collectively helps bring about; one day, we suddenly realize we have recovered what was lost. The ongoing search for new myths by which to live is such a historical force. Moreover, this historical imperative creates powerful psychological pressures. To perceive events of the moment, such as the Gulf War, as merely about oil or the "new world order" is to miss a "big picture" that reaches back to antiquity and includes dreams of heroism and the love and protection of gods who knew from where we came and to where we are headed. This heroic quest for meaning is the logic underpinning recovery discourse and its rhetorics. The following theory is an outgrowth of ideas presented and developed in the previous discussion.

A Theory of Recovery Discourse

Recovery goes on continuously. Its eruption into the public imagination and consciousness, however, is attributable to a disruption in established bonds and self–Other perceptions, a disruption that can be developmentally traced. For example, racial recovery rhetoric is a special instance of a more generic process, the outgrowth of several important events and dynamics stimulated, in part, by the crisis in identity and the relative failure of the Black Power and civil rights movements of the 1960s and 1970s. Four events had broad relevance:

(1) shifting rhetorical conditions, the perceived loss of white voice at home with regards to race and gender and abroad with respect to political economics;

(2) the experience of intragroup violations resulting from a break in the collusive racial bond;

(3) the intermeshing of liberation efforts and discourse among various disenfranchised groups, resulting in such transitional metaphors as the "Rainbow Coalition"; and

(4) the emergence of postmodernist discourse as a dominant rhetoric.

These elements, viewed as the preconditions of racial recovery rhetoric, serve as a backdrop for the proposed theory of recovery discourse.[3]

The Theory

The loss of collective meaning, or certitude, heralded the advent of a new and continuing struggle to recover what was lost in the breakdown in believable communication about reality or values. As life continues, it does so in a more constrained and privatized world; the individual replaces the group; and from the perspective taken here, this privatization leads to at least four interconnected phenomena:

(1) The individual becomes both speaker and listener for self in a way unprecedented in the past and becomes the central architect of self-creation.

(2) To the degree that it is change- and growth-focused, this self-communication carries the seeds of its own continued alienation or privatization.

(3) The attempt to reconnect with the Other (however understood) continues to be problematic since the dialogic dimension, so essential to healthy self–Other understanding and growth, is compromised by the resort to logic like, "Well, we each have our own opinion," and, "After all, it's my life and who's living it?"

(4) Recovery itself becomes configured as a heroic discovery, as the next few paragraphs show.

First, the experience of betrayal and violation revolves around sacrifices and previously constrained choices. This is the "loss phase" of recovery.

Second, the struggle with contradictions and exploration of previously tabooed options leads to the discovery that one can function outside of the previous relational matrix. This is the "recovery through discovery phase."

Third, the identification of and joining with persons having a shared experience of violation and betrayal serve as the "recollusion phase," expressed as a clash of "contemporaries" and "consociates" (Gresson 1978). Consociates are those with whom we have a "real" relationship based on shared experiences and struggles. Contemporaries, by contrast, are those with whom we share a historical attribute like race, class, or gender. In a transitional, or postmodern, society, we rely upon consociates to validate our recovery choices; we are unable to believe in the availability and support of another merely because of a shared historical accident. Because of the strain of a privatized reality, a consociate will also ideally be a contemporary. Otherwise, one chooses the consociate over the contemporary. Exceptions are those persons driven to remain committed to the traditional ways in spite of the increased likelihood of personal damage (Fiske 1980). From the logic of this stance, for example, a Black woman, unable to find the Black man she prefers, may choose a white man whose values, beliefs, and behaviors make him the "comrade" and the Black man the "ex-comrade." The dynamic is the same, of course, with a Black woman like Monique who prefers a given white man but loses him, then defines him as "ex-comrade" (like the Black man), and identifies with the white female who sees her as a strong, successful victor over male betrayal. This phase relies significantly on what I call "transitional metaphors" (Gresson 1987), which are discussed in the next section.

Fourth, self–Other healing rhetoric, expressed as continuities of cultural (and racial) care, resolves the historical and pragmatic problems of group (racial) loyalty and persisting oppression (racism, sexism, classism). This is the "heroic reintegration phase." Earlier, Audre Lorde's notion of "Black Mother" explained the particular sources of strength and wisdom the narrator as self–Other inducer relies upon. As Lorde indicated, the "Black Mother" is not the patriarchal white father; and her gifts are enlarging rather than constrictive, creative rather than destructive. Recalling this point, reconsider now a passage cited earlier from *The Female Hero,* in which Pearson and Pope observe:

> Both male and female heroes begin the quest for wholeness and selfhood by risking the violation of conventional norms, including conventions about appropriate sex-role behavior; both learn not to manipulate and restrain other people; and both reach accommodation with the best qualities as-

sociated with men and with women, integrating strength with humility, independence with empathy, rationality with intuition, and thought with emotion. (Pearson and Pope 1981, 15)

This is not, however, the archetypal hero of white male mythology; this is, so to speak, the hero as nonwhite male patrician. To carry out this version of heroism, moreover, the hero relies on two special rhetorical weapons: the *transitional metaphor,* to promote self-soothing during discovery and recovery; and *rhetorical reversal,* to induce the Other to accept the change and join with the new self in forging a better, healthy reunion. These two rhetorical strategies are central to the theory of recovery. The next section first elaborates upon these tools and their specific roles in the recovery process; then it presents a model of racial recovery rhetoric derived from the theory.

Reversal and Transition in Recovery

Rhetorical Reversal

Earlier we identified the rhetoric of "reverse racism" or "reverse discrimination" as a generic rhetorical recovery strategy. While this tactic has gained a special prominence in white recovery discourse, it is hardly restricted to this discursive arena. Reversal is a pivotal tactic with a most interesting logic. It pertains to the power to name, define, and negotiate reality. In the 1960s, Blacks engaged in such behavior around the notion of "Black." Before the 1960s, this word held largely negative connotation for most American Blacks, but by seizing and embracing the word "Black" and investing it with positive value, Blacks engaged in a most significant form of reversal. One of the major reflections of the power shift — at least, symbolically — occurred when whites no longer told Blacks the meaning of words and Blacks defined and redefined meanings according to their own values and interests. It is, for instance, now a part of Black folklore that Quame Toure (Stokely Carmichael) told the white press, "Black Power means whatever we say it means."

Blacks have assumed a different oppositional style in recent decades, focusing increasingly upon elaborating the nature and liberational role of Black literary and cultural theory and criticism (Awkward 1988, 7). In conjunction with this shift, white women have increasingly assumed the vanguard challenge of white male appropriational tactics. The struggle for "self"-control has been essential to this challenge of the canon. For example, "making reversals" is a major feminist strategy. In their article "Women Take Back the Talk," Cheris Kramarae and Mercilee M. Jenkins have enunciated it as follows:

> One strategy employed by feminists is to make the negative positive. Mary Daly calls herself a *hag*, which formerly meant "an evil or frightening spirit." She asks, evil and frightening to whom? Others make positive reference to themselves as witches and spinsters, to stress the importance of their having control over what they are called and how they are treated. This can be done successfully with most of the words men use to describe women because the majority of these words have slid semantically to a derogatory sexual meaning.
>
> Still other women make the positive negative, thus transforming reality. For example, some experiment with the division of the world into "women" and "nonwomen," a reversal, of course, of the category scheme which has been used by "nonwomen." (Kramarae and Jenkins 1987, 140)

Kramarae and Jenkins describe contemporary feminist efforts to reclaim language, but the sense of reversal I have in mind originates from the oppressor. Blacks like Harold Cruse, Angela Davis, Molefi Asante, Alice Walker, and Malcolm X, and white females like Elizabeth Cady Stanton, Betty Friedan, Adrienne Rich, and Mary Daly are but a few of the critics who have addressed this aspect of reversal. For example, in his speeches, Malcolm X noted the press's capacity for, and propensity toward, reversing meaning. Responding to a question regarding a telegram he sent to the then-leader of the American Nazi Party, Malcolm observed:

> The entire press was aware that it was sent. Nothing was done about it; they wouldn't print it. . . . The so-called liberal element of the white power structure never wants to see nationalists involved in anything that has to do with civil rights. And I'll tell you why. Any other Black people who get involved are involved within the rules that are laid down by the white liberals. And as long as they are involved within those rules, then that means they're only going to go as far as the liberal element of the power structure will endorse their activity. But when the nationalistic-minded Blacks get involved, then we do what our analysis tells us is necessary to be done. (Malcolm X 1970, 44)

For Malcolm, the oppressor (the press) could reverse reality merely by imposing silence, cutting off public knowledge of alternative, conflictive facts and realities. A similar view of reversal has been central to the work of Mary Daly, the radical lesbian-feminist theologian. In *Gyn/Ecology,* she declared that patriarchy equals reversing and identified it among "the games of the fathers":

Despite all the evidence that women are attacked as projections of The Enemy, the accusers ask sardonically: "Do you really think that *men* are the enemy?" This deception/reversal is so deep that women — even feminists — are intimidated into Self-deception, becoming the only Self-described oppressed who are unable to name their oppressor, referring instead to vague "forces," "roles," "stereotypes," "constraints," "attitudes," influences." This list could go on. The point is that no agent is named — only abstractions. . . .

Whenever Hags hear the terms *trivia, trivial, trivialize,* these should function as reminders of the omnipresence of Reversal, whose ultimate meaning is re-versing of life-engendering energy, symbolized by the Goddess, into necrophilic Nothing-loving. . . .

In such a situation it is difficult to even imagine the right questions about our situation. Women struggling for words feel haunted by false feelings of personal inadequacy, by anger, frustration, and a kind of sadness/bereavement. For it is, after all, our "mother tongue" that has been turned against us by the tongue twisters. Learning to speak our Mother's Tongue *is* exorcising the male "mothers." (Daly 1978, 8, 29, 79, 330)

Daly's vision is not postmodern, properly speaking, and yet she pursues — as do most liberation rhetors — a postmodernist stance vis-à-vis the dominant discursive group: white males. Still, Daly's position, itself part of the dominant (white) discourse, fails to illuminate a profound truth: any oppressed group — not only or principally white females — can become a victim of reversal and thereby lose the capacity to name the oppressor. A larger view of reversal, partly instructed by Daly's insight, assumes that anyone may be an oppressor, and anyone may experience oppression. From this view, we can diagram the following sequence:

PERCEIVED LOSS → RECOVERY BEHAVIOR → RHETORICAL REVERSALS

Central to the theory of recovery developed here, this sequence declines to isolate a given group or person as "true victim," and for an important reason: each person is genuinely capable of experiencing self as victim of the Other. Thus, each human and each group is capable of disidentifying with the Other and uttering a reversal. This possibility partially underlies the very rhetorical quagmire Christopher Lasch described. In a discussion of William Ryan's *Blaming the Victim* (1976), Lasch writes:

In the preface to the revised edition, Ryan apologizes for devoting the first edition largely to the plight of Black people and the poor. He has come to see that almost everyone is vulnerable to disaster: to "catastrophic illness"; to the "deliberate manipulation of inflation and unemployment"; to "grossly unfair taxes"; to pollution, unsafe working conditions, and the "greed of the great oil companies." (Lasch 1984, 67)

The point is not that various individuals and groups have no real differences in their experiences and life chances, but that all people may know vulnerability. The view of rhetorical reversal proposed here — and Ryan illustrates it in the passage referred to above — is that one needs to be understood in terms of a rejection of one specific form of vulnerability because one *is* vulnerable in another sense. This, then, is the implicit logic of recovery rhetoric: "I may disclaim vulnerability on the grounds that I am vulnerable." An excellent illustration of this reasoning appears in the epigraph to chapter 4: "Many Black men . . . exaggerate their oppression in order to gain a woman's sympathy and exploit her emotions, transforming her into a passive shadow that ultimately is left alone to struggle, suffer, and weep."

Whether accurate or not, whether based on her personal experience or not, in this passage, Linda White shows how reversal and vulnerability come together to contextualize — to motivate and mobilize — the recovery project. Five interrelated dynamics seem closely associated with rhetorical reversal:

(1) the experience of a personally debilitating loss of one's share in a collective hegemony, whether deserved or not;

(2) a public — first personal, then collective — effort to recover the pragmatic and moral losses;

(3) a gradual convergence of the public and private actions and analyses;

(4) their dual justification and legitimation by various factions within society through negation of the previously reigning rhetorical situation; and

(5) the gradual emergence of a reconciliatory, more inclusive formative image, purged of the former negativity of the lost moral context.

Both the oppressor and oppressed may participate in this tactic of recovery rhetoric; thus, either out-group members or members of the oppressed group may direct reversals at the oppressed. The relative differences in history and real differences in power, however, ultimately make such rhetorical arguments less than persuasive. Several illustrations of this argument have already appeared, perhaps the most notable instances being Julius Lester's suggestion that Blacks oppress him as much as whites and that he would fight them both to be free, and Eartha's characterizing an experience she had with a white woman as an instance of Black oppression.

These types of reversals that "fly in the face of history" pose certain problems, especially in narratives. A major part of the difficulty may be the gender difference in narratives.

Reversals in Narratives: A Gender Perspective

One way to understand the reversals and their relation to narrative as a vehicle for self–Other persuasion is to consider the gender difference in storytelling. As Kramarae and Jenkins maintain:

> Strategically, women's stories are designed to create an atmosphere of support based on a sense of a shared social reality. This reality is not reified in the culture as men's reality is. So the point of the story or joke is created or discovered jointly in the immediate context.... We are spinning our relationships as we spin our stories as we spin our reality. Through our storytelling we give our own meanings to our experience and through our joking we reverse men's reversals and turn the social order rightside up.... Bonnie Immerman's study of published lesbian personal-experience narratives illustrates this self-affirming quality and shows us the value of personal narratives to "debunk expert knowledge" and provide "alternative role models." (Kramarae and Jenkins 1987, 146)

Recent communications research findings largely support this stance (see Carter and Spitzack 1989). Thus, a critical issue for the proposed theory is the gender of the listener and storyteller. Each brings important presuppositions to the discourse. Consider, for example, Audre Lorde's reversal of the personal-choice *topos* described earlier. Although she and other Black women used this notion to defend their break with the racial collusions of the past, interpretations of the meaning of their action seemed to differ significantly from those of actions associated with Black males. Recall, in fact, that a major source for the Black sexism debate of 1979 was Robert Staples's comment that Black women seemed to share a flawed logic and confusion in their discourse about male-female choices and responsibilities. This debate suggests that the reversal ("personal choice cuts two ways") may have quite different purposes as rationale and narrative event when applied to a male rather than a female.

From this view, my interpretations of the three earlier narratives are precisely that: *my* interpretations, complete with my own projections. No doubt, Monique, Eartha, and Akia would describe both their and my presence in the narrative differently from the way I have. For this reason, a male elaboration of the narrative as a conciliatory action invites gender bias. Such a bias, moreover, may require an alternative approach like the one Mary Daly attempts in her work.

Recognizing the possible significance of gender to narrative function does not mean that women cannot misuse the reversal with men. The constraint on the reversal tactic — one that postmodernism seems to neglect, if not negate entirely — is history. History compelled Audre Lorde to observe that white oppression has forced Blacks to relate as woman and man in a special way that whites and Black feminists cannot negate by fiat. This is why, moreover, she remained vulnerable to the "ex-comrade": they have a shared history and have shared secrets that cannot be ignored or dismissed. As a tool in the service of the narrative, the reversal must not violate this shared history.

A parallel — and critically important — argument applies to white feminists who, in an ironic twist and reversal (recall Gardner's statement on p. 8, above), assume that their identification with women of color as women neutralizes their brutality toward all people of color, even the men. Audre Lorde challenged this kind of reversal behavior when she observed that white women share with white men, as the dominant group, a capacity for destruction of Blacks that must be closely monitored and managed.

In short, reversals that try to ignore the fact of connection in order to achieve a sense of recovery present problems. They stand in danger of rhetorical failure to the degree that they ignore history and the vulnerability it creates. The reversal in the story fails when it ignores the persistence of *vulnerability*. Again, Lorde's words are instructive: "There already is an additional vulnerability to each other which is desperate and very deep." This is the meaning of Kenneth Burke's observation that the Black as "Negro" and "human" cannot be separated (Burke 1968, 193).

This is why the Other intrudes into the narrative as both listener and validator. When the narrative rejects a *vulnerability* attributable to a shared and collusive history, several problems ensue; of these, the main one is the endangering of the dialogic mending of broken discourse. Though the narrative may draw upon "enlargement" as a *topos* for rejecting traditional loyalty mandates, privatization predominates. The earlier narratives illustrated some of the negative aspects of such privatizing. Still, the privatizing process can be constructive and instructive.

Because even monologic narrative attempts to influence the Other's control, it invites a certain degree of participation by the "Other" (Gresson 1978). When this "Other" is a traditional or socially created mirror of oneself, the language of choice stresses "natural affinity" and being "hereditary allies." When, however, the "Other" represents a private or existential bond — one forged in the present moment — the immediate (though not necessarily the ultimate) designation frequently finds expression in the language of *collusion,* contrived association and action.

It is in narrative writ large that we can see evolving this search for new ways of connecting. We must find ways, as well, to encourage this evolution, and the psychology of narrative and dialogic inquiry seems ideally suited for this task. With the assistance of this approach, we may one day find more ways of transforming the plight of those persons who find their only means of resolving untenable collective contradictions is through their privatization of "public troubles" into personally valid stories. The individual is not alone, however, even in a private narrative. Linguistic means of sharing fears and isolation exist. The self–Other metaphor described in previous chapters is one such rhetorical tool and may relate to a collective and, at times, private vision. As mentioned, I have previously used the term "transitional metaphor" to describe this rhetorical effort at self–Other persuasion and support (Gresson 1987). A brief review of this notion can provide fuller appreciation of the emotional and relational appeal of recovery rhetoric.

The Transitional Metaphor as Recovery Trope

Traditional societies, seeking to manage the uncertainties of life and contain the accompanying anxieties by playing out prescribed roles, rely upon myths and ritual symbols. Modern societies, especially pluralistic ones, also rely upon such mechanisms to explain, predict, and control the anxieties accompanying sociocultural change. Transitional metaphors pertain to both sources of anxiety: those deriving from the experience of life per se (death, hunger, intimacy, betrayal) and those that accompany modernity (ethnopolitics, global political economics, the prospect of nuclear holocaust, planetary chemical pollution).

The transitional metaphor is a word or expression that recapitulates the primal awareness of the "loss of the womb" (the secure, warm oneness with universe and mother) and the efforts to grasp this separation in a cognitive-emotional manner. This formulation gives rise to a wide variety of expressions. For example, some pertain to being "in between," as (1) "between the devil and the deep blue sea" or (2) "between a rock and a hard place." Others transcend this "place" by hinting at both the primal loss and the anticipation of some degree of recovery. Here, for instance, is a lyric fragment from a contemporary Negro spiritual: "Mother and father have gone on, . . . sister still living in sin. . . . "

These illustrations reflect the "transitional mode of awareness" (Farber 1979). David Winnicott (1953) noted that "transitional objects" were connected to imagination and other cognitive functions through the infant's evolving capacity for symbolization. Symbolization enables the individual to move toward an inner, self-soothing capacity: an abstracted replacement of the security of mother, family, social group. The "transitional mode of awareness" pertains to a collective rather than individual sense of circumstances and an attempt to manage this collective sense. Consider, for instance, this widely seen bumper sticker:

> Prevent the Nuclear Winter
> Support the Nuclear Freeze

Other, more traditional illustrations of this "transitional mode of awareness" include:

(1) Take it easy;

(2) Be cool, man; and

(3) Hang in there, baby.

These expressions are intended to be soothing, comforting supports. They are in sharp contrast with metaphors (like "nuclear freeze") that emphasize the creation of a technology capable of cosmic annihilation. Yet both types are concerned with "transitional anxiety." In another form, such metaphors emphasize life span shifts or changes:

(1) The child is father to the man;

(2) Out of the mouths of babes; and

(3) Once a man and twice a child.

Paradox, or the balancing of contradiction, is critical to these metaphorical forms. The idea is not merely to enlarge meaning through the illumination of relatedness between two or more events or phenomena. When one chooses to break with an established norm, one invites both guilt and anxiety; and experiences of oneself as "bad" versus "good" commonly occur. Nor is it always easy to identify what in the self is "good" and "bad," desirable and undesirable. For the mature adult, choosing from among conflictive identities has often been difficult but still possible; for the young child, such a choosing can be psychologically impossible and can result in "splitting" people, particularly parents, into all-good and all-bad representations. Of course, when one is forced to make such an inaccurate assessment, one's own self-image is affected (Blanck and Blanck 1979; Mackey 1984). Societies that encourage the creation of negative and positive stereotypes (Jew, Black, homosexual) contribute to such "splitting" behavior — hence the idea of self-hating Jews, Blacks, homosexuals, and so forth (Gresson 1982). Some transitional metaphors seek to deal with the anxieties and related cognitive-affective experiences associated with the management of what Goffman (1963) has called "spoiled identity." For example, the recent rise of the expression "Brown people" to reflect pride in Black-white parentage suggests a desire to deemphasize both the traditional insistence that mulattoes are Black and the rejection of one's biological connection to the "racist master." This effort to retell the story of racial ancestry is, moreover, a powerful clue to the specific relevance of race to the recovery project. It also offers an excellent vehicle for illustrating how one can use the recovery theory as a source for specific models of recovery rhetoric. The next section offers an example of one perspective of racial recovery rhetoric. Though not the only way of understanding narrative, racial history, and recovery motive, the model does account for many current events and unfolding developments within the African-American community that are often neglected by other perspectives, notably certain psychological and political analyses.

A Model of Racial Recovery Rhetoric

The proposed model emphasizes three dimensions: (1) racial heroism as rhetorical condition; (2) the *topoi* of redemption and heroism; and (3) racial self–Other metaphors as transitional.

Racial Heroism as Rhetorical Condition

James B. Stewart has written:

> Few of the writer-performer-producers of the rhythm and blues music of the 1960s continued to explore the same themes in the 1970s. One who did is Stevie Wonder, who, in fact, extended the celebratory format to include the progeny of a viable Black male-female union — the Black child — in "Isn't She Lovely" and "Ebony Eyes." (Stewart 1979, 196)

In a related discussion, Rhett Jones said:

> The attempts of Black folk in the United States to understand the way in which they have been defined by others and by themselves is no idle intellectual exercise, but rather an essential step in the struggle for Black liberation. It is only after Blacks have sufficiently understood the ways in which Africanity has been conceptualized that they will find it possible to construct definitions of self on which all Black folk can begin to agree. (R. S. Jones 1983, 7)

The narratives presented earlier revealed both sexism and racism as recovery motives. The passages opening this section remind us of the twin features of this complex problem. First, a break has opened in the historic oneness of Black man and woman. This break has not touched all Blacks; nor has it gone unchallenged. This is evident in Stevie Wonder's refusal, symbolically, to defect from the Black family. Yet Stewart's point is well taken: few Black musical creators follow the lead of Wonder; and even more important, evidence suggests that the Black community itself might be yielding to a real, but less than comprehensive, relational rift between Black male and female.

One illustration of this dynamic shift in the Black community's presumed self-assessment occurred at the Massachusetts Institute of Technology in 1983. Each year, the university radio station there presents the top hits of the year. On this occasion, the disk jockey observed that the number two hit of the year was Stevie Wonder's "Ebony Eyes," as sung by Smokey Robinson and Rick James — the old and the new guard. But the number one hit of the year was, almost prophetically it seems, a song entitled "So Afraid It's Over," sung by One Way — a song depicting the breakup of Black romantic love and family.

Stewart offers a sobering conclusion to the possible media representation of the tensions within the "Black family" as race:

> The potential implications of such a situation are mind-boggling. To the extent that people accept the proposition advanced by Ben Sidran that "music is not only a reflection of Black culture, but to some extent, the basis on which it is built," and further, that individuals appreciate the over-arching importance of the family in any culture, it is imperative that necessary steps be taken to ensure that the social commentary on Black male-female relationships contained in Black music again displays a direct correspondence to the feelings and aspirations of its constituency. (Stewart 1979, 196)

Stewart announces a vitally important goal for a "collective" constituency — that is, from a perspective committed to the perpetuation of an Afrocentric identity and collective liberation agenda. Not all Black scholars, however, share a similar sense of, or concern for, an Afrocentric constituency. More important, it is not clear that anyone knows precisely what the feelings and aspirations of *all* African-Americans are in this regard. This possibility brings us to the second feature of the complex racial recovery problem: how to attain a collective identity from the perspective of the individual.

This shift of definition underlies the argument Rhett Jones makes in his essay on Black self: that the pursuit of a collective identity can be achieved only after Blacks attain a fuller understanding of how whites historically defined them and how they want to relate to these definitions. This task is one of recovery because it means Blacks must dialectically confront various complex possibilities: returning to an ancient Afrocentric identity; retaining large aspects of the African-American identity that has emerged over the past four hundred years; or abandoning these aspects of identity for a hybrid, postmodern American identity. These choices reflect Black vulnerability.

Blacks as "Black" are vulnerable to white — that is, vulnerable to the white power structure and dependent on its continued patronage for survival and sustenance. But there is another vulnerability, one to other Blacks. Audre Lorde (1981) exposes this very vulnerability when she confessed her fear before the "ex-comrade" (Black men) when discussing feminist concerns. This particular dimension of vulnerability, if used optimally, renders one apologetic, compassionate, and available for transcendence of the present, but only when one can acknowledge this vulnerability as such.[4]

Because of the need to deal with a dual vulnerability, Black persons as rhetors must be ironists. They must induce both fellow oppressees and the oppressor to share this plight and its likely consequences: failure, flexibility, folly. Lloyd Bitzer illustrated the sentiment this position of vulnerability evokes in his account of the exigency characterizing the genuine rhetorical situation:

> An exigence is an imperfection marked by some degree of urgency; it is a defect, an obstacle, something to be corrected. . . . Exigence is the necessary condition of a rhetorical situation. If there were no exigence, there would be nothing to require or invite change in the audience or in the world — hence there would be nothing to require or invite the creation and presentation of pragmatic messages. When perceived the exigence provides motive. (Bitzer 1980, 26)

The Black person's rhetoric of recovery carries a similar theme. The central exigency of the "Black condition" is the vulnerability constituting its genesis and intergenerational adaptation to white racism and oppression. This vulnerability inheres in the fact that to "buy in to Blackness" yields oppression and to "buy out of Blackness" yields oppression. Liberation thus becomes an unattainable illusion though one shared, to be sure, by all humans. Racial recovery rhetoric thus concerns itself with a perpetual ritual of vulnerability management; this is what we typically mean by the allusion to Blacks as "the premier pragmatists." This emphasis on pragmatism, however, has diverted attention from the ironic posture of Black recovery discourse. A closer consideration of the irony in Black communication yields some interesting communicational patterns and preferences. Black heroism is thus defined as management of these tensions and contradictions.

The *Topoi* of Redemption and Heroism

Within racial recovery discourse, irony inheres in the need to use and transform the obvious facts of ambiguous power and vulnerability as the enduring twins of the "Black diaspora." The trope of Uncle Tom is the historical and heroic metaphor within this discourse. Esu, the African trickster with two mouths (Gates 1988), represents the contemporary Black counterpart of Uncle Tom. Together, they remind us of the primacy and persistence of the ironic in life. Each conveys a notion of the Black hero. But Black heroism becomes most evident today within the four major *topoi* and four tropes of recovery rhetoric. Here are the four major *topoi* of recovery rhetoric: myth, messianism, magic, and mysticism. Racial recovery discourse is a rich repository of the reasoning inherent in these *topoi*. Even though those persons "in recovery" seek to conform other realities to their own, a need persists to "make sense" to the Other. The persistence of these four topics of recovery rhetoric indicates that persuasion, despite frequent disavowal, remains a primary concern of the recovery hero. A brief illustration of the four *topoi* of recovery discourse partially clarifies this point. (Table 2 summarizes the four *topoi* and the relevant tropes.)

Myth. This *topos* focuses on past collective collusion as the basis for persuasive images. Racial myths focus on stories and characters that somehow "keep the dream alive."

Messianism. A shared sacred legacy of obligation to continue caring for the Other(s) is the basis for this *topos*. Heroic delivery from the enemy is the central theme.

Magic. This persuasive theme focuses on fantasized, shared (mythological) formulas as the keys to controlling the Other. Magic occurs during and around the archetypal journey back to the past and the use of routinized practices to achieve wholeness.

Mysticism. Mysticism focuses on a privatized or fantasized, non-shared vision of the (possible) future as a rationale for action. Here the privatized vision reigns, and one's persuasiveness inheres in quickening that force within each of us that understands that "life" and "I" could, may, and shall be Other. From this view, mysticism is a kind of privatized magic: "You may not know my way of flying, but you can conjure up your own experience of flying."

These *topoi* are interrelated by a shared logic and vulnerability and

Table 2

Major Rhetorical Features of Racial Recovery Discourse

Representative	*Topoi*	*Tropes*
Gates (1988)	MYTH	*Signifyin(g) Monkey* (Metaphor)
Moses (1982)	MESSIANISM	*Uncle Tom* (Metaphor)
Naylor (1988)	MAGIC	*Race Heroine* (Other-Metaphor)
Lester (1982)	MYSTICISM	*Black Mystic* (Self-Metaphor)

usually occur as rhetorical choices in the face of contradiction from within and without. Previous studies remark an awareness of one or more of these features in Black discourse. Soundra O'Neale (1986), for example, includes mysticism as one of the rhetorical devices Black female novelists choose to depict their Black female characters.[5]

These *topoi* imply that the constrictions racial oppression places on character development are such that "racial liberation" means, in part, the opportunity to choose from a variety of provocative self–Other representations introduced and developed in stories and narratives. Here, too, the self–Other metaphor becomes apparent as a central rhetorical and transitional feature.

Racial Self–Other Metaphors as Transitional

Racial recovery rhetoric is rich with transitional metaphors, and Cheryl A. Wall's anthology on the criticism of Black women reveals several (Wall 1989). Most notable is an essay by Mae Henderson (1989), regarding whom Wall says: "Heteroglossia and glossolalia, Henderson's tropes for intertextuality and revision, are defined in terms of Bakhtin and Gadamer as well as in terms of the religious practices of the Afro-American sanctified church" (Wall 1989, 12). And what is Henderson's Black trope? Speaking in tongues.

Regarding her metaphor for Black women's reality, Henderson reasons:

[B]lack women must speak in a plurality of voices as well as in a multiplicity of discourses. This discursive diversity, or simultaneity of discourse, I call "speaking in tongues." Significantly, glossolalia, or speaking in tongues, is a practice associated with Black women in the Pentecostal Holiness Church, the church of my childhood and the church of my mother. In the Holiness church . . . , speaking unknown tongues (tongues known only

to God) is in fact a sign of election, or holiness. As a trope it is also intended to remind us of Alice Walker's characterization of Black women as
artists, as "Creators," intensely rich in that spirituality which Walker sees
as "the basis of Art."

    Glossolalia is perhaps the meaning most frequently associated with
speaking in tongues. It is this connotation which emphasizes the particular, private, closed, and privileged communication between the congregant
and the divinity.... Speaking in tongues, my trope for both glossolalia
and heteroglossia, has a precise genealogical evolution in the Scriptures.
(Henderson 1989, 22–23)

    Henderson sees Black women writers and critics as sharing the dual
gifts, to speak and interpret multiple tongues: the former speaks, the
latter interprets. Her description clarifies the heroic task described here
thus far around recovery of self and Other. Observing that Black women
writers seek to remain on the margins, to be the "insider-outsider," Henderson quotes Gadamer: "There is a kind of experience of the 'Thou'
that seeks to discover things that are typical in the behavior of [the
Other] and is able to make predictions concerning another person on
the basis of a [commonality] of experience" (Henderson 1989, 36). It is
also noteworthy that she begins her essay with these lines from Audre
Lorde's "Sister Outsider":

> I am who I am, doing what I came to do, acting upon you like a drug
> or chisel to remind you of your me-ness, as I discover you in myself.
> (Henderson 1989, 16)

    Mae Henderson relates the transitional quality of the metaphor to
the narrative context by emphasizing the self-contained (read as self-
soothing) aspect of the gift of tongues. This gift remains public and
connective, inducing motive. She confirms this by citing Audre Lorde,
a woman at the core of the recovery discourse agenda among Black
women, the race, and the species. Thus, the circle is, rhetorically speaking, complete. As we recall, the self-soothing feature is linked to drawing
strength and courage from acknowledging one's vulnerability and seeking choices and options that make sense in this condition. One familiar
with the work of the Gestalt psychologists, and particularly the work
of founder Fritz Perls, will sense the parallel between the Lorde's poetry
and Perls's famous saying:

> I am not in this world to please you;
> You are not in this world to please me;
> You do your thing and I'll do mine;
> And if we come together, that's fine.[6]

This connection between Perls's "existential-phenomenological" theory of treatment and Black writers like Lorde and Henderson reflects a convergence between racial recovery rhetoric and a form of psychotherapy popular during the radical 1960s and 1970s. The association is captured in the explanation of "polarities," a central concept in Gestalt psychology:

> As humans grow in families and society, the tendency is to develop and value those characteristics and attitudes that stimulate approval (such as generosity, passivity). The consequence is that the opposites (polarities) of these attitudes and characteristics are cut off from both awareness and expression so that significant aspects of the self are denied. The Gestalt process aims at the patient making contact with what he has rejected and to re-win those natural qualities (self-interest, assertiveness) of his person. (Rosenberg 1978, 297)

The oppressed (Black) person, seizing freedom, will naturally gravitate toward the self-expression identified in Gestalt psychology. Moreover, this return to, or recovery of, what Freud called "primary narcissism" is self-validating, self-reinforcing. Since the experience of vulnerability teaches the folly of premature or reified commitment to any one value or idea, one must find additional reason and support for consoling the self — one must be "marginal," must act in the given situation as if it is the only one. Henderson's choice of speaking in tongues as the self-metaphor for Black women is shrewd since it allows her both to take this pluralistic posture toward the Other and to identify this stance with a biblical source.

To focus briefly on this point of the sacred and theonomy, recall that this chapter began with a passage from Becker's *Beyond Alienation*. One part of that passage reads:

> [T]heology confirmed psychiatry, and showed us that man cannot stand alone with his meanings; but theology showed us something more: that the truly free man will reach for free fellow men, and ultimately for theonomy on which to base his highest strivings.

In other words, the species seems determined to go beyond self in defining a "final authority" for its actions. Henderson does precisely this in her choice of a metaphor. Yet there is something more here: choices that can be validated only by deities who seem not to speak directly to the masses must await some final judgment day. In the meantime, we must accept whatever the individual does at face value. One, therefore, finds an exit to a most difficult situation: satisfying self and Other.

Of course, when one does not satisfy the Other, one can always explain the Other rhetorically as lacking the mystical vision. Lester uses this very rhetorical ploy when he dismisses those Blacks who take issue with his apparent collusion with Jews (see chap. 2, above). In his words, "The mystical experience is as incomprehensible to the non-mystic as the Black experience is to non-Blacks" (Lester 1982, 85).

In this phrasing we see how one uses the sacred to persuade the self immediately and to set up the structure for persuading those others who, likewise, are prepared to sacralize personal decisions and claim that the tongues in which one speaks are "known only to God."

A multiplicity of factors make up the power of recovery rhetoric: biological, deistic, political, economic, and cultural imagery ready the individual to seize the opportunity to act, and certain times are especially ripe for this recovery activity. This fact will become clearer in the two chapters to follow, particularly in chapter 9 where we meet Henry Louis Gates, the Black postmodernist literary scholar who has apparently found a way to weave these various imageries into a postmodernist tapestry of racial rhetoric.

Conclusion

In chapter 2, I quoted Orrin Klapp about the convergence of the "identity crisis" among white and Black Americans. Klapp took the stance that most Blacks would probably endure the agony of a personal identity crisis if they could acquire the material goods enjoyed by most white Americans. History has proved him partially correct; those who were on the short list of privileged Blacks have largely embraced the identity crisis of the white majority. This is why many contemporary African-Americans can sincerely ask, What or who is Black? Prior to the 1960s, one would have known what "Black" was just as most whites would have known what "racism" is. But times change. This is why contemporary white recovery rhetoric — the white man as victim — may be seen to converge with some of the more privatized recovery experiences and expressions of Black Americans.

Racial loss for white Americans is significantly moral and symbolic. Still, individual whites, particularly males, may experience themselves as "less privileged" than Blacks, women, and other designated groups who have received some privileges once restricted to only white men. Important here is the convergence of Black and white vulnerability and the resulting efforts to regain what has amounted to an "imbalance of the moral order."[7]

In his description of the phases of a rhetorical situation, Bitzer writes:

A few situations persist because the exigencies are deeply embedded in the human condition. War and peace, triumph and tragedy, slavery and freedom, life and death, guilt and innocence — such universal or archetypal exigencies are ever present and account for situations perpetually forming. (Bitzer 1980, 35, 36)

As noted in chapter 1, Elliott Rudwick and August Meier have argued that Black violence against whites typically ends with Black acquiescence: Blacks yield to the anger and power of white sadism. This is Black pragmatism. The recent rise of Black conservatism seems to be merely a contemporary illustration of this pragmatism.[8] Black pragmatism has thus become a dominant *topos* for contemporary Black recovery discourse.

This understanding of Black pragmatism, when examined by the reasoning inherent in Bitzer's position, yields a disturbing yet accurate portrait of much of contemporary Black identity discourse. Several major works now aim at answering what was once moot: Who is Black? From this view, Black recovery is essentially about finding a way to re-ingratiate self to the white power structure. This theme brings us to a consideration of an implied connection: white recovery action and the discourse of the "new world order."

In my research on Black women's commitment rhetoric, I found four interrelated dimensions making up the evolution of an alternative or counter exigency (Gresson 1985b). I call these dimensions of the dialectic of personal racial growth:[9]

(1) uttering the unutterable: "Sometimes I feel angry because they [unemployed Black male youth] are all we have to choose from";

(2) experiencing connection but difference: "I can't be worried about the race; I care but I have to live for me";

(3) reassessing the unutterable through self–Other compassion: "I just feel bad for Black men; I think they ought to start thinking about themselves as individuals, as persons, not as categories"; and

(4) establishing an enlarged, more balanced self-ideal: "When I got a chance, I took some [compassion, love, care] back for myself."

This particular pattern of Black self–Other tension tells us something of the rhetorical challenge facing the collectivity, but it does not help us to see "the big picture." In chapter 1, I cited Celeste Condit to the effect that the contemporary emphasis on privatized morality — such as that which evolves from poetic and rhetorical narratives — allows an insufficient perspective on the public discourse that ultimately shapes morality. I share this view, and I believe that one can achieve this larger rhetorical perspective with the theory of recovery presented in this chapter. One can apprehend the theory itself and the primary recovery rhetorics within the current debates around affirmative action and the potentially liberating discourse of deconstructionism. The convergence of white and Black visions of recovery, expressed as "Black-white collusion," can be found in these two discursive arenas.

Using theoretical notions developed so far, I intend to explore the recovery communications embedded within the most celebrated instance of "Black deconstructionist discourse": Henry Louis Gates's *The Signifying Monkey*. But to understand better the rhetorical situation giving valence or power to this particular expression of Black postmodernist deconstruction, one should first observe a larger picture of the contemporary white recovery project.

Application of this theory and model to white and Black recovery efforts helps situate contemporary American race relations within the most inclusive political, psychological, and philosophical context. It also suggests the critical descriptive and interpretive role of contemporary rhetorical theory and criticism. Ideally, a rhetorical perspective will arise to parallel the emerging unifying race myths and temper the efforts to camouflage the brutal destructiveness of aggression clothed in such rhetoric as that of the "new world order."

8

White Recovery of Moral and Heroic Voice:
How to Say "Yo' Momma!"
When You're Already "the Man"

❖

Dialectical irony implies a bondedness in which the ironist realizes
her freedom only through unmasking the pretensions of her "vic-
tim," but in which the victim regains his subjectivity only through
being ironized. To see someone as the victim of irony is to see that
person, relative to oneself, as submerged in unreflective absolutism.
— Richard Brown (1987)

Postmodern society generates folly. It is folly to claim that by hitting men
as often as men hit women, women can be "batterers" in the same sense
as men are. It is folly to claim that the Soviet Union's demise means
that capitalism is good and that God is on capitalism's and not com-
munism's side. It is also folly to cry "reverse racism" and claim that
Blacks, Hispanics, poor white ethnics, and other disenfranchised groups
have turned the tide of oppression and now oppress privileged white
men in some wholesale fashion. Yet folly reigns. And an ironic twist has
occurred in race relations and related areas involving historically oppressed collectivities: the oppressor is now the oppressed, and the victim
is now the villain.

In chapter 1, I described the deconstruction of oppression. This chapter returns to that theme but enlarges and examines it using the theory
presented in chapter 7. More specifically, this chapter employs the idea
of "rhetorical reversal" to indicate how the symbolic and substantive
dimensions of racial reempowerment seem to be occurring; it also discusses the particular rhetorical strategies employed. We can begin with
the symbolic and conclude with the substantive arenas; but these two
domains exist in a state of mutuality, each instructing and imitating the
other. To illustrate the symbolic domain, the world of contemporary pop

163

music presents us with the meteoric rise of a white male as the reigning "King of Rap." To illustrate the substantive domain, we can adduce both the Supreme Court and the media's management of racial incidents. Before taking up Vanilla Ice, however, I will review and briefly illustrate the dimensions of rhetorical reversal.

A Model of Racial Recovery Rhetoric

Rhetorical Reversal:
A Postmodern Rhetorical Strategy

Harold Isaacs opens his volume *Idols of the Tribe* with a story of a young Italian politician from Newark, New Jersey, trying to recover from the recent election of a Black mayor by the city's Black majority:

> This young ward politician has come to see that brandishing arms and threatening violence — as some of his political elders were doing — would not work in streets the whites no longer ruled. He was casting about instead for ways of negotiating a modus vivendi with the new kings of the jungle. He told about an encounter he'd had on a television panel show with a prominent Black militant leader. Without other preamble, the Black stabbed a finger at the Italian-American and said, "You're a racist son of a bitch." Without blinking, the Italian-American replied, "You're damned right, and so are you, you racist son of a bitch." (Isaacs 1977)

This passage illustrates rhetorical reversal — that is, the neutralization of a historical or factually based trope by the misuse of its moral power in relation to self. In the case Isaacs presents, it is used by an Italian-American who neutralizes the term by essentially saying to the Black man, "Yo' Momma!" "Signifying" has borne many meanings, but psychologically, they all relate to a need to handle matters with *irony* — to renegotiate the terms of endearment and the conditions for relatedness.

In the scenario described by Isaacs, we get two important insights: (1) part of the personal power of the storyteller derives from finding another with whom to share the story; and (2) collective power evolves when the other takes the story and carries it forth. I will return to this idea later when I discuss the famous Earl Butz racial slur incident. The key idea here is that whites still retain the power to negotiate around "voice" and "voicelessness." The liberation movements of the 1960s and 1970s revealed important changes in the way men of power would continue their domination of the weak.

The Italian-American politician revealed deep anxiety toward such change, and he attempted to control it. He thereby reminded us, as well, that few surrender their perceived privileges without a fight. This is no singular revelation. History repeatedly shows it. Recall that at first Esau plotted Jacob's death after his loss of power. The message of Genesis is that a change of heart is vital to the persistence of the species. It is why Esau forgives Jacob's treachery. But few of us live in mythic fairy tales. Our struggle must continue, and short of major global reconstruction, we have little evidence that the more powerful will willingly show compassion and justice for the disenfranchised.

Thus, what we seek to find in the narrative of the Italian-American from Newark is not a change of heart but a change of tactic. He might be willing to change his attitudes and values. He might be only trying to defend himself from a perceived, unmotivated attack. Both of these possibilities address the essential tension: the once-powerful must find a way of relating without the old "cultural weapons"; and this necessity introduces a rhetorical crisis of recovery. How the actor ultimately comes to relate is essential to the initial structure of the crisis he faces. Thus, the immediate need is for a change of tactic for maintaining control, and this is the source of the rhetorical dimension of recovery of racial hegemony.

The discourse of white recovery suggests the following sequence:

(1) Power shifts along racial lines (such as those that have characterized the 1960s in America and the 1990s in South Africa) create anxiety, confusion, rage (turned inward), and anger (turned outward).

(2) The incumbent leaders are perceived as traitors by members of the once-dominant group. The discourse is one of loss of entitled privileges. (The soothing of these passions during such periods becomes a major task. We saw this task underway recently with Nelson Mandela's repeated insistence that Black South Africans will not overwhelm and destroy white South Africans under democratic governance.)

(3) When a renormalization process occurs like the one that took place in the United States over the last decade, the discourse of loss persists but gradually gives way to a discourse of recovery.

(4) This discourse of recovery takes on several ironic rhetorical elements identified and conceptually interrelated in a way that helps to explain more dramatically and pragmatically certain perplexing language features and logics.

(5) These features include the following dimensions and dynamics:

a. public (collective) efforts to recover the pragmatic and moral losses;

b. private renegotiations of the original hierarchical arrangements in daily life;

c. a convergence of the public and private actions and analyses;

d. their dual justification and legitimation by various factions within the society through negation of the previous reigning rhetorical situation; and

e. the gradual emergence of a reconciliative, inclusive formative image, purged of the negativity of the lost moral context. We see this reconciliation in the "Rainbow Coalition" metaphor, with its emphasis on unity of differences.

These elements taken together constitute "rhetorical reversal," a process that takes place on two interrelated though distinct levels. Through the operation of these elements, white Americans have gone a long way toward recovering two myths — social messianism and manifest destiny — compromised by the conscience and imagination of the 1960s.

Rhetorical Reversal: Its Dimensions

These events provide the backdrop for the self-induced and Other-sustained sense of "righteous indignation," or "moral outrage," underpinning rhetorical reversal. Three distinct though interrelated dimensions appear with this process.

1. *The Violation: Negative Stereotyping.* Here we have a charge that the Other has refused to accept one's actions at face value or allow for the possibility of acquiescence. This charge often resembles "the privatization of morality," where an individual is seen as the primal site of good and bad deeds. For example, a white gang member claims that an attack on a Black in a predominantly white neighborhood was over territoriality, not race. In another case, a young man writes to the editor of a local paper that an incident in which a group of Black women were harassed by a group of white males was "sexism" not "racism." The violation occurs because of an implied intentionality rooted in a collusive bond: the white person, for instance, is aroused by the Other's — a Black's — act of defining the situation.

2. *The Assertion: "Blaming the Victim."* This aspect of the reversal is characterized by an outrageous charge that the real perpetrator of hostilities is the historical victim, not the historical villain.[1] Rhetorically,

however, it is merely regaining a control of meaning, making and invoking a *topoi* of "innocent of all guilt" for historical crimes — especially when accused by a "historical victim." This argument is reinforced by a postmodernist inversion of "innocent until proven guilty" since now the jury resides within, and is at one with, the accused.

3. *The Recovery: Disavowal of Moral Complicity through Historic Privilege.* Here we have a refusal to associate one's current privileged place in society with historic inequities that persist in current individuals and institutions. Thus, we see a refusal to acknowledge that white American wealth rests upon exploitation, especially of other races, classes, and genders, and that it continues to reproduce essentially the same patterns as existed under, say, slavery. Such a disavower has no shame nor sense of blame — hence, no moral obligation — around the plight of the oppressed: "they" are "individuals" just like oneself, capable of making it or failing just like oneself. This stance, of course, allows one to trivialize the Other's historic and structural differences.

Frederick Douglass, the slave turned abolitionist, observed that power concedes nothing not demanded of it. He seems most accurate: we find little evidence that parents, teachers, priests, or dictators give up their relative power without an argument. We might elaborate upon Douglass by observing that what has been lost will often be recovered "by whatever means necessary." Earlier we saw in Ronald Reagan's inaugural speech something to this very effect: "It is right to dream large dreams." What ought one to do to retain power, especially when history tells a story of greater kingdoms than ours falling with time? How does one defy aging, history, death?

Vampirism is one answer to this question, and the actual answer is, in fact, a variant of vampirism: taking the moral integrity and thus the root *topos* of the victim. This is hardly a new idea; it is the essential meaning of cannibalism.[2] Nor is this cannibalism absent from the more mundane and commonplace events of daily life. We can see a special case of vampirism through the prism of the rhetorical reversal technique.

Recovery as Symbolic Reversal: The Case of Vanilla Ice

Here is how a recent article on contemporary developments in the world of so-called rap music ended:

> Though he embodies the macho swagger of most rappers, his is a sanitized, nonthreatening rap, a suburban version presented with crisp diction and Disneyesque dazzle. Purists don't like it and some older rap fans find it

too slick, but the screaming white girls who make up his core audience certainly respond. At a time when rappers like Public Enemy and KRS-One struggle to reach mass audiences with earnest and powerful raps about poverty, self-reliance and the need to overcome societal roadblocks, it's almost perverse that the most popular rapper is a sexy white man whose lyrics rarely stray from good-time concerns. (Moon 1991)

This article focused on a rap star called Vanilla Ice. But who is this man, and why is he so important to the country and to the pursuit of an enlarged understanding of white recovery activity? The reviewer, Tom Moon of the Knight-Ridder newspapers, invests a great deal of detail in his discussion of Vanilla Ice, a twenty-two-year-old from a middle-class, white Texas town who had, within a few months, sold seven million copies of a rap album. Moreover, despite the scandal associated with his rise to fame, he has continued to gain fans among young whites, particularly but not exclusively female. By placing his recent activities within the rhetorical reversal framework, we can see the recovery message in Vanilla Ice. We can begin with the violation: his felt loss and his move to recover it.

1. *The Violation.* Most rap stars are Black or poor inner-city youth from Hispanic backgrounds. However, we are told about Vanilla Ice that

he went to great lengths to obscure his suburban Dallas upbringing. He and manager Tommy Quon — who discovered Ice at a talent contest at his Dallas club, City Lights — created an anti-hero's life story that left many scratching their heads.

In his initial bio — which was revised last month after press accounts refuted many of its claims — this rapper said he grew up near a Miami housing project, went to the same high school 2 Live Crew's Luther Campbell attended, was seriously wounded at least once, and won hundreds of trophies in motocross racing. . . .

But in a *Rolling Stone* article last month, his mother seemed confused by her son's gang references. Certainly, she said, she "wasn't aware" of the stabbing that Ice said "drained half of the blood from my body." (Moon 1991)

2. *The Assertion.* The previous extract also strongly implies that Vanilla Ice sees himself as the real victim, that the Other is essentially a fraud rather than victim. But it is most evident in Vanilla Ice's own description of himself and the Others (read as Blacks):

During an October interview, he elaborated grandly on these points, and explained that true rap fans could tell that he was from the streets: "The reason you don't see as many white people in (rap) is because rap comes from the streets. When I'm on stage I feel the same way as Black people feel, I can tell by the way they're moving. I grew up with mostly Black kids from the neighborhood, got into the same trouble they did, listened to the same music they did. (Moon 1991)

These are powerful and telling lines . . . and lies. Vanilla Ice asserts (1) that he need only say that he has a particular plight to convince others to treat him in the same way as they treat the Black person as victim; (2) that the real differences between his and Blacks' life histories and life chances are irrelevant; and (3) that the differences between him and the Other are collapsible by personal fiat. He knows that he feels as Blacks do; therefore, he is free to fabricate a self and negate the reality of the Other as a separate and different type of self. This is precisely what the Italian-American politician, confronted by a Black militant accuser, did: exercised a right to collapse the real differences between their respective forms of racism.

To be sure, this "bio-embellishment" is largely "show-biz hype" with its own long-standing history. But when whites portrayed Blacks in the entertainment of yesteryear, that portrayal said something about the values and norms of the period. The same is true in the present case. Vanilla Ice is more than an idiosyncratic idol of the white female teenager: he is symptomatic. Indeed, several successful movies of the past decade have returned to the "Black face" to make the point that for a white to break back into the game, he must be "Black."

This portrayal of white as Black suggests that "Blackness" is arbitrary and negotiable. It also provides the ultimate rationale for why and how Blacks and whites can come together under the banner of "nonracial self" or "racelessness." (The painful irony is that "Blackness" has always been negotiable. Thus, the double bind: one really ought to let "Blackness" go, and one really ought to "be ashamed" to give it up so readily after all that "Blacks" have given to make the folly and lie a palatable reality. This is the ultimate sham and shamefulness of oppression: one will be "politically incorrect" whatever decision one ultimately makes.)

To be "freed" of "race" after so many hundreds of years of persecution solely because of this quality is a great relief, then, for Blacks. But there is more: it gives whites even greater relief and release to hear "race" and "racism" are dead. To be given reprieve from guilt and responsibility without surrender is every postmodernist's birthright. Vanilla Ice pursues his birthright by claiming another's, and we will always have our Jacobs.

But the key dynamic propelling Vanilla Ice's self-consciously assertive recovery of his rights is a racial recovery motive rather similar to what we once called "racism." It is similar, for example, to that spirit of opportunism that inspired the imaginative white male in Boston in 1990 to kill his pregnant wife in a Black neighborhood, accuse a Black male, and *induce* the mayor, police force, and city to fall in frenzy upon the Black community. Nor is this use of stereotyping to "retribalize" the races restricted to isolated incidents. Before getting to the third reversal feature of Vanilla Ice, it will be helpful, then, to take a quick detour through film, which supplies an excellent clue to the pervasiveness of the "retribalization" process.

The movie *Rocky* presents the saga of a working-class Italian from Philadelphia who wants the glory of being a champion of the boxing ring. We all can identify with his story. But if we consider it from a recovery perspective by examining the images the movie emphasizes, the story takes on new meaning. In five *Rocky* sequels, Rocky progresses from being the loser's hero to becoming first a racial hero, then a national hero, then an international hero: in the first movie, Rocky gains the respect of the boastful Black champion, Apollo Creed, by fighting him to a draw. In the sequel, he defeats Creed. In the third movie, he wins Creed's affection, loyalty, and assistance as he battles another Black, Mr. T. In the fourth installment of the saga, Rocky returns to the ring to defeat a Russian demigod after the Russian kills Apollo Creed, always the American loyalist, in the ring. (Note that Rocky won the Russian heart well before the 1990s.) In the fifth, and presumably final, installment, Rocky does his intergenerational generative bit: he guides a young white prodigy, a young man who just happens to be, in real life, the only serious white male contender for the heavyweight championship since Black men began dominating the ring in the 1960s.

Rocky, like *The Godfather*, is mostly just good entertainment. But there is an important though subtle and understated recovery mission and message in this particular saga. Some other films have been less subtle in the recovery message.

For example, in the movie *Soul Man*, a white male refused entrance to Harvard "paints himself Black," buys an Afro wig and some gold for his neck, and goes off to Harvard, courtesy of affirmative action. He is so persuasive that he becomes a hero and even wins a beautiful Black woman, who cannot, of course, tell he "ain't the real McCoy."

Though a comedy, *Soul Man* is reminiscent of *The Stepford Wives*, a drama about white New England husbands who kill their feminist wives. The newest member of the group, a Black man, arrives at the very end of the movie, after the white wives have been destroyed and replaced by automatonic replicas. Presumably, the Black wife will get her "treatment" too.

These two movies pursue the idea that the white man, denied his birthright, must recover it. Nicer than skinheads and more polished than the Klan, the presumed audience for such movies as these is being told a story: loss can be recovered. But does Vanilla Ice really relate to this fictionalized violence toward Blacks and women? And how does his behavior symbolize a collective rather than private recovery?

Vanilla Ice symbolizes White Power, the Italian-American who takes on the Black militant in Harold Isaacs's story. He is the Rocky who defeats the loud-mouthed, Black heavyweight champion (an apparent composite of Muhammad Ali and George Foreman) before he goes on to defeat the Russian hero, with the Black champion and his trainer back in their proper place as his seconds.

Moreover, it is precisely the "inability to know he's faking" that makes Vanilla Ice a race hero. He explodes the myth of Black musical superiority and its companion myth, that "Black suffering" is related to "soul." We have even more direct evidence that Vanilla Ice is a central (and sexual) symbol of the white recovery project: he has already been described as Elvis Presley's replacement.[3] But Elvis did not have to remove a "Black champion"; Vanilla Ice did.[4]

As table 3 shows, a developmental and dialectical sequence operates here. To understand this aspect more fully, however, we need once more to return to the article on Vanilla Ice, this time focusing on the third reversal feature, the refusal.

3. *The Refusal.* Here is what Tom Moon tells us:

> Ice's music is derivative in the M. C. Hammer tradition. It depends on simple, repetitive beats and uses vintage pop hits for melody and structure. Lyrically, Ice's raps are nothing special. The best ones offer an update of the "girls and cars and fun" theme that the Beach Boys made their trademark. ... Tellingly, what Ice omits from his rap is perhaps its most important element, its advocacy, its relevance to modern life. Even the most lurid and violent raps by Black artists address specific audiences and real-life conditions. That shred of truth gives them their strength and resonance. And the pop raps of DJ Jazzy Jeff and the Fresh Prince make sly social commentary. (Moon 1991)

Moon exposes, in these lines, the irony: Vanilla Ice does indeed address a specific audience — white men who believe that Blacks, women, gays, Jews, and others have stolen their birthright. Those millions of white

Table 3
An Illustration of the Recovery of White Voice:
The Case of Male Music Idols

RECOVERY CLIMATE		
1950s	1970s	1990s
CULTURE HERO Elvis Presley	Michael Jackson	Vanilla Ice
CULTURAL BASE Rhythm & Blues	Rhythm & Blues	Rap/R & B
DOMINANT VOICE WHITE	MINORITY	NONRACIAL*

* White voice and nonracial voice are effectively the same in a white-dominated society. "Color" is an obsession only for the "colored" and "the white gatekeepers"; others are free to disregard color or race, to believe in the factitiousness of the ideology of subjective equality and universal suffrage.

women who swoon over Vanilla Ice convey merely a part of the message. From a recovery perspective, they are only an incidental audience; they are the "spoils of the victor." Nor is it stretching a point to make the comparison to Elvis.

That Vanilla Ice resembles Elvis Presley is clear to all who recall that "The King" was a white man whose "gift" — his body movement — was similar to, yet different from, those of the Black entertainers he imitated. But more can be gleaned from the association with Elvis: (1) the unquestionable dominance of the white voice in the 1950s and early 1960s meant that only a white man could be a culture hero. Few have ever questioned that Elvis (or Larry Bird after him) was a great artist. But he was only one star among so very many. Yet he was the white star in a world of Black stars. Like Tarzan in the jungle, he had to be "king." By the late 1970s, however, a Black man could hold this role, provided he could capture the white imagination and be Black but more. Michael Jackson did this.

A gifted Black child star, Michael Jackson, like Donny Osmond before him, belonged to a family of talented people. (At one point, the Osmonds and Jacksons had competing television shows.) But Michael emerged as culture hero, or "king," over other mortals. Some saw him as Peter Pan, others as the Pied Piper. For most, however, he had become a sort of "racial eunuch": deprived of the features that suggest Black manhood, Michael Jackson qualified as a hero for millions of screaming young white females. (He could even appear on the cover of the tabloids as a mate for Brooke Shields and father of her child.)

Clearly, to achieve this status, Michael had to sacrifice. His loss symbolized the preparedness of some Blacks to trivialize their "old Black selves" by rejecting aspects of self traditionally associated with "Blackness." Jackson's loss also prepared the stage for the recovery of a white male as the reigning "king of music."

Vanilla Ice embodies this recovery. Elvis Presley, by contrast, symbolically allowed whites to continue their reign. But Vanilla Ice is helping them recover a crown that involves much more than music. Blacks dominate popular music in much the same way as they dominate basketball and football. Though white men largely own these sports as professional activities, a white man must fight to participate on the court and field. Vanilla Ice fought for his place in the entertainment sun, his "piece of the action." But to own "a piece of the action," a man must "pass" — he must possess something that allows him into the game. The fabricated Vanilla Ice biography is, of course, a stereotype, but we can ask rhetorically (with Tom Moon), "But really, what does it matter? Despite — or maybe because of — the allegations, Ice's popularity has skyrocketed."

Vanilla Ice's behavior is important because it provides a means for achieving the convergence of personal and collective recovery as racial hegemony. Upon this exposure, the rhetoric of recovery appeared in his apology. His imitation of a stereotypic biography of "Black genius" both affirms and negates the moral ground previously underpinning the Black voice: racial suffering has heightened the Black man's passions and encourages his spontaneity and musical giftedness to find expression without the inhibitions accompanying white civility. That is to say, Blacks have *soul.*

By feigning the history of poverty and wretchedness of urban, minority life, Vanilla Ice imitated the larger societal drama: *white male as racial victim.* This imitation implies Blacks have substantial power and magic; that Blacks are worthy models for whites. But this imitator also negates the alleged basis for Black achievement in music and similar areas of entertainment by appearing to succeed merely by creating a fictitious history of social oppression and struggle for survival — and "proving" that even a white male can be a great "rapper."

Vanilla Ice's cheerful willingness to affect the wretchedness of "Blackness" to achieve the glory of "rap star" represents a break with the past that saw Blacks as valueless and symbols of weakness. In his rejection of the ancient stereotypes he claims a "Black bio," thereby puzzling his mother and those others who may continue to prefer white to Black. Still Vanilla Ice effects no solid break with the larger social order; rather, he becomes the white male who believes that minorities get all the breaks and that one must be like Blacks and other minorities to get so much as an even chance. Through imitation, Vanilla Ice regains a certain racial hegemony. The white man's rise to the top (in this case, of the rap world) recapitulates the rise of the Black rap star. The white star is thus at once purged and victorious. This is the heroic recovery of racial hegemony.

Vanilla Ice's career reflects a reversal of meaning that informs the logic behind the various white recovery rhetorics. Recent developments in academia and the Supreme Court enlarge the scope of this analysis and further suggest how white recovery of voice has significantly (re)silenced the Black voice. Consider for a moment white recovery in the political and social rather than cultural arena. It is, after all, the convergence of symbolic with substantive power that makes the white man awesome — and differentiates him from the Black, brown, red, or yellow man in the contemporary world.

Recovery Discourse as Rhetorical Condition

Practical men and women understand that "getting in the first word" beats "getting a word in edgewise." In the realm of communication, Asante and Atwater (1986) called these built-in advantages "rhetorical condition." Reminiscent of Marshall McLuhan's reflections on the mass media as the message, Asante and Atwater wrote, "What we are saying is that structure constitutes a parallel message indicating the idea of a rhetoric of form about the rhetoric of words." This notion pertains to hierarchies and inequities and helps describe the rhetorical context within which race rhetoric as recovery rhetoric has evolved. The critical point in Asante and Atwater for this discussion is an allusion to the ideological aspect of hierarchical discourse: "[H]ierarchical discourse which seeks to maintain its hierarchical position is supported by ideology. Without the ideological context, the discourse is vacuous, empty, a hollow form without power" (Asante and Atwater 1986, 170).

The individual seeking to recover or retain a sense of hegemony requires more than just privatized validation. Privatized reality is alienated discourse. It reflects the absence of communion and thus the absence of power. It is precisely when one finds through ideology a connection to others that one can move toward justification, righteous indignation, and political (re)empowerment. But individual incidents, while important, do not adequately address larger societal needs regarding the loss and recovery of hegemony in discourse. After all, "while the condition may be negotiated by the communicators, different rhetorical situations produce different conditions because the inherent power relationships change from situation to situation" (Asante and Atwater 1986, 171). How does one learn that one's individual negotiation has "collective merit"? That is, how is one able to join one's own feelings and emotions to the collective level? What is the transformational code?

Humor as Rhetorical Condition

We have been viewing narrative as the preferred vehicle for persuasion. But other vehicles — satire and humor, for example — also serve to persuade. From this viewpoint, satire and humor are rhetorical conditions, and humor is particularly important in this regard. Humor has considerable cultural significance: it encodes many subtle, sacred, and shared meanings for a group. Humor has, moreover, a decidedly aggressive feature, as such various scholars as Henri Bergson, Sigmund Freud, and Theodore Reik have observed. It is also true that African-Americans have held for centuries a unique place in American humor. In fact, a special drama evolved out of the sharing of a racist joke during the postradical 1970s.

In 1975, the secretary of agriculture, Earl L. Butz, was exposed as having told a racist joke involving the "prime and solitary pleasures and pursuits of Negroes" — namely, food, leisure, and sex. Butz later said that he had heard the joke from a midwestern colleague and merely shared it with his white colleagues on a private plane ride back to Washington, D.C. When Butz was forced to resign, many critics and supporters lined up to have their say. Perceiving the reactionary nature of the white American response to an incipient move toward eliminating racism, Klumpp and Hollihan observed:

> Ritual is not only the essential process of reaffirming a piety, but also the process of a rebirth through which ideology may be changed. Whether an event precipitates a conservative ritual reaffirming an old ideology or a new ideology depends on the rhetoric surrounding it. Earl Butz argued that he was simply repeating a joke heard earlier from a midwestern politician. The rationalization is believable, and of course that is the point — Earl Butz's sin was the failure to stifle his innate cultural bias. (Klumpp and Hollihan 1979, 19)

Butz suffered a failure to conceal, but his was also an expression of the way in which humor promotes the recovery of voice. Butz probably told the truth. But the deeper and more profound truth is that humor provides a vehicle for reestablishing racial hegemony without having to be identified directly with the act of aggression; after all, it's just a joke. The rhetorical power of humor inheres in its seeming neutrality. In this case, it allowed the speaker to redefine a racist act as a joke, a simple social sharing of an acknowledged "nonfactual" but "funny" bit of information. This is the hegemonic dimension of humor, and this particular use of humor reveals the hegemonic status of race relations in America: one may commit a racist act and deny it as such because the aggression is concealed in a chameleonic communication.[5]

This ability to act racist without bearing the racist label is the equivalent of recovering racial hegemony. Klumpp and Hollihan's analysis of the Butz controversy supports this argument. In particular, they point to this instance of the recovery process: Butz repeated what he had heard fully intending to establish and extend identification through the sharing and covalidation of an old value. As Klumpp and Hollihan point out, one may not consider the exposure of the racial slur or the subsequent debates and forced resignation as changing the overall situation since the social structure underpinning such thinking remains in place. Additionally, Klumpp and Hollihan maintain that this split of private and public racism permits personal racist acts to persist because no one demands sincere change.

Moreover, another, more critical form of collusion operates here. This more critical collusion is the shared stance that no continuity exists between the public and personal behavioral domains. Yet it is precisely this shared stance of nonrelationship that sustains both objective (public) and subjective (private) actions of racism. Only on certain occasions can the collusive bond be exposed and understood as such. Humor exposes subjective and objective racism. This form of collusion is precisely what gives the professional wrestling match its symbolic value and persuasive power. A brief examination of the essential drama of the pageant known as professional wrestling helps illustrate the collusive communication I have been describing.

The Wrestling Match as Rhetorical Condition

Professional wrestling has a basic form: good versus evil in a world where the odds favor evil. Most wrestlers, therefore, are cast as either good or evil. (In their carnival world, the wrestlers themselves call the good guy a "face" and the bad guy a "heel.") In professional wrestling, the referee is the judge; he (women seldom serve as judges in professional wrestling) stands for justice. But justice can be conveniently blind, and the referee often sides with the "evil" wrestlers. This unholy alliance is, in fact, what stacks the odds in favor of evil. By managing, routinely, to miss blatant "illegal acts" — actions perfectly evident to the audience — the referee induces the audience to identify with the "face."

Presumably, the members of the audience associate these acts of unfairness and judicial complicity with events in their own lives. Roland Barthes has described "the world of wrestling":

> But what wrestling is above all meant to portray is a purely moral concept: that of justice. Justice is the embodiment of a possible transgression.
>
> It is therefore easy to understand why out of five wrestling matches, only about one is fair. One must realize, let it be repeated, that "fairness" here is a role or a genre, as in the theater: the rules do not at all constitute a real constraint; they are the conventional appearances of fairness. So that in actual fact a fair fight is nothing but an exaggeratedly polite one. One must understand, of course, here, that all these polite actions are brought to the notice of the public by the most conventional gestures of fairness: shaking hands, raising the arms, ostensibly avoiding a fruitless hold which would detract from the perfection of the contest. (Barthes 1972, 21–22)

Barthes's description comes remarkably close to the paradigm Klumpp and Hollihan depicted wherein the president asks for the resignation of Earl Butz. This technique, moreover, is routinely employed. For instance, CBS once suspended its popular humorist Andy Rooney for repeating Butz's error; and ABC Sports forced "Jimmy the Greek" into early retirement for the same reason. In each of these cases the public took sides precisely as they had in the Earl Butz case, and the central claim in each instance was a denial that racism had been the intent.

In wrestling, such responses by the actors are significant because they ultimately echo the official stance. Thus, in the wrestling match, a "heel" uses some foreign substance — say, salt or ring resin — to disable his opponent. The referee claims not to have seen this ruse despite the cries of the spectators and the disabled "face." The "heel" denies wrongdoing, and the referee supports him. In the real world, we see an excellent illustration of a wrestling referee in recent Supreme Court actions.

At the conclusion of a recent *reversal* of an earlier landmark case, Justice Thurgood Marshall accused several of his peers of "selective amnesia" and of insulating "an especially invidious form of racial discrimination from the scrutiny of the Sixth Amendment." Marshall, a Black justice and member of the body voting on the earlier landmark case, declared the spirit of the previous decision violated. Like Chief Justice Earl Warren, Justice Marshall belonged to the "Old America" where racism was official policy; thus, he knows that the presence and effects of racism have not essentially changed over the past four decades. In an earlier time, this condition would have been clearly accepted as the case. But times change.

Table 4
Rhetorical Reversal and the Supreme Court: A "Case" of Recovery

	RHETORICAL SITUATION	
	1954	1990
RHETOR	Chief Justice Warren	Justice Scalia
RHETORICAL REVERSAL	[Segregation] generates a feeling of inferiority in their [Blacks'] hearts and minds in a way unlikely ever to be undone.	Justice Marshall's dissent rolls out the ultimate weapon, the accusation of insensitivity to racial discrimination — which loses its intimidating effect if it continues to be fired so randomly.

Earlier, we adduced the popularity of Vanilla Ice as evidence that times change and whites no longer accept the notion of racism as a given. We also saw that Vanilla Ice trivialized the historical meaning of racial protest embodied in reggae and rap music by creating a fictitious biography to support his imitation of Black rap stars and that Vanilla Ice's rhetoric is paralleled by official recovery actions and rhetoric. Observe these comments of Justice Antonin Scalia, who voted with the majority in the case Justice Marshall criticized as encouraging racism:

> Justice Marshall's dissent rolls out the ultimate weapon, the accusation of insensitivity to racial discrimination — which will lose its intimidating effect if it continues to be fired so randomly. (*New York Times,* January 23, 1990)

Table 4 clarifies Scalia's response as reclamation or recovery of rhetorical hegemony.[6] Unlike Chief Justice Earl Warren, who is of another era, Justice Scalia conveys a resistance to the idea of white aggression and dominance as "racism." Previous generations of whites may have resisted any characterization of their racism as inhumane destructiveness, but they at least knew what racism was and that they condoned and committed racist acts. Scalia's stance implies (as have several recent Supreme Court reversals of the Warren Court) that racism has become rare, existing in the actions of a few whites and the minds and random racist rhetoric of rather more Blacks.

Negotiation of Meaning
and the Erosion of Moral Responsibility

Like the wrestling referee, Justice Scalia is an actor in and an icon of an unjust institutional structure.[7] He reaffirmed not only a popular belief that many actions by whites that harm Blacks are not necessarily "racist" but also the refusal of whites to feel fear or guilt for behavior they do not consider racist.

When labeled as racist, such behavior is now posited as idiosyncratic, and the incidents are isolated. This sentiment has given rise to a new form of rhetoric, the rhetoric of the self. It draws its justification, righteousness, and efficacy from the presumed privacy of personal experience and privatized meaning. Its emotional fuel is (1) a historical sense of betrayal by society and (2) an existential sense of violation by the *negative stereotyping* and moral indictment inherent in traditional racist rhetoric. As humor provides an opportunity for private but shared sentiments to find expression, so a stance like Justice Scalia's offers an opportunity for imitation and illustration of the thesis.

Vanilla Ice's recovery behavior is symbolic. The Supreme Court's recovery actions are binding and substantive. Together, the symbolic and substantive are destructive. Nowhere is this more evident than in the recent reloss of the Black voice.

The Press and the Loss of the Black Voice

A large state university newspaper provided the following account: a group of white males had a confrontation with two Black males. One of the white males was cited for "criminal mischief." He denied the incident was racially motivated, adding with presumed sarcasm, "Anything between a Black guy and a white guy is considered racially motivated." A Black person who was attacked said, "They called us niggers a couple of times. I guess I really can't say what they were thinking about. It might have been racial. I don't know" (*Daily Collegian* [Pennsylvania State University], February 13, 1990). The critical factor here is the uncertainty characterizing this exchange. It is now possible to portray interactions — even physical conflict — between persons of different race without "race" being a collectively recognized factor. The Black male *becomes* uncertain of the meaning of events. This is much as it was historically: whites control the "definition of the situation." The difference is that now power is exercised unofficially. White law enforcement officers, university officials, and the news media are the power brokers in this drama; they can and they do deny the relevance of race in an altercation. Their silence, to recall Malcolm X and Mary Daly, is the reversal.

These events parallel Justice Scalia's ruling; and a shared message is offered: racism is essentially dead, and Black persons are as likely as white persons to receive fair treatment from a random sample of jurors or find themselves in a "friendly fight." The destructive power of the denials involved in this drama parallels the wrestling match where the spectators and the "face" know the truth but cannot gain a favorable ruling from the referee. This is the meaning and experience of loss of racial voice for African-Americans at the close of the twentieth century.

Meanwhile, the recovery of the white voice occurs as only an aspect, albeit an important aspect, of a larger recovery process. The African-American shares in this larger recovery as American, but loses voice as a member of an oppressed social group. Before we take up the precise nature of the recovery and loss for African-Americans, con-sider one final illustration of the contextual features of this recovery of meaning-making that characterizes the American imagination of today.

A recent issue of the *Centre Daily Times* (State College, Pa.) reported that during a campaign speech a white, female gubernatorial candi-date called the state governor "a redneck Irishman from Scranton." Her spokesman responded on her behalf with the following rationale: "She said it. I do not characterize it, as it is being characterized, as an ethnic slur. I don't consider it one [and] I'm Irish and from Scranton" (*Centre Daily Times*, February 13, 1990).

The candidate's refusal to acknowledge the pejorative ethnic mean-ing in her comment reflects a privatized stance. But the appearance of someone who supports this privatized meaning is the real concern, for that person is helping the candidate to escape from a frame of historical guilt and personal responsibility to a "nothing means nothing" stance. This kind of support is a problematic, but nonetheless meaningful, fea-ture of discourse in postmodern society: words and meanings are now negotiable. Thus, one is responsible ultimately to a privatized lexicon validated by significant Others singled out for their capacity to share this vision: the individual's right to say and do as he or she pleases and redefine (renegotiate) meaning because of the loss of collective language and meaning.

Postmodernism as Privileged Recovery

The condition created by the death of "official racism" is the need to define the meaning of various persistent instances of "racist behavior."

Since the mere fact that one taunts or hurts a "nigger" no longer constitutes individual and collective acts of racism, one needs a validational context. This validational context has to meet two interrelated requirements with respect to human activity: (1) racist actions on the part of a public figure must be seen as private actions that may or may not reflect personal racism; and (2) racist actions on the part of private citizens must be renegotiable as episodic and free of a collective underpinning. Together, these two requirements pertain to the symbolic level of voice recovery — that is, the legitimation of the persistence of private beliefs regarding the "true nature" of things and the dramatic renegotiation of this belief.

The media constructed their coverage of Jesse Jackson's "Rainbow Coalition" campaign for the Democratic presidential nomination so as to maintain the idea of Blacks versus whites (Gresson 1987). The *New York Times, Los Angeles Times,* and *Washington Post* all reported on the "birth and death of the Rainbow Coalition" in a way that invalidated it as a basis for coalescing. In several instances, the leads of the articles reporting campaign events were misleading; in other cases, the headlines were inflammatory. Most important, however, was an evident determination to dismiss the coalition as a racial fantasy, to polarize the coalition along racial lines, and, ultimately, to reduce it to nothing more than symbolic "Black pride."[8] These events strongly suggest that a major white recovery strategy has been to deindividuate the African-American.

"Deindividuation" means to make "undifferent." For example, the military, parochial schools, and hospitals make, respectively, all their recruits, students, and patients dress alike. They make individuals look as much alike as possible in their clothes, hairstyles, the possessions permitted in the sleeping area, and so on. This is deindividuation, and it serves to "play down" that which, like wealth and family origin, makes one different from another. Both rich and poor wear white gowns in the hospital; both rich and poor wear uniforms in the military and in parochial school. And yet some differences remain. We know that a poor white or Black is more liable to be an infantry person than the child of a billionaire; we know that students who attend "City Catholic High School" are liable to be poorer than those who attend Loyola or Notre Dame High.

But why is *deindividuation* an important concept? It helps us, in the present instance, understand how Blacks and whites in the twentieth century have found a common identity yet remain different. It helps us, for example, understand how both Blacks and whites may wear Jordache jeans or Reebok tennis shoes despite the fact that Blacks earn on average less than half of what whites earn in this country and that Black families' collective net worth is a mere fraction of white wealth. It also helps us start to see how this move toward "nondifference" invites one to forget differences in both the past and the present, and probably in the future.

In fact, leaders of various oppressed groups have historically fought this condition. Jews historically tend to forget their victimization by Gentiles. Thus, several organizations — B'nai B'rith and the Anti-Defamation League, to name two — exist specifically to remind the world, and especially the potentially complacent Jew (called the "ambivalent American Jew" by the Israelis), that "it can happen again" and not to deindividuate too much.

In short, the oppressed remain forever in danger of yielding even as they get up off their knees. The peculiar predicament of Clarence Thomas before the Senate Judiciary Committee again suggests itself: here we beheld a "self-made" Black man about to join one of the most elite clubs in America, and he had to concede that the stereotype of the Black male as bestial sex figure had frozen him forever into submission to the Other. Thomas, nonetheless, symbolizes those Blacks, notably male, who gain national prominence by taking controversial racial stances — Julius Lester, William Wilson, Thomas Sowell, Shelby Steele, and Glenn Lowry being among the most prominent and familiar. These men share a common plight: the accusation that they collude with the white man's agenda. To varying degrees, each has tried to address this accusation, but none has found a totally persuasive narrative. A notable effort, however, at least in his scholarly persona, has come from Henry Louis Gates, Jr.

The next chapter explores Gates's narrative style as he has addressed the challenge of postmodernism and the African-American. That chapter considers these two questions in particular: Has he delivered Black literary theory from, or into, the jaws of white recovery? And is his invitation to hide within the void of Black postmodernism collusion or creative management of Black vulnerability?

9

Henry Louis Gates's
The Signifyin[g] Monkey as "Signifying":
How to Persuade as a Postmodern
When You've Been Warned Not To

❖

Critics eternally become and embody the generative myths of their culture by half-perceiving and half-inventing their culture, their myths, and themselves. . . . Aware as I am that rhetoric makes uneasy kin of us all, I also realize that a greater access to such means makes some rhetoricians seem more kin than others. We are currently party to myths of a nonself because rhetoricians of this myth are privileged. One can, however, always refuse to be a part of a deconstructionist collective.

—Houston A. Baker, Jr. (1984)

My reading of his [Houston A. Baker, Jr.'s] manuscript convinced me that in the blues and in Signifyin(g) were to be found the Black tradition's two great repositories of its theory of itself, encoded in musical and linguistic forms. This book [i.e., The Signifying Monkey], in so many ways, was written out of my deep regard for Houston Baker's critical presence. . . . I have written this book to analyze a theory of reading that is there, that has been generated from within the Black tradition itself, autonomously.

—Henry Louis Gates, Jr. (1988)

In 1990, the *New York Times Magazine* acknowledged a "new star" of Black studies: Henry Louis Gates, Jr. The proximate reason for this canonization was the widely publicized efforts several major universities had made to recruit him following the attention and acclaim his book, *The Signifying Monkey: A Theory of African-American Literary Criti-*

cism, had received. In 1988, an elite circle of scholars deemed Gates's book "important," and in 1989 it won an American Book Award.

Not all response to Gates's success has been positive. Some African-American scholars have accused the white establishment of trying to shape the popular imagination of Blacks through a selective praising of writers, like Gates, whose scholarship extends beyond the borders of the text. For this group, the style and substance of Gates's work have been "too white" or too easily usable by those whites seeking to maintain political and cultural hegemony vis-à-vis Blacks. Critiques of Gates have, in fact, ranged from suggestions that he is a blatant opportunist to hints that he is an unwitting pawn in the hands of ill-meaning whites. Gates himself addressed this oppositional perspective in a contribution to the *Chronicle of Higher Education:* "Today, the errant scholar can be reproached as a collaborationist, accused of unwitting complicity with the ideologies of oppression" (cited in Winkler 1990, A8). Of what does Gates's scholarship consist, and why is it so controversial? This chapter addresses these questions.

Gates's argument is really quite simple: Blacks have used a secret racial language of their own to enhance self and the Other as mate, child, sibling, friend, enemy, and master. Moreover, Blacks have shared with each other an awareness of this language and its use, as well as a set of rituals intended to pass it from one generation to the next. Though Black American, this language reflects an African origin. The Africans embodied their wisdom of the essence of life (including a vision of how to manage its contradictions) in the trickster-god Esu-Elegbara; African-Americans have evolved a related trickster, the Signifying Monkey. The essential quality of this shared tradition is a vision of the fluidity of life, and the dynamic transformation of this vision within the African-American tradition is seen in repetition and revision.

Because Black writers share this language, they often employ it as standard for developing themes, plots, and characters. It is, therefore, possible to use the understanding one has of the commonsense use of this Black language to examine what it is that Black writers do. Moreover, since it is most likely generic to the human condition, this language may upon inspection show similarities to Western figures of speech and help inform Western literary theory and criticism.

We must now ask, What about this theory made it a source of wide acclaim and even wider controversy? The answer is partly, but not principally, related to the book's overt achievement: a development of a theory of African-American literary criticism. The book's covert message of Black recovery — Blacks must constantly play the ambiguous and adaptive trickster — is the preconscious basis for both its acclaim and its rejection. To appreciate this stance, one must see the book as an attempt to resolve the contradiction of affirming a racial and social identity in a world suffering an identity crisis. Like the fairy tale, *The Signifying Monkey* is a message and a model of recovery.

The message is both "motivated and unmotivated," to use Gates's own expressions for intentional and unintentional activity. By calling the book a "fairy tale," I focus on its efforts to "escape a curse." It achieves this through its core argument: much of (Black) life is characterized by first repeating what we have learned, then revising it in accordance with our individual experience, abilities, and visions. This is essentially a recapitulation of the separation-individuation process applied to African-Americans described elsewhere (Gresson 1982; 1985b; 1987). More precisely, Gates's theory of Black literary criticism amounts essentially to a theory guiding one in the process of examining intertextuality, the way Black authors read and rewrite each other.

As a fairy tale, Gates's book resembles no other fairy tale quite so much as "Sleeping Beauty," where the good witch, unable to reverse the death spell cast by the wicked witch, comes forth to declare that the death is really nothing more than a long sleep from which the princess will be awakened by her prince charming. Meanwhile, everyone in the kingdom will sleep as well, and no one will age during this period.

This return to folklore for his theory enabled Gates to find a way out of the mandate to be an Afrocentric survivalist and an American individualist: in fine postmodern fashion, he heeds the words of Houston Baker to eschew postmodernism by calling upon a particular African myth and tradition. The two tricksters of this mythic tradition, Esu and the Signifying Monkey, are decidedly postmodern in their worship of irony. It is, of course, irony that undergirds so much of current postmodern discourse (R. Brown 1987). But Gates does not say this, partially because to expose himself would be to compromise the "magic" of his effort even though one cannot quarrel with his scholarship. Moreover, Gates seems only partially motivated in his repetition and revision of Baker.

To understand this argument, we must first examine the book as we examined the earlier narratives — not so much to collapse the differences between text and narrative as normal speech or conversation,[1] but rather only to indicate that *recovery* is central to the author in both genres. This chapter focuses for three reasons on both the book and the discourse it has generated. First, *The Signifying Monkey* is a preeminent though still unappreciated example of recovery rhetoric. Second, the responses it has stimulated are themselves aspects of the recovery process and indicate the societal impact of racial recovery activity. Third, this book and the controversy surrounding it converge with and illuminate the larger American recovery project.

The Text as Recovery Narrative

Houston Baker, Jr., as Rhetorical Occasion

Houston Baker, Jr., published *Blues, Ideology, and Afro-American Literature: A Vernacular Theory* in 1984. It was widely hailed as an important book by a major Black scholar and literary critic. Critics were not surprised to find Baker's book at times "impenetrable" and "deconstructionist." Baker, after all, held an endowed chair at the University of Pennsylvania, and the cognoscenti all along expected that he might move African-American literature into the deconstructionist camp. As one reviewer, Roberta Armstrong, put it:

> A deconstructionist analysis of Afro-American literature is perhaps the next logical step in literature . . . that is unabashedly self-referential. . . . Baker establishes the blues as a vernacular paradigm of American culture; his arguments are convincing, as he relates slave narratives and folk tales to the blues. [Yet] . . . many contemporary literary critics and scholars risk going unread because their language is often impenetrable to even the most eager student. . . . Much of the theoretical framework Baker constructs is unduly cumbersome — which is why he is really at his best when he is dealing directly with literary or blues texts. (Armstrong 1987, 149)

Given the wide familiarity with Baker's style and scholarly bent, it is interesting that he begins his book with a kind of chastisement of Gates and other Blacks writing in this postmodernist tradition. From the tone of the first epigraph to the present chapter, one would hardly expect Baker to write what some found to be so clearly deconstructionist or postmodernist in persuasion. Noting that Robert B. Stepto, Gates, and Baker have all been "accused of dismantling the Black subject when they bring contemporary theory to bear on their readings of Black texts," Valerie Smith expressed considerable surprise at this tone (V. Smith 1989, 42–43). As she went on to note:

> For Joyce Ann Joyce, however, Gates, Stepto, and Baker have all adopted a critical "linguistic system" that reflects their connection to an elite academic community of theoreticians and denies the significance of race for critic and writer alike. The intensity of this debate among Afro-Americanists is underscored by the fact that Joyce's essay occasions strikingly acrimonious responses from both Gates and Baker. (V. Smith 1989, 43)

This puzzlement regarding Baker's apparent contradictions increases when we read Gates's own reaction to the book. He says he was inspired by it and found in it essentially the "twin" to his own theoretical effort, and he also seems to be disclaiming that his own book, *The Signifying Monkey,* is a deconstructionist work. Just what is going on here?

The answer is relatively simple on one level: both Gates and Baker have been viewed, correctly or incorrectly, as undermining the effort to bring Black and minority values, experiences, and voices to the mainstream without having to "transpose" them in ways that lose the collective uniqueness forged by racism. This is an in-group sore spot — albeit an inevitable one — that reaches back to William Julius Wilson's *The Declining Significance of Race* (1978), a book that inspired a major debate around "Black betrayal and opportunism" (Gresson 1982). Also, both of these scholars have earned the right to write postmodernly — especially if such writing is largely reserved, in Baker's words, to "a privileged and elite" literary group.

Both Baker and Gates are, in short, engulfed in the ambivalence and double binds implicit in the "twoness" of which Du Bois wrote in 1903 and so many have echoed since: on the one hand, these two men stand apart from the "mass of literary critics" — both have had elite educations and elite appointments — yet both are heirs to a Black scholarly and literary tradition that has increasingly striven to be self-reflective without falling prey to the recovery of white voice described in the previous chapter (see Asante 1983).[2]

Houston Baker seemed to disclaim membership in the elite club even as he wrote a book within its paradigm. Consider his own words:

> My revisionary project is also one of reclamation and invention. . . . The story of spirit work is a unifying myth. It provides coherence to both the autobiographical self and the general Afro-American cultural enterprise described in the following pages. One might say that it is my own narrative for confronting the disappearance of culture and the self announced by postmodernism. My intention . . . has been determinately rhetorical. . . . My revised critical project . . . comes to signify me (and on me) in the same way that "tradition" or "deconstruction" writes both a creative practice and the practicing traditional or deconstructionist critic. The import of my own cultural coherence, therefore, can be stated as a hypothesis about critical practice in general. (Baker 1984, 6, 7)[3]

Baker took on a most interesting task. He attempted to write a recovery book. In short, he seems to have chastised Gates and other Black deconstructionists for undertaking the very project he himself undertook. The even larger irony is that he could not write the kind of book he wanted to write without aspects of deconstructionism because the descriptions and destructiveness now associated with postmodern deconstructionism are precisely the forces so many, including Baker, rely upon in constructing and validating their own narratives.

What Baker actually does is call forth a rhetorical reversal. His symbolic effort is Afrocentric; his substantive effort seems postmodernist. But most critical to this discussion is the fact that Gates took Baker's spirit of recovery, much as Jacob took Esau's birthright and blessing in the Genesis story, and made it his own. We must believe Gates when he says he holds Baker in high regard: Gates's intellectual debt is to Baker's 1984 recovery project, a project that both failed and offended. It failed adequately to convey his own narrative persuasively even though he spoke brilliantly, even seminally, of narrative, myth, signifying, and autobiographical and rhetorical self. It offended because he was determined to take a "Black rhetorical stand."[4]

Gates's book too was a recovery piece. He targeted, however, not the deconstructionist camp with which he remains identified. Rather, Gates targeted the "offending" Baker and "the race" that had signified on him and made him say, "Yo' Momma!" This response — thoroughly Black, as Gates himself observed in delineating his theory of intertextuality — is both the vehicle and the tenor of *The Signifying Monkey*. It is also one of the most powerful scholarly illustrations to date of the postmodern text as recovery rhetoric. Having reviewed the text in terms of the recovery sequence, we can proceed to consider the larger rhetorical framework with which it is identified.

The Rhetoric of *The Signifying Monkey* as Recovery

Violation, Loss, and Withdrawal: Gates's Narrative — the Story of Repetition and Revision

The intriguing fact from a rhetorical perspective is that Baker attempted to serve two masters, whites and Blacks, without benefit of the *wisdom of the Black vernacular*. This wisdom, however, is precisely what Gates calls upon: Gates's genius, what sets him apart from and allows him to trope upon ("cap on") Baker, is his return to and recovery of a "Black story." In short, he seems to recover the vernacular. True to the mandate of the contemporary race hero, Gates manages to say persuasively and without giving immediate offense "Yo' Momma!" to both Blacks and whites, friends and foes.

He does it by arguing for an African-American rhetorical strategy, traceable to African origins, that embodies the pluralistic imperative: "The Black vernacular has assumed the singular role as the Black person's ultimate sign of difference, a Blackness of tongue. It is in the vernacular that, since slavery, the Black person has encoded private yet communal cultural rituals" (Gates 1988, xix).

These sentences deconstruct the African diaspora: Gates reduces or "deconstructs" Black history since the middle passage to a "Blackness of tongue." Moreover, Gates's theory surgically removes this "Blackness of tongue" by characterizing the African vision embedded in the trickster, Esu, as ambiguous, superfluous, and negotiable. (Later, we shall see that symbolically this surgery occasions the reloss of Black voice, since without the "Black tongue" there can be no Black voice.)

By executing this deconstruction of the African diasporic vision, after being told by Baker and others to refrain, Gates functionally says "Yo' Momma!" — a response structurally equivalent to the Italian-American saying, "You, too, are a racist son of a bitch," to the Black militant. But Gates does more: he proceeds to write a book that echoes and reechoes "Yo' Momma!" over several hundred pages.

No trivializing or simplistic reduction of Gates's effort is intended here. His is a remarkable rhetorical act, particularly in view of the fact that Gates's effort was, like Baker's, essentially a private-public matter: "spirit work," "unifying myth," and "autobiography converging with African-American heritage."

Ironically, the criticism now beleaguering Gates is precisely the criticism that prepared the way for his emergence as a race and culture hero: that is, an Afrocentric stance — which emerged following the revolutionary 1960s — toward white scholarship, particularly as it relates to Blacks and other perceived victims of Western cultural and political imperialism. Scholars writing within the parameters of Afrocentrism understood and incorporated aspects of the critical theory underpinning deconstructionism. They rarely write or relate, however, from within the discursive communities variously identified with deconstructionism. This is the message of W. Lawrence Hogue in *Discourse and the Other:*

> As I have stated earlier, the value of these Afro-American critical studies lies in the fact that . . . [t]hey establish a critical matrix that receives Afro-American texts more favorably, that defines the worth of Afro-American literature within an Afro-American cultural context. But what these Afro-American critical studies fail to take into consideration is that Afro-American myths, definitions, and linguistic structures are not "natural" in their use by Afro-American writers or by the dominant American

literary establishment. They are produced.... Afro-American myths and conventions are inextricably tied to the production of Afro-American texts that in turn determine which images or representations of the Afro-American will appear before the American public. (Hogue 1986, 21)

Gates's larger importance, then, is that he wrote a book of racial recovery one could relate, without significant tension, to the European world vision. Jacques Derrida, a primary proponent of postmodernism, indirectly says this in his cover blurb for *The Signifying Monkey:* "It is rarely the case that work *on a marginalized corpus* makes such a contribution simultaneously to linguistics, rhetoric, and literary theory" (emphasis added). Embedded in Derrida's comment is a clue to the recovery role Gates's book has played in the continuing struggle to discover a new set of myths by which to live. Gates has become through this achievement the leader of the new integrationist spirit.

Martin Luther King, Jr., was the last major Black associated with this role. Molefi Asante maintains:

Indeed what Martin Luther King, Jr. had seen as the dilemma of Negro Americans had now become the dilemma of the entire nation. And so even after the assassination of Malcolm X in 1965, King kept trying to resolve the dilemma of the split between the white and Black nation and the internal split between Black and Black. (Asante 1985, 12)

Gates's book appeared after integrationists had failed in a long attempt to identify a collectively compelling metaphor. Baker addressed the task in a problematic way that celebrated Blacks apart from whites. Gates *chose* a metaphor of irony, the Monkey, long a source of tension, shame, and chiding between whites and Blacks. (For whites, Blacks were the monkeys who ate bananas and scratched under their armpits and followed the white Tarzan obediently through the jungle trees.) Gates turned this metaphor of race into a generic vision of humankind, the Black expression of the "World Navel" (J. Campbell 1968). Here is how Gates used the rhetorical reversal most brilliantly: like Mary Daly, who called herself a "Hag," Gates called Blacks writ large a "Signifying Monkey." But he transformed this Monkey, a thing of white ridicule, into Esu, primordial trickster who, as Black or white individual, dares tell white and Black critic alike to "Kiss my...." No! better yet, "Yo' Momma!"

In a way, then, Gates accomplished what even Martin Luther King, Jr., had failed to do: "integrate" Blacks and whites beneath a common generic vision. Moreover, he achieved it, rhetorically, through the discovery and recovery of a lost trickster, Esu. Gates thus became the master ironist, for within the rhetorical figure of irony dwells the transformation Baker had sought.

Irony and Integration:
The Monkey as Compelling Metaphor

Before the publication of his book, Gates had been urged to find his way back to the fold. We might call this the "Afrocentric mandate." Recall that Julius Lester had also been given this mandate, and he reacted by taking an adversarial posture: "If I have to fight Black and white I will." Gates seemed to share Lester's perspective. But he differed in the expression of his stance: he was decidedly "Black" and encoded his opposition in a story of his discovery of the "real deal."

As we have already seen, this kind of value imposition characteristically leads to intragroup conflict, and the notion of signifying is a more or less civilized way of handling the predicament. The basic form of this management is "Yo' Momma!" Within my own cultural tradition this expression meant that a difference of opinion had reached an impasse. One person had succeeded in making the other "look bad" (in the vernacular, he or she had been "capped on"), and only two options remained: suffer the defeat or raise the stakes by denigrating the Black mother long held sacred among African-American men (and not altogether unlike the paradoxical adulation given the white woman as "Miss Ann"). Hence, the expression "Yo' Momma!"

To raise the stakes this way, however, could be risky. It gave the adversary only two options: to cave in to the ultimate insult or to fight, possibly to the death.[5] Returning to the Italian- and African-American described by Harold Isaacs, we see the white male, rendered relatively voiceless in a newly "Black majority town," whose stance is now one of "victim's power." He must counter an accusation of racism with words, not physical blows; yet he must also let the speaker know that things have reached a point of ultimate solutions. In saying that he and the Black man are both racists, he is essentially saying, "Yo' Momma!" But he went on to offer a truce: "Well, now that we're agreed on that, can we see what else we might agree on?" (Isaacs 1977, x).

Gates, likewise, had to see what else could be agreed on, and his answer, rhetorical and narrative in form, was *signifyin(g)*:

> The Black tradition is double-voiced. The trope of the Talking Book, of double-voiced texts that talk to other texts, is the unifying metaphor within this book. Signifyin(g) is the figure of the double-voiced, epitomized by Esu's depictions in sculpture as possessing two mouths. There are four sorts of double-voiced textual relations that I wish to define. (Gates 1988, xxv)

The story Gates tells using the Black "double-voiced" metaphor has four episodes, each pertaining to a relational crisis: whites and Blacks; and Blacks among themselves. He identifies them as

(1) tropological revision — the manner in which a specific trope is repeated, with differences, between two texts;

(2) the speakerly text — extended dialectical discourse among dialects within the vernacular tradition;

(3) talking texts — intertextual critique; and

(4) rewriting the speakerly — unity and resemblance.

Here Gates moved the essentially tension-filled mandate to another level: "I will show you how deconstructionism itself is generic to — and recapitulates — both African and African-American life."

Gates crafted this theory in an impressively scholarly fashion, but his motive is personal. The motive inheres in the criticism both he and Baker had received and in Baker's ironic "disaffection" from the deconstructionist camp. Gates's rhetorical triumph consists in demonstrating that Esu and the Signifying Monkey are related — he calls them cousins — and that the repetition and revision dynamic permeates Black vernacular conversation and literary history.

Thus, Gates solved the riddle Isaac posed to Esau: to serve tradition while shedding the yoke from his neck. Gates does this by recovering, through discovery, a generic tradition — God, Abraham, Isaac, Esu-Elegbara, and the Monkey — wherein the latter two act simultaneously as a "new chain of being" and deus ex machina. Before examining this aspect of Gates's rhetorical style, we must consider the structure of the book generally and particularly its "heterogeneous styling."

The Signifying Monkey as Heterogeneous Stylism

Gates's book has something for everyone, which is part of the meaning of Derrida's comment quoted earlier. Gates wrote a volume that speaks to various discursive groups. Its many themes address the need to be "pluralistic" and "inclusive." One also recognizes in Gates a man of broad scope — a sense, as we shall see, not wholly in the reader. The heroic metaphors Gates associated with himself and the media associated with him invite this experience of him. But the "variety" feature becomes most evident and effective in the structure of the book itself.

One may see *The Signifying Monkey,* then, as a single theme repeated in four ever-expanding places: (1) preface, (2) introduction, (3) part I:

"A Theory of the Tradition," and (4) part II: "A Reading of the Tradition." His preface, for example, states the thesis in simple, everyday terms and images. His audience seems to be his family and friends, particularly those who may be daunted by the book's technical sections. In anticipation of the technical sections to come, Gates writes:

> Finally, it is fair to say that my brother, Paul, is the inspiration for this book, because it was he who once asked pointedly just when I was going to write a book that our parents (and he, an oral surgeon) could understand. If I have once again failed to do so, then once again I apologize. (Gates 1988, xiii)

Similarly, in his introduction, Gates states the thesis for his audience: this time, those Black and white scholars concerned with cultural hegemony and the neglected integrity of the Black aesthetic. Here again, he offers a disjunctive that amounts to *signifying* — that is, speaking in riddles, or "with tongue in cheek":

> Lest this theory of criticism, however, be thought of as only Black, let me admit that the implicit premise of this study is that all texts Signify upon other texts, in motivated and unmotivated ways. Perhaps critics of other literatures will find this theory useful as they attempt to account for the configuration of texts in their traditions. (Gates 1988, xxiv–xxv)

In part I, where Gates presents the thesis writ large, he seems to pursue a rhetorical technique of persuasion by overwhelming the reader — that is, offering much and claiming to be able to offer even more. Look, for example, on page 168: "One could easily write an account of the shaping of the African-American tradition"; on page 249: "[L]et us examine just a few of scores of examples"; and on page 123: "I could list several other examples of Signifyin(g) revisions in the tradition, both motivated and unmotivated."

Passages like these prepare one to see signifying everywhere in everyone and everything, which is possibly Gates's goal. This tactic finally brings a reader back to the yin and yang of life, and this is what enables Gates ultimately to employ the "trope of tropes" as a universal quality. What he has really described so well in nearly three hundred pages is the "separation-individuation" phenomenon: the idea that all of life is a continuous separating and rejoining. He has found a way of identifying something truly generic to the Black tradition that may inform the white world: *chaos, cosmos, contradiction.*

Critical to the overall project, this heterogeneous stylism projects the ambiguity of life that Esu embodies. But Gates's finest persuasive stroke is the exploitation of his own role as "archaeologist," his self-metaphor.

Observe for a moment its textual and persuasive presence. In chapter 1, Gates reproduces a dozen or so African artifacts, strategically placed to remind the reader that Gates has "discovered" a Pan-African link.[6] To understand this complex but important interconnection, we can turn to the related but differentially emphasized descriptions of Esu offered by Joseph Campbell and Gates.

Recovery through Discovery: Gates as the Hero with a Thousand Tricks

Gates says, "[I have] disclosed the Black vernacular tradition which theorizes about itself in the vernacular" (Gates 1988, xxi). He describes his task in these terms:

> Whereas Esu serves as a figure for the nature and function of interpretation and double-voiced utterance, the Signifying Monkey serves as the figure-of-figures, as the trope in which are encoded several other peculiarly Black rhetorical tropes.... I am ... concerned to demonstrate that the Monkey's language of Signifyin(g) functions as a metaphor for formal revision, or intertextuality, within the Afro-American literary tradition. (Gates 1988, xxi)

Gates apprehends and applies Esu's gift. Through this interpretation, one can achieve a richer reading of Gates himself and can come to see how the rhetorical task (of which the Black messiah theme is but one expression) can be achieved. Let us begin with Joseph Campbell in *The Hero with a Thousand Faces*.

Campbell sees that the "effect of the successful adventure of the hero is the unlocking and release again of the flow of life into the body of the world" (J. Campbell 1968, 40). He also says that among the lessons of the great myth-stories one is central: the transcendent force of life is bigger than the particular visions of truth, right, and beauty we choose to cherish. "The World Navel, then, is ubiquitous. And since it is the source of all existence, it yields the world's plenitude of both good and evil. Ugliness and beauty, sin and virtue, pleasure and pain — all are equally its production" (J. Campbell 1968, 44). To illustrate his point, Campbell calls upon none other than Esu:

> This difficult point is made vivid in an anecdote from Yorubaland (West African), which is told of the trickster-divinity, Edshu. One day, this odd god came walking along a path between two fields. He beheld in either field a farmer at work and proposed to play the two a turn. He donned a hat that was on the one side red but on the other white, green before and Black behind [these being the colors of the four World Directions; which is to say, Edshu was the personification of the center, the *axis mundi*, the

World Navel]; so that when the two friendly farmers had gone home to
their village and the one had said to the other, "Did you see that old fellow
go by today in the white hat?" the other replied, "Why, the hat was red."
To which the first retorted, "It was not; it was white," insisted the friend,
"I saw it with my own two eyes." "Well, you must be blind," declared the
first. "You must be drunk," rejoined the other. And so the argument developed and the two came to blows. When they began to knife each other,
they were brought by neighbors before the headman for judgment. Edshu
was among the crowd at the trial, and when the headman sat at a loss to
know where justice lay, the old trickster revealed himself, made known his
prank, and showed the hat. "The two could not help but quarrel," he said.
"I wanted it that way. Spreading strife is my greatest joy." (J. Campbell
1968, 45, 46)

This powerful story has many meanings. Among them is the folly of
taking things too seriously or being too certain of the real. What a story
for the contemporary world with its confusion and contradiction! What
a consolation! Now consider Gates's description of the trickster, which,
by the way, does not seem to benefit from a reading of Campbell:

Scholars have studied these figures of Esu — and each has found one or
two characteristics of this mutable figure upon which to dwell, true to
the nature of the trickster. A partial list of these qualities might include
individuality, satire, parody, irony, magic, indeterminacy, open-endedness,
ambiguity, sexuality, chance, uncertainty, disruption and reconciliation, betrayal and loyalty, closure and disclosure, encasement and rupture. (Gates
1988, 6)

Both Gates and Campbell touch on the idea of recovery though neither
deals with it explicitly. Still, the story Campbell tells is one of recovery, and Esu (or Edshu) represents recovery through discovery of the
nonnecessity of the things held as necessary.

This talk about tricksters is, as Gates makes clear, talk about assertion and aggression. He embeds this idea within a complex discussion of
parody and pastiche. For example, he emphasizes, for rhetorical effect,
the notion of "deeply admired antecedent," which he applies specifically
to Alice Walker's feelings for Zora Neale Hurston and the manner in
which she "repeats and revises" (Gates 1988, xxvi). His argument —
low-key in its utterance, but pivotal in its ideology — is that a break
with tradition need not be interpreted as violent or intentionally unkind ("unmotivated troping" is the concept he introduces to convey this
stance).

Moreover, as we saw, Gates seems unaware of Campbell's uses of
Esu — Gates's citation of authors dealing with the trickster borders on

overkill, yet none comes anywhere near Campbell's description. Still, from a certain perspective, his possible "amnesia" (later Gates says he forgot he had once read about Esu while on a journey abroad) is important: Campbell's tale of Esu leaves little room for seeing Esu as other than the "god of deconstructionism" he is. Gates describes Esu as everything but deconstructionist.

To call Esu a deconstructionist deity would dispel the spontaneity and "unmotivated" renegotiation implied in the archetypal journey and recovery. Thus, the most disruptive descriptor Gates employs in the earlier passage is rupture. But we need not accuse him of sleight of hand. Others have done this, but the greater significance in his work is the recovery project wherein we see the convergence of at least three separate though related lines of development: Black female narratives of self-recovery, the recovery of white voice, and the pursuit of a self-healing societal process. We now turn to the analysis of Gates's work as recovery rhetoric and the discursive environment to which he belongs.

Analysis

Gates's Self-Metaphor: The Literary Archaeologist

Gates's "self-metaphor" is that of archaeologist/culture hero. He has "dis-covered" Esu and the Monkey. Moreover, Gates is Esu; he is the Signifyin(g) Monkey. Earlier, we noted the rhetorical tactic of including in his book photos of several African artifacts, mostly figures of Esu from his personal collection. To appreciate this linkage of book with man, return to the *New York Times Magazine* profile of Gates:

> In 1982, a year after being dubbed a genius by the MacArthur Foundation, Gates was again in the news (and his picture graced the pages of *People* magazine), when he announced *he had rediscovered the first novel published by a Black person in the United States. This coup established his talent for a special kind of literary archaeology and, in his mind, justified the MacArthur Grant*. Gates, who came across a tattered copy while browsing in a Manhattan bookstore, studied the century-old census reports, obituary notices and county records to verify the race and gender of the author [a Black woman named Harriett E. Wilson]. His work extended the scope of the Afro-american literary tradition by more than thirty years. (Begley 1990, 49; emphasis added)

Having seen Gates project himself as an "archaeologist," are we surprised to find him extending the African-American trickster, the Signifying Monkey, back to its African ancestor, Esu-Elegbara? In both the preface and introduction, Gates emphasizes the "path to discovery," his own "archetypal journey" backward. (The artwork and schematics he includes add weight to the argument by illustrating his archaeological bent.) The array of examples he presents — music, poetry, visual art, and tales and stories from Africa, the Caribbean, and elsewhere — gives one a sense of the primal and the primacy in what Gates has (re)discovered:

> In a curious way, which I was to realize only much later, my discovery of Esu was a rediscovery; for my supervisor at Cambridge, John Holloway, had forced me to read Frobenius' *The Voice of Africa*, a decade ago, and it was there that I first met Esu-Elegbara. But it was the Afro-American tradition that generated the concept of Signifyin(g). (Gates 1988, ix, xx)

In this passage Gates shows himself at Cambridge. He is, in short, openly an elitist. But one finds a hint of mystery here, too, for he was "forced" — like Jonah, Paul, Huck, and most heroes — to embark on a journey. The trip to England and Europe is but an aspect of The Journey. More important is the theme of *discovery*.

But why does he emphasize the word "rediscovery"? To answer this, we must examine the notion of hero, but not the narrow notion of European man as hero. Remember that Gates's recovery project is to bring something like integration to the Black-white dynamic. What kind of hero does this require? In their important book, *The Female Hero in American and British Literature*, Carol Pearson and Katherine Pope observe: "An exploration of the heroic journeys of women — and of men who are relatively powerless because of class or race — makes clear that the archetypal hero masters the world by understanding it, not by dominating, controlling, or owning the world or other people" (Pearson and Pope 1981, 4, 5).

Here we have a crucial insight into the hero as woman or "powerless" person. This hero is unlike the archetypal hero, who is white, male, and upper-class — say, a Teddy Roosevelt who "speaks softly and carries a big stick." The Black man as hero must use words well: *the essence of signifying*. Gates tells us both that Blacks have done this forever and that he is a Black signifier, elite connections notwithstanding: "I wish to do so [define and use the notion as he does] because this represents my understanding of the value assigned to Signifyin(g) by the members of the Afro-American speech community, of which I have been a signifier for quite sometime" (Gates 1988, 51).

He also declares that he can understand the nature of the "discourse of the Other" (Hogue 1986) and use it to his ends. He does this in his "deconstruction" of signifying: he makes it a vacant vernacular transaction by downplaying the racial conflict — the Black frustration and aggression — at the core of signifying. The point is not that repetition and revision fail to represent Black social history or the African genius accurately. Rather, Gates's deconstruction achieves precisely what Bernard Bell (1988) observed as atypical of Black postmodernist writers: the privatization of racism.

Gates achieves this privatization in his imitation of Esu, validating yet negating the passion within the Afrocentric vision. For instance, he seems to be playing games when he first discounts white theory, then goes on to say in various places in the text essentially what he says on page xxiii:

> Naming the Black tradition's own theory of itself is to echo and rename other theories of literary criticism. *Our task is not to reinvent our traditions as if they bore no relation to the tradition created and borne, in the main, by white men.* Our writers used that impressive tradition to define themselves, both with and against their concept of received order. We must do the same, with or against the Western critical canon. To name our tradition is to rename each of its antecedents, no matter how pale they might seem. To rename is to revise, and to revise is to Signify. (Gates 1988; emphasis added)

What takes place in this passage leads one to imagine four-sided hats with different colors. This sensation also encourages one to see tiny, colored bunny rabbits playing in briar patches like those one finds in the racially violent stories of B'rer Rabbit and his friends.[7] In this passage, all his racial self-asserting aside, Gates surrenders to the white literary tradition. He yields hegemony; he replaces Black within, beneath, and under white; and he raises this action, this decidedly pragmatic gesture, to a theoretical or abstract level.

In short, Gates's journey, so the story goes, led him to Esu-Elegbara, and this trickster's message — given by the ancient African gods — is radically existentialist: it emphasizes the self as being ("existence") and history, sacrifice, loyalty, truth, integrity, and beauty ("essence"). (The last three are later constructions.) Thus, the Black man is free to choose, to negotiate, to forgive, and to forget the past and all its reifications. If the Black man now finds himself on the side of conservative white academia and government, so be it. If the times now seem right for forgetting the original "middle passage" and forging yet another, just do it. For the true self-metaphor — Gates's, mine, yours — is ultimately that inspired by Esu, speaker of many tongues.

We are hardly surprised to learn that Mae Henderson, who characterized the Black woman artist as one who "speaks in tongues," was reacting to an intertextual invitation from Gates in her own effort at repetition and revision:

> The critical paradigm that Mae Henderson devises...answers the challenge Henry Louis Gates issues in *Figures in Black*. The critic of Afro-American literature should not, Gates says, shy away from literary theory, but rather "translate it into the Black idiom, renaming principles of criticism where appropriate, but especially naming indigenous Black principles of criticism and applying these to explicate our own texts." "Speaking in Tongues" does just that. Heteroglossia and glossolalia, Henderson's tropes for intertextuality and revision, are defined in terms of Bakhtin and Gadamer as well as in terms of the religious practices of the Afro-American sanctified church. (Wall 1989, 12)

The invitation in Gates's narrative is similar to, but distinguishable from, the one we find in his theory. The appeal of his theory is that very heterogeneity that has forced pragmatism upon the African-American as his or her chief self-metaphor. And is not the lesson of "multiple tongues" ultimately pragmatism? Then what of Gates's theoretical work? How is it to be contextualized as rhetorical message?

Gates's Theoretical Work

First, many significant discussions of most aspects of Gates's theory have already come forth. Indeed, he centered little of the book on presenting new knowledge, whether in regard to the figures of literary criticism proper or to the special readings generated about the canonical texts he discussed in *The Signifying Monkey*. On the contrary, the central and brilliant feature of Gates's effort inheres in his integration of various myths, theories, criticisms, and scholarly efforts into a *critical recovery epic*. In a motivated spirit, Gates has constructed a story of self-recovery that links the two dimensions of loss — Black and white, African and European — that Joseph Campbell and Wilson Moses introduced. In this way Henry Louis Gates becomes the symbolic convergence of the race and culture hero, as is evident in his encounter with the Other.

The Other

Who is the Other for Gates? Clearly, one of the Others is a Black writer like Alice Walker, who epitomizes, in personal and public life, the literary and vernacular traditions he has ascribed to Esu and the Monkey.

> Finally, Walker's decision to place *The Color Purple* in a line of descent that runs directly from *Their Eyes* by engaging in a narrative strategy that

tropes Hurston's concept of voice (by shifting it into the form of the epis-
tolary novel and a written rather than a spoken vernacular) both extends
dramatically the modes of revision available to writers in the tradition and
reveals that acts of formal revision can be loving acts of bonding rather
than ritual slayings at Esu's crossroads. (Gates 1988, xxviii)

Gates here tells a story about what Black tradition — as vernacular and
as art form — has provided as a preferred option. Although his work is
poetic and therefore complete (Lucaites and Condit 1985), his message
and plea are not poetic but rhetorical, and they invite completion. In
this sense, his work is a prelude to the encounter with the Other that
proceeds from narrative inducement.

Simply put, then, here is Gates's message of invitation to the Other:
What Alice Walker has done, you can do. You can break the collusive
racial bonds described by Audre Lorde. You can pursue your personal
interests and live out your lives just as Julius Lester says. You can do
all of this, and yet remain bound to tradition. You can do it because
Blacks — first in Africa, then in America — understood the primacy of
irony and the principle of repetition and revision.

Gates's choice of Alice Walker as an important Other serves ultimately as recovery work for the race divided against itself. By turning
to Walker and showing how she models repetition and revision toward
Zora Neale Hurston, Gates implies how the broken bond can be symbolically healed. He has found a way of symbolically beginning this
healing that, as we have seen, must come from the broken collusive
bond.

As a Black man living the "personal choices" that partially inspired the break described by Audre Lorde (1979; 1981), the Black
male's choice of white female, Gates's orientation toward Black women
as Other is particularly significant. Too few Black men choosing to
live outside traditional Black intimacy have been able to connect with
Black women who have done the same. Gates proceeds in an interesting way: he connects the need for Black female storytellers identified by
Mary Helen Washington to the racial need for an enlarged definition
of "Blackness." In the passage just cited, for example, we both see and
sense an immediate parallelism to Washington's sentiments:

Washington: "Because of these writers, there are more models of how it is
possible for us to live, there are more choices for Black women to make,
and there is a larger space in the universe for us."

Gates: "Walker's decision... both extends dramatically the modes of
revision available to writers in the tradition and reveals..."

If Gates has captured both the form and flow of Washington, it is neither dishonest nor derivative. It is *signifying*. It is also transformative, for it gives him, as Black man, more space, too: including the exercise of deconstructionism and the right to be the "new star of Black studies."

We are speaking here, of course, of a resolution among Black male and female of the personal-choice themes: the Black male has taken for himself what he wanted, including white women, and the Black woman has done the same. Blacks have become, in this way, "ex-comrades."[8]

Perhaps Blacks will never return to the shared racial collusions of the past. But evident even now is the drive to find an alternative way of relating, a new collusion and bond. In the language of literary criticism, "intertextuality" is the concept that describes and charts the progression toward this renewed bond and collusion. Earlier we saw that Henderson's "speaking in tongues" metaphor seems to belong to this particular discursive project. There are other examples as well. Gates himself offers one illustration in the final chapter of his book where he offers his interpretation of how Walker illustrates his theory of repetition and revision by her imitation and modification of Hurston's style and subject matter (Gates 1988, 249). One aspect of Gates's argument is that some of Walker's characters derive from Hurston. This attributed connection supports his theory that Walker signifies on Hurston as Blacks generally do with each other. But in an endnote, Gates writes that Walker did not interpret her sources as he had; still she wrote him the following: "But your version is nice, too, and my version is so confusing" (Gates 1988, 280).

Here are two points regarding this exchange: first, Gates is positive in his regard for Walker's work, in general, and her Pulitzer Prize–winning novel, *The Color Purple,* in particular. Many Black males, however, found this book disturbing and accused Walker of colluding with whites in depicting Black men negatively. Bernard Bell conveys a literary view of this concern in his recent history of the Afro-American novel: "The best but most problematic of Walker's novels is the Pulitzer-Prize winner. Less compelling as critical realism than as a folk romance, it is more concerned with the politics of sex and self than with class and race. Its unrelenting, severe attacks on male hegemony, especially the violent abuse of Black women by Black men, is offered as a revolutionary leap forward into a new social order based on sexual egalitarianism" (B. Bell 1988, 263).

Gates's theory of Black literary criticism essentially says, however, that Walker's novel represents *continuity,* that it is to be seen in terms of the connection with Hurston, a connection Bell also notes but chooses not to emphasize. Thus, the social message or rhetorical message regarding the loss of the collusive bond or its participation in the white recovery project is irrelevant.

Meanwhile, Gates's treatment of Walker sidesteps the larger societal drama they both "star in": each has been called brilliant by whites and a white collusionist by Blacks; each has received the high honors whites give to only certain Blacks. This understanding helps inform the intertextual dialogue around Walker's narrative: "But your version is nice, too, and my version is so confusing."

Recall for a moment the conversation with Eartha. She, too, expressed confusion around her narrative development and showed appreciation for a benign interpretation. The point is Gates's argument for intertextuality as the arena and the process where racial differences are resolved through repetition and revision seems valid, but it also exposes the fact that the collective narratives proffered as representative of the evolving Black American are contrived; selected speech communities get the opportunity to say what "Black is" and to describe what is happening. The research by both Soundra O'Neale (1987) and W. Lawrence Hogue (1986) reaches this very conclusion. The exchange between Gates and Walker seems to support this observation further; it also points us toward the second point: Gates's mission is iconoclastic with respect to certain aspects of "traditional Blackness."

Gates as Ironist and Iconoclast

Gates's theory is about literature, but it is also about life. The theory, after all, supposedly reflects what is "autonomously Black." What Alice Walker says to him directly is therefore no trivial matter. Hence, he needs to connect his stance to her in a way reminiscent of Eartha's conversation with the Black male at the white club in Newport. Gates's description of motivation is connected to this concern with interpretation. Thus he talks of actors as "motivated and unmotivated" revisers of tradition, essentially a transposition: Gates has said Blacks in the barbershops and on the streets signify on each other and that this also occurs in Black literary theory (and presumably white literature as well). In this representation of Black revisers we see another Other — the race.

Something silent and uncanny transpires between Gates and the Other as "the race." We get a first glimpse of this when he says:

[Black literary discussion] is a meta-discourse, a discourse about itself. These admittedly complex matters are addressed, in the Black tradition, in the vernacular, far away from the eyes and ears of outsiders, those who do not speak the language of tradition. I shall suggest reasons for this penchant of the Black tradition to theorize about itself in the vernacular. My attempt to disclose the closed Black vernacular tradition is meant to enrich the reader's experience of reference and representation, of connotation and denotation, of truth and understanding. (Gates 1988, xxi)

Recalling the meaning of the "outsider as hero," Gates intends to disclose that which is private and secret. It may seem merely a harmless effort to "recover" something lost: the right to be human. But it means "ritually destroying" the race. Consider how he visualizes Black survival:

My father has mastered Black language rituals. He is not atypical. It is amazing how much Black people, in ritual situations such as barbershops and pool halls, street corners and family reunions, talk about talking. Why do they do this? I think they do it to pass these rituals along from one generation to the next. They do it to preserve the traditions of "the race" (Gates 1988, xx)

Let there be clarity regarding "the traditions of 'the race'": Black people came to this continent in chains and survived by becoming one family — a "Black family." This has been mainly a fictional family, but a family nonetheless. As whites lost their myths, so did Blacks. This is the combined message of Campbell and Wilson Moses. Individual Blacks have validated this message in their choices of mates, politics, sexuality, social lifestyles, and so forth. By exposing the language symbolically conveying the rituals and traditions constituting the traditional "Black family," Gates exposes the contradiction. In this connection, Richard Brown (1987) observes that irony and dialectic convey the poverty of language to reveal the emerging truths shaping the lives of contemporary humankind. By asserting that Blacks had a tradition already in place for "ritual slaying," Gates partially validates "breaking the bonds" by allusion to an inherent wisdom, the two tricksters: the first defied all efforts at closure on a life necessarily characterized by irony, betrayal, duplicity, and ambiguity. The second taught a technique for breaking away: repeat then revise.

Repetition and revision are fundamental to Black artistic forms, from painting and sculpture to music and language use. I decided to analyze the nature and function of Signifyin(g) precisely because it *is* repetition and revision, or repetition *with a signal difference*. (Gates 1988, xxi; emphasis added)

The key idea here is "with a signal difference." But, if Gates is right, clearly some substantial slaying is involved. For ultimately, neither Esu nor the Monkey is a nice guy. Each brings a terrible toll with his message of possibility.

The Signifying Monkey does this as well. Gates has woven a view of Black life drained of the *racial* violence and pain. This is the deconstruction, and this is why his book and he, to the degree that it is his own narrative, are flawed and without evidence of dialectical enlargement. Recall Thomas Benson's observation on Malcolm X's life and autobiography: "What makes Malcolm's life a drama — an enactment of conflict — *rather than a mere growth is the presence of racism, the agency of constriction, domination, and injustice*" (Benson 1974, 3; emphasis added).

Benson's sense of the African-American's action matrix is in close harmony with that of the clinician and family-therapy theorist Elaine Pinderhughes, who saw the complexity in terms of the contradictions the powerless inherit, so to speak, from the dominant social order:

> In being excluded and kept separate, and in being the recipients of much of the tension, conflict, contradiction, and confusion that exists within the system, they provide stability for their benefactors. . . . In becoming system balancers and tension relievers in the social system, victims must learn to live with stress, conflict, and contradiction. They must find ways to cope with the powerlessness that gets mobilized. Coping responses vary from time to time and from victim to victim but become the essence of the culture that people develop. (Pinderhughes 1983, 333)

Here Pinderhughes describes the adaptation required of all African-Americans. Contradiction here emanates from this collective survival effort. Contradiction also comes, however, from the interpenetration of motives and needs as various identifications evolve within the same person. Signifying is certainly repetition and revision; but it is a truncated dialectic. It beats up on the self and the Other as helpless victims of oppressions too painful to enjoin. This is why it differs from Esu: *Esu* is ubiquitous power; *signifying* is the victim's power.

In neglecting the real tensions and tragic violence generic to both Esu and the Monkey, Gates reveals the privatized quality of his work. It is significantly silent on the theme of racial hegemony. His theory suffers, for even when he approaches the theme of violence, he does so with a problematic politeness. But this delicacy should hardly surprise us. Gates's success (recall Derrida's praise) is his integrative ability. His genius as scholar and his cultural value lie in this ability. Thus, the frequent allusions to white scholarship in language that is hardly "separatist" even when he declares that he has "written a book to analyze a theory of reading that is there, that has been generated from within the Black tradition itself, autonomously."

We do not have here the whole truth. Signifying is a response to power. Esu is power. Signifying, as Rhett Jones reminds us, is closer to a different historical experience: "Afro-Americans had to be satisfied with hidden informal methods of social control. While whites were creating and celebrating white heroes, Blacks had to content themselves with feeble little tales about the doings of rabbits" (R. S. Jones 1988, 35).

We have lost the traditional basis for racial collusion: "We are in this together and are one and must remain steadfast against the savage racists." This was both necessary and a potential benefit to Blacks and others as well. But we cannot achieve the potential gain of the lost racial collusion — the experience of freedom as a human — by privatized resolutions of racism's persistence. This persistence and privatization, unfortunately, are very much the dominant reality, and this is why the issue of collusion looms large among politically inclined African-Americans.

Collusion, Intertextuality, and Other Themes

Writers like Audre Lorde remind us of the losses and the emergent arrangements. But the suggestion that some benefit more than others from certain stances regarding what has been recovered implies a recollusion. Within the Black literary tradition, this recollusion has emerged as a discussion of "intertextuality," the acknowledgment of specific "Others" as "friend" and "foe" in one's own vision of reality.

This aspect of intertextual discourse appears to be a historic tendency. "Repeating and revising" — or signifyin(g) — represents Gates's effort to face the future: the loss and recovery. Gates convinces by ambiguity, Esu's gift. He identifies with the trickster-god, an element in his style noted by both critics and friends. Sacvan Bercovitch, a professor of English at Harvard, reportedly said: "[Gates has] found a way of asserting the existence of a separate Black American tradition, and of asserting this in a way that places the Black American literary tradition at the cutting edge of literary theory. [M]any skeptics believe that Gates has merely found a gimmick" (cited in Begley 1990, 49).

Though some are dissuaded by this style of persuasion, it is precisely this quality that attracts others and is, moreover, precisely what the culture hero brings back to the tribe: an example of the way to survive with style in an oppressive yet malleable world. Survival in the "academic jungle" is the key to Gates's appeal to the minority audience. This survival consists in being heard and taken seriously — being used (and in turn using, as Gates uses the universities trying to woo him) according to the way in which one wants to be used.

Gates's detractors generally miss the central rhetorical recovery aspect of his discourse, its "race hero" feature that consists in building a believable myth out of the contradictions of one's life and the human condition. Gates spells out his mission:

> I am not interested in either recapitulating or contributing to this highly specialized debate over whether or not speech act *x* is an example of this Black trope or that. On the contrary, I wish to argue that Signifyin(g) is the Black trope of tropes, the figure for Black rhetorical figures. I wish to do so because this represents my understanding of the value assigned to Signifyin(g) by the members of the Afro-American speech community, of which I have been a signifier for quite some time. (Gates 1988, 51)

This is recovery discourse. This is reintegration discourse. This is heroic discourse. Gates here dismisses the need to negotiate his credentials and emphasizes his right to assert self before both the mainstream discursive communities and the marginal discursive communities. His message is "ritual slaying" for the one and "ritual bonding" for the other. But which is for which? History provides an answer, at least for the moment. Gates has joined the mainstreamers. Such would seem to be the message of Valerie Smith (1989) and some other of the Black female critical theorists. Likewise, Gates's own observation, cited earlier, points to this conclusion: "Today, the errant scholar can be reproached as a collaborationist, accused of unwitting complicity with the ideologies of oppression."

True enough, but the "errant scholar" may indeed be a collaborationist. After all, even Audre Lorde, surgical and persistent critic of Black folly and contradiction (particularly among men and homophobic Blacks), allowed that one remains forever vulnerable before the former comrade. Surely Gates can see this. And if he acts as if race is passé, has he not indeed said "Yo' Momma!"?

"Pluralism" and "diversity" are the reigning rhetorical *topoi* of intercultural relations. Though such visions as Hogue's and Asante's are both cogent and critical for a traditional revolutionary ideology, they do not reflect the principal motives of a heterogeneous society still largely dominated by an increasingly smaller racial-ethnic group. Nor does an Afrocentric stance adequately include the dominant literary elites. Gates's book represents an attempt, true to the spirit of the age, to be "all things to all men." His success is debatable. But the typical critique has been insufficiently attentive to the recovery aspect of his work, even though much of his appeal is attributable to precisely this feature. His successful integration of the creative fragments of previous scholars accounts for his ultimate persuasiveness. More important, he has used the vulnerability of Black studies, particularly its myths of homogeneity of value and vision, to discredit aspects of that scholarship.

Conclusion

We will finally see Gates's work as a remarkable effort to address the new world condition from a rhetorical perspective, which is why both white and Black scholars respond to it. Furthermore, Gates is insensitive neither to Black tradition nor to racism per se. For instance, Asante recognizes Gates's insights into the contemporary and historical plight of the Black person and the rhetorical challenge this plight presents. Asante even quotes Gates in this context:

> The recording of an authentic Black voice — a voice of deliverance from the deafening discursive silence which an enlightened Europe cited to prove the absence of the African's humanity — was the millennial instrument of transformation through which the African would become the European, the slave become the ex-slave, brute animal become the human being. So central was this idea to the birth of the Black literary tradition in the eighteenth century that five of the earliest slave narratives draw upon the figure of the voice in the text — of the talking book — as crucial "scenes of instruction" in the development of the slave on the road to freedom. (Asante 1988a, 123; citing Gates 1985, 10–11)

But Asante and Gates diverge at this critical place: postmodernism's ahistoricism. Thus, in the very same discussion, Asante continues, "Blackness is more than a biological fact; indeed, it is more than color; it functions as a commitment to an historical project that places the African person back on center and, as such, it becomes an escape to sanity" (Asante 1988a, 125).

With this statement Asante's and Gates's racial differences — as well as that between Blacks who would be "human" rather than "Negro" — become clear: for Gates, all that remains of "Blackness" is a "Black tongue." This is why his vision can be postmodernist. But the question one must ask is: What is a Black person whose "Black tongue" has been silenced? This question awaits an answer, and the current struggle among Blacks who would support or disclaim Clarence Thomas illustrates, pragmatically, the importance of this question.

What, then, can we say about Gates's work? It is a narrative of the heroic quest we each must undertake in a transitional society. His selection of Esu and the Signifying Monkey is perceptive and persuasive. Still, Gates is currently locked in battle with members of the Afrocentric community. He denies that his work, or, more precisely, his stance with regard to Black studies, is capable of being misused. But times change and so do alliances.

The rhetoric of collusion is ultimately a conversation with the self, a self-soothing exchange. A few Black scholars (e.g., Gresson 1978) have previously addressed this conversation. I consider it the "message and the massage" of recovery discourse. It is the rhetorical tactic of the "transitional race person," a person whose essential vulnerability is intensified in the attempt to make meaning in a transitional society. Donald N. McCloskey put it well: "[It is] rhetoric that is unusually aware of itself as rhetoric" (McCloskey 1985, 118).

Critiques of Gates's work, or of the man, that remain wedded to the so-called politically correct vision will serve only to fuel the growing backlash against area studies. It is important that *The Signifying Monkey* be seen for what it is rhetorically, for this is the place where the important scholarly stance has been taken. As a Black man whose choices threaten to place him outside the traditional context, Gates is as compelled as Monique or Eartha to give an accounting of himself. I believe that he does just that, and his approach is brilliant: he invokes the Black man's own tricksters, Esu and the Signifying Monkey, to legitimize his stance. Thus, his work is *heroic*. He has succeeded, in a fashion, in creating a statement regarding the mutability of choice and has discovered a traditional Black god who shares his vision. His work, as discovery, is complete. His narrative, if it be so, is poetic. He has provided a "closed story."

Criticism of the man and his work beyond the text remains valid and necessary. But such criticism must be seen as such. As for the book itself, Gates already expects it to be troped. Such a troping would include an effort to acknowledge signifyin(g) as an important but impotent weapon in a postmodern and postnuclear age. Placed in its time, Gates's book seeks to recover a part of the "Black self" — lost in the diaspora — through Esu-Elegbara. It signifies the postmodern African-American struggle to survive in a race-conscious, race-dominated society.

10

Loss and Recovery Revisited

❖

We are privileged to be participant observers of another great experiment by Western humanity upon itself: an attempt to build upon the obsolescence of both love and hatred as organizing modes of personality.

—Philip Rieff (1966)

Joseph Campbell was not the first to see or describe the "loss of the coordinating myths" of the Western world. Before him, Friedrich Nietzsche, Søren Kierkegaard, Sigmund Freud, and Hannah Arendt had described much the same "human condition." Nor was Campbell's vision the most celebrated articulation of the human plight: Jean-Paul Sartre's "Existence precedes essence" and Philip Rieff's "psychological man" have both received more public notice. Still, Campbell's assessment remains uncannily prophetic: humanity seeks to recover what it has lost.

Within the pages of this book I have tried to isolate some small part of this recovery project so that we might more closely assess its possibilities and problems. I have been particularly concerned with the role of race and gender in this drama because these are among the most important and potent categories dominating American understanding of gain and loss.

But these categories, like love and hatred, have been increasingly challenged in postmodernist America: it is clear that a society that is increasingly pluralistic in racial and ethnic composition cannot continue to visualize itself as "white" or "black." From this view, "race" is obsolescent. But it is precisely at this point of obsolescence that the recovery motive reintrudes into the public discourse. And loss is the name of this recovery discourse.

209

Loss and the American Psyche

Writing in the late 1970s on educational policy in America, David Cohen made the following observation regarding the theme of loss: "But the sense of loss may persist not only because it is an objective feature of modern social experience but also because it is a subjective feature of the way moderns view experience. Loss may seem important as much because it is a central theme in modern culture as because it is a fact of social reality" (Cohen 1976, 568).

Recently in a classroom discussion on African-American education, a middle-aged woman — a master teacher who had taught for nearly twenty years in rural Pennsylvania — described the white (male) experience as "having everything taken away from them." Although she could see and name the anxiety this stirred in the hearts of the whites she knew, she could not see that loss may beget anxiety and anxiety may beget recovery actions.

It is precisely this myopia regarding the anxiety underpinning much current white discourse on race that I have examined in this book. I have been arguing that the anxiety pluralism creates for whites has stimulated whites to talk increasingly to each other about race and racism even as most seem to deny they play any major part in American life. This denial is ubiquitous; Bernard J. Lee has viewed it in these terms:

> In the United States experience today, we seem — as a piece of national creature anxiety — unable to admit our limited role among the nations of the world, our inability to control destiny. In short, like J. Alfred Prufrock, we see the moment of our greatness flicker, and we are afraid. Nations do come and go. Only a snake says, "Well, maybe not. Perhaps you can be eternal like God." Today that temptation has become a terrible, terrible danger — an incredible recess of darkness. (Lee 1990, 52)

In the above we are reminded that the sense of loss runs deep. But the important lesson is not the presence or persistence of a recovery commitment. Rather, it is the implication such a motive has for the changes we must make in the ways we talk and relate to each other regarding matters racial.

The New White Racial Narrative

A short time back a student came to speak with me: a working-class mother of five males between fourteen and twenty-three, she introduced herself largely by telling me stories of her struggles with other white, but upper-class, female teachers insensitive to the poor white woman; with abusive boyfriends, including her own fourteen-year-old, who treats his little girlfriends like "trash"; and with the expanding presence and power of the KKK in the school district in which she works. Because of her wisdom, experience, and efforts to survive by returning to get her college education, she is perhaps more vulnerable than many similarly situated women; and therefore, like the wretched heroine of Tennessee Williams's *A Streetcar Named Desire,* she counts on "the kindness of strangers" like me. And she talks: "White men are so angry; my twenty-three-year-old son can't get a job. He comes home and says, 'Mom, they told me not to even apply, they need a minority. I understand that the Blacks need a chance, mom, but . . . ' And I know he's trying, but it's hard for them to see how things really are."

I can feel the intense pain of the jobless white male: I had eight Irish Catholic brothers-in-law; they were good, decent men. I saw them in moments of triumph and tragedy, joy and sorrow. I watched them struggle with a hard earth, a changing technology, a cold and cruel business world. They were hardly "the Man." And yet they were "the Man." Because they cannot see their privilege when they are in such pain, they deny the presence of privilege. Even some Blacks have taken the part of whites because they too see the pain so many white people are in at this point in our country's history. For example, Shelby Steele's *The Content of Our Character,* a recent best-seller, is significantly a story of white pain. Although I feel he is misguided in his overkill of Black exploitation of white guilt, I believe that he has also seen the pain whites are in. Where I differ with Black writers like Steele, who seem to validate whites at the expense of Blacks and other minorities, is over their neglect of the power of white men to take care of their own interests.

This power is well-documented. It seems almost too obvious to comment on. To understand why a young Black college student might doubt a racist act is racist, we must examine the way in which the media and powerful white interest groups have manipulated the images, beliefs, and messages about who has attained what in the past three decades and at a cost to whom. A largely white media constructs the preferred image of "Black men" by selective reporting of crime, violence, and evil in our society.

But the greater challenge is the seductiveness of the new white racial story. Many whites have constructed personal racial stories that invert aspects of the Black racial story. They reject the inherited story that Blacks, Jews, and others are inferior; they now experience and believe the story that Blacks and others are *privileged.* Because they see and hear images of Black success — Michael Jordan, Michael Jackson, Whitney Houston, Clarence Thomas — they "feel" that all Blacks have the power and opportunity to be model successes. Because they see many of their own family and friends suffering, they believe white men have had to pay for Black success. This is a new white racial story. In this new white racial narrative, moreover, the white male is victim.

A major objective of this book has been to describe the novel as well as traditional qualities of this view of the white male as victim and to relate it to the precise way in which he now conceives of and communicates about racial matters. But American society is not necessarily controlled by a single power group; there are many competing interest groups whose successes vary from time to time and place to place. The competing private and collective interests of different groups of Blacks also influence what is believable. The stories that Blacks themselves tell about themselves have become one of the most powerful threats to belief in the traditional racial narrative.

A Heterogeneous Black Racial Narrative

The narratives presented in part III reveal sexism and Black male abandonment of the race as two such contradictory enemies to Black racial survival and collective liberation. I have suggested too that the frequently cited tension between male and female (Hoch 1979) has affected the African-American couple; a crucial, underexamined, and nonresolved rift in the collusive bond has (re)opened between Black man and woman. This rift has occurred concurrent with, and in relation to, the larger, societal crisis in identity. The confluence of these racial and societal crises has confused understanding and analysis even more.

In this book I have proposed a rhetorical (communicational) approach to describing and interpreting these crises. It represents both whites and Blacks as concerned with recovery. For whites, this is largely a matter of reestablishing both material and cultural hegemony, although significant oppositional creativity is occurring among white feminists, gays, lesbians, and other such collectivities.

The recovery effort for Blacks, though fused to these other oppositional liberation thrusts, is far more complex because it entails — as it always does for the oppressed — fusing individual and collective identities and fates, even when these may not be the same. Thus, Blacks must dialectically confront various complex possibilities: returning to an ancient Afrocentric identity; retaining large aspects of the African-American identity that has emerged over the past four hundred years; or abandoning these for a hybrid, postmodern American identity.

Twin stumbling blocks have arisen to complicate this task further. On the one hand, recognizing their own vulnerability and the divisiveness among African-Americans who now experience a heightened sense of heterogeneity over their homogeneity, whites have evolved a strong, increasingly more institutionalized rhetoric of white victimization. A number of Blacks, moreover, pursuing their own visions of racial and personal liberation, have, perhaps unavoidably, strengthened this rhetorical stance.

Blacks, on the other hand, have begun to repolarize around the meaning of, and obligations to, "Blackness." Divergent views along political and ideological dimensions have always presented major problems. Now, as well, an increasingly distinct gulf between Black "haves" and "have-nots" seems to be affecting Black self-care (Glasgow 1980). Thus, several competing, often contradictory rhetorics have evolved, most notably the rhetoric of abandonment, a broad-based cultural response to the felt loss of those who have served as caregivers and nurturers of society (Lorde 1979; Miller 1976). As it pertains to the felt loss of traditional Black female nurturing, this rhetoric is understandable. This orientation, however, reflects a deep and, until recently, neglected area of intragroup relations: relational justice for the most vulnerable.

The rhetorical agenda for Blacks must include a recovery-sensitive ideology at both the individual and collective levels. This rhetorical task pertains ultimately to regaining control of the rhetoric of liberation and coalitional communication, which presupposes a real and broad-based connectedness not readily belied by constant intracollective contradiction. We can see that this is a psychopolitical task. We are clearly speaking of the need to find a good fit among personal and public experiences, ideologies, and psychologies. The task means finding ways of changing the cultural contradictions that distort human individuation and compromise reintegration subsequent to psychological (re)birth. For Black Americans, this task involves coming to terms with a historical wound (enslavement and continued racial vulnerability) and relational contradiction (the ways in which we have shared in our own abuse and betrayal).

The rhetoric of Black female abandonment deflects one from this critical developmental task. The cultural contradictions against which many Black women struggle, both intra- and extrapsychically, point to the perennial wisdom that the best psychological and cultural choice for Black people is a renewed intragroup compassion grounded in an ever-expanding sensitivity and commitment to the world community.

The rhetoric of personal choice signifies a break from a historically vital but changing racial bond. This rhetoric constitutes a betrayal, but it is, as well, a kind of coming of age. The rhetoric of self-recovery, spawned partly by a shameless rhetoric of personal choice, is both understandable and, probably, inevitable. Self-recovery, moreover, is necessary and can be creative. It need not foretell racial suicide or premature demise. Already we see signs of a synthesis afoot. We see this in the rhetoric of enlargement. We find such rhetoric throughout the Black Power movement ideology, notably in Martin Luther King, Jr., Stokely Carmichael, and Malcolm X (Gresson 1977; 1978). In more recent times, it has appeared in Michele Wallace's assertion that "criticism is an act of love," Alice Walker's "womanist" vision for the species, and Audre Lorde's metaphoric observation that there is a redemptive "Black Mother within us all" — Black, white, female, and male.

Enlargement, however, cannot occur as sleight of hand. It cannot be gerrymandered into vitality and integrity. It must be dialectically derived in the context of an existential, day-to-day struggle. More precisely, it must be part of a global, species-specific maturation. But it requires, as well, that we acknowledge the persistence of racism and that we collectively begin the systematic rebuilding of a healthier, more inclusive set of formative images. We must delimit these images enough to inspire identification and involvement, yet make them expansive enough to embrace the integrity of the world community.

Richard Brown says irony can facilitate the public "experience and resolution of ambiguity and contradiction" (R. Brown 1987, 190). But this larger project cannot take place without the individual's ultimate growth, and that ultimate growth is tied to "returning to the collective." Recovery is ultimately concerned with reintegration with, or reconnection to, the group. This may be a clue to the rhetorical format of larger, broader based encounters and dialogues toward relational justice and reconnection. In this sense, we all need to keep talking.

Notes

❖

1: Race, Rhetoric, and Recovery

1. For a fuller discussion of this scholarly concern with the individual versus society in the struggle to control individual choice, see Gresson 1982, esp. chap. 2.

2. Here I wish to note that the current discourses around "essentialism" and "totalization" are not unrelated to my tasks nor ignored in my discussion, although I seldom draw attention to these terms in my discussion. Moreover, I am well aware that these terms challenge the idea of an *essentialist or totalizing* "recovery" project or agenda. Clearly, from such a view, my own project might seem uninformed; yet I would argue that it is precisely the essentialist-antiessentialist struggle that contextualizes the recovery project I describe: the recent resurgence of an antiessentialist perspective is merely the latest expression of hegemonic recovery within patriarchal society. I argue that the impulse to transcend essentializing and totalizing agendas largely benefits the ruling class: the spaces created for "empowerment" and "growth" through nonessentialist activity, in many instances, amounts to the weak "capping on" the weak. For an excellent example of the plea against essentialism, see Michael Eric Dyson (1993); for a powerful critique and exposure of the reactionary potential of antiessentialist criticism, see Tania Modleski (1991).

3. The theme of edification and its relevance to the narrative form has been increasingly discussed by authors concerned with individual responsibility and civility. For instance, interpreting Richard Rorty's (1979) ideas regarding edification, René V. Arcilla (1990, 36) writes: "As we edify ourselves in response to events that befall us — including childhood traumas, what history teachers tell us, love letters we struggle to compose, medical tests we suffer, chance chats, etc. — we develop our ability to weave contingent but consistent stories of the course of our lives.... Edification thus means the process of accounting for the events of one's life as a chain of fateful choices, however constrained, that enable one to celebrate, before death, the history of one's originality."

4. The idea of the Black male as "worse than the white male" was a critical proposition. I believe that it is most important to understand that the moral forcefulness of the idea received its impetus and believability from reports — narratives — emanating from Blacks, both male and female, from other oppressed groups like Jews and Latinos, and from white females. The white female, identified with both the powerful white male and the less powerful women of color, could and did introduce an idea, "Black male as villain," that was believable

when she could reveal his gender arrogance in political matters and his sexual brutality as lover and mate. The narratives of both Monique and Eartha reveal instances of such Black male brutality toward white women and the resulting gender bond. Still, bell hooks (1981), among others, wrote of the historical collusion between Black male and white female. A radical reading of antiessentialist discourse would dismiss notions of "racial collusion" and "racial history" as some totalizing or imminent historical construction that must or ought to underpin racial realities. It is precisely the rhetorical quality of this newer scholarship that signifies the recovery task as transracial uplift.

5. The recovery task for whites has been to reverse the shame and moral culpability accompanying the public admission of the immorality and destructiveness of racism in this country. This recovery task, however, has been part of a larger national recovery mission. We saw this national recovery mission recently portrayed in the manner in which the Gulf War was executed by the president and the U.S. military and in the support America — Congress and the "Yellow Ribbon movement" — provided the men and women who fought. A significant part of this war ritual was aimed at vindicating the moral demise and cowardice that characterized the Vietnam era. A notable aspect of this war and the victory celebrations at its conclusion was the insistence that Blacks and other minorities were not being misused in the war. The composite picture of the Black and minority presence was one of total and full integration. In fact, the two major televised celebrations after the war — the HBO special with Whitney Houston and the Barbara Mandrell special with Bee and Cee Winan — prominently displayed the Black presence as a *smaller but integral* part of the American recovery of moral fiber. Part IV presents a fuller discussion of this white recovery effort because it is the motive and matrix within which Black liberation discourse — the empirical material for this inquiry — has evolved during the past decade.

6. Biblically, this term signals "the end of the world" — the final conflict between good and evil, God and Satan. More generally, today the term is often used to signal widespread death and destruction: doom. As such, it contains little of the hopeful expectation of the imminent final victory of good over evil. I use the term to suggest the sacred aspect of the imagined battle between good and evil: "Black liberation," or "racial uplift," as it was earlier viewed, has long carried a messianic aspect; likewise, the English settlers very much saw God and Satan at the center of their liberation efforts. It is in this sense, then, that the term "apocalypse" is often today invoked as a signal of danger of a sacred character.

7. For an excellent treatment of the Los Angeles riot of 1992, particularly its participation in the recovery project taken up in this book, see Robert Gooding-Williams (1993).

8. Using the concept of "dialectical irony," a parallel argument has been advanced by Richard Brown (1987, 3–4):

> Irony is a metaphor of opposites, a point of view that distances and derealizes what is taken as real in order to permit the realization of new meanings and forms. Irony is thus the uniquely dialectical trope, in that the resolution of its opposites is left to its public. To be ironic, irony thus

demands participation and completion by its auditors. Such participation *is enlightenment and freedom.*

9. Allow me a word here about the narratives to follow and their place in the study: I collected the narratives as part of a study on Black female racial commitments. I presented this research as a theory of Black female psychological development in narcissistic society (Gresson 1985b), but none of the narratives was reproduced in whole in that study. I collected these nearly fifty narratives during (1) training situations in which I was a psychology intern; (2) clinical situations in which I was the psychotherapist; (3) community action situations in which I served as consulting adviser; and (4) situations of close friendship and personal counseling.

I use five narratives in this book. Two of the five women are former students who became close friends at some point after they had completed their study with me; two of the women were university and mental health center colleagues; and one was the daughter of another female colleague.

My close association with these people is a critical and desired circumstance in this study. In each case, these women were trying to convince me both to understand and to affirm their decisions and developing attitudes regarding Black men and the conflictive racial choices they and some other Black women had made. For them, I was a reflection of the crisis of the race: a successful Black man who had once married a white woman. I was also a Black man they cared for. Finally, I was a Black man whose failure with regard to Black women was most ironic because I seemed to care about the plight of Black women. Akia once said to me in this regard, "Damn, Aaron! If you can be so insensitive to Black women with all your reading of Black women's literature and feminist values, what does that mean for the rest of Black men?"

The question was rhetorical. It reflects how that woman used my circumstances and behavior both to persuade herself that she was making the right choices and to induce me to see the salience of her choices. In short, the narrators used me to contextualize the racial (cultural) meaning of their own analyses and actions around racial commitment. Likewise, they used my own racial contradictions and weaknesses to clarify their pain, despair, and anger.

From one perspective, the character of my involvement with these women and my use of their narratives to enhance my own narrative — and, to a degree, career — are essential evidence of the appropriative problematic inherent in current debates around the possibility of a genuine Black male feminism. My own study was begun prior to the major statements of this discourse, and had I been privy to them, I might have abandoned the project. Clearly, I was aware of some Black females' displeasure at my agenda; and I did proceed with the support only of Black women who affirmed the task and my assumption of it. Still, I wish to record here my ongoing uncertainty that I, defined by whatever categories available, ought to "interpret" others. For a recent and important discussion of this topic, see Michael Awkward (1988, 5–27).

2: Black Male Recovery

1. By designating "whiteness" as a value, I seek to contextualize it as a distinguishable ideational element that white Americans conscientiously in-

ternalized and that nonwhites sought to approximate in their own character formations. For an important historical and economic account of "whiteness" so understood, see David R. Riediger (1991).

2. Here I am closing in on an essentialist tension: the very need to insist on unity in values betrays the absence of an essential wholeness or oneness. And yet I am very much cautioned from embracing the Black antiessentialist position. I am cautioned first of all because I distrust the frequent collusive re-actionary outcomes of such positions: they rarely apply to the pragmatics of the less privileged; they seem to be hurled outward toward a "straw villain" (the essentialist). Second, and related to the above, I suspect that antiessentialism is largely disinvolved with the pragmatics of "identity-building" as something serious to the survival of the disinherited. To be sure, there is a collectivist agenda at stake and in development in such cases, but they differ immensely from the "grassroots" realities I have in mind. In this connection, I am reminded of a passage from a brilliant study by Tania Modleski (1991, 22):

> I worry that the position of female anti-essentialism as it is being theorized by some feminists today is a luxury open only to the most privileged women. I worry about the consonance of this position with the ones being advanced by certain white male poststructuralist intellectuals who have proclaimed the death of the subject: if Nancy K. Miller is correct to counter proclamations about the death of the subject by insisting that "only those who have it can play with not having it," could we not also say of anti-essentialist feminists that only those possessing vastly wider options than the majority of women living in the world today can play at "being it" while theorizing themselves into the belief that they are not it?

3. This type of thinking reveals the desperation felt as a result of the Black desire both to achieve and to retain group cohesion throughout history. The permissiveness of the 1960s merely resurfaced a deep and deadly chasm.

4. The basic failure of Blacks to achieve a critical, political understanding of the role of group power in American life is a central theme in the classic volume by Harold Cruse (1967).

5. For a conceptual discussion of this neglect of Black father-daughter inquiry, see R. L. Taylor (1976).

6. Andria's narrative also brings us face-to-face with the collusive nature of antiessentialism: the bond she and Julia forge is created largely from a shared rendering of the "Black male body" as danger. This pragmatic essentialism is precisely what occurs in any bonding situation; and it is the failure to address this fact that renders some antiessentialist discourse inauthentic and incorrect.

7. I do not mean to infer that women cannot and do not freely choose each other as sexual subjects. Rather, I want to indicate here that often misogyny and patriarchalism are intimately connected to sexual choices. This is certainly true in Andria's case. In this regard, Susan Willis (1987, 160) writes that in *A Color Purple,* Alice Walker's "utopian vision is predicated on the transformation of the two most significant determinants of a woman's domestic life: sexuality and economics. Lesbianism gives Celie the means for transforming her body, previously defined as an object for use, into the site of her pleasure and her means for giving pleasure to another. It transforms her bed and bedroom, previously

defined as zones for the reproduction of male domination and the economic expropriation of women, into a context for discovering new bases for social relationships." Thus, we might see Andria's "concern with respect" as very much linked to a larger discourse and concern. For an extremely important discussion of the lesbian factor — notably lesbian sadomasochism — in undermining and transforming patriarchal gender relations, see Modleski (1991, 135–63).

But there is yet another aspect of lesbianism that bears comment here: Black lesbianism and Black homophobia. Patricia Hill Collins (1991), elaborating on Barbara Smith, Audre Lorde, and others, has addressed the importance of Black women and men examining more deeply the fears, and their sources, beneath their oppression of women who deeply, and perhaps exclusively, love only other women sexually. For a major Black feminist writer on Black lesbian themes in literature, see Barbara Christian (1985, esp. 199–210).

8. Black women experience this severance as abandonment, physical and mental abuse, and other forms of disrespect. During the height of the conflict between Black men and women, Aretha Franklin, the "Queen of Soul," popularized a song with which many Black women identified. The song was called "Respect," and the sisters routinely sang it to their men and to each other.

9. The recent interest in mulattoes and their place, practical and potential, within American society illustrates this point. The reader is referred to F. James Davis (1991) and Joel Williamson (1980). For a discussion of the class issue, the reader might consult Manning Marable (1980).

10. Although some African-American scholars and critics address the issue of "forbidden fruit" and its contribution to increased miscegenation, this topic has been generally undertreated. Perhaps the best statement of the issue appears in Frantz Fanon (1967).

3: Black Women's Recovery Narratives

1. I developed this perspective in *The Dialectics of Betrayal* (Gresson 1982). Building on Albert Memmi's observation that Freud tried to teach the Jews that they had to abandon aspects of Judaism if they were to be fully free of the oppression of anti-Semitism, I argued that Blacks are also trapped by the limitations imposed on them by racism and that they must reject certain oppressive adaptations to racism in order to be more fully human.

2. Patricia Hill Collins has written in this regard: "Literature by Black women writers provides the most comprehensive view of Black women's struggle to form positive self-definitions in the face of denigrated images of Black womanhood. Portraying the range of ways that African-American women experience internalized oppression is a prominent theme in Black women's writing" (Collins 1991, 83). Collins identifies a variety of other tropes — drugs, alcohol, excessive religion, madness and denial — Black women use to combat the negative images propagated against Black womanhood. The point is that the range of stories being written enables Black women to choose one or more preferred models of Black womanhood as either actuality or option. This is precisely the liberatory meaning of "killing the sacred cow" that Mary Helen Washington connects to Black female storytelling.

3. Alice Walker, like Henry Louis Gates, Jr., has had a career that recapitulates the sequence I am calling "the rhetoric of recovery." As I will argue later, a major aspect of this configuration is the propensity to "discover" forgotten insights; this propensity, as Joseph Campbell notes, is the hallmark of the "culture hero."

4. Elsewhere I used the term "transitional metaphors" to describe this self-soothing, self-comforting behavior (Gresson 1987). A brief return to the story of Esau may help illuminate the link between self-recovery and self-soothing: after Esau had heard his father out, he first had to acknowledge his brother as "lord" and then decide whether to kill Jacob or surrender to his lordship. His initial impulse was to slay Jacob. But he could not go to his parents or the elders for support in this plot: he was alone, and he had to find a way of consoling himself. I view the language of self-consolation as "transitional" in the sense that it is a private dialogue, a language of the self, one that is used until the self recovers others to stand in place of that "inner self" that Alice Walker identifies as within each of us. Symbolically, this "twin self" is the equivalent to God and Isaac, who enabled Abraham and Esau to escape their bondage.

5. This concept, "in recovery," is a part of the vernacular of addiction recovery literature. I use it here to suggest a convergence between this traditional usage and the larger societal condition of addiction and need for recovery. This is not an altogether new application of the concept. But it is an unusual one.

6. The observations of Asante and Duncan suggest one possible focus for an integrative, critical, methodological approach — that is, an approach responsive to morality, motive, and methodology. As this approach pertains to metaphors of race, we can find ways of apprehending descriptively, and acting upon relationally, the unfolding "drama of holism" we might anticipate from within the African-American community. For example, Michael Jackson and Jesse Jackson are complex, dialectical illustrations of this larger societal dynamic. Using different aspects of themselves, they have expanded their "formative images" (Gresson 1978) to include the larger society. In this way, one emerges as the "cultural hero" of the "new generation," and the other becomes a serious candidate for president of the United States. How their proponents talk about their postures (with such expressions as "the Rainbow Coalition," for example) parallels the narrative activity of the women soon to be introduced. All are engaged in a creative act of collective identification.

7. For a clinical discussion of Walker's ideas in this passage, see M. A. Z. Kamau-Collier (1990, 28–37).

8. This fracture was symbolized first by the rhetoric of personal choice (Black males) and then by the rhetoric of self-recovery (Black women). Though larger than the clash of the sexes and broader than the issue of interracial intimacy, these parameters — gender and miscegenation — became the basis for the subsequent disenchantment among various discursive communities of African-Americans. But the drama was not so simple. There were few massive abandonments across various previously tabooed barriers. Most Blacks remained within the constraints of traditionalism: believing themselves an oppressed people who had achieved some degree of liberation but still had a long

way to go. Others, however, moved fully into alternative lifestyles, including miscegenation, politicized or combative homosexuality, rugged individualism, and capitalism. But others were more puzzling. They had made changes in their lives but retained a clear and firm sense of traditional identification. Moreover, they often insisted that they were even "better" members of the group now that they had achieved a degree of separateness.

9. From the term "sensitive," I infer that the rhetor means tolerant, understanding, and supportive.

10. In chapter 9, I examine Henry Louis Gates, Jr., as a premier instance of a Black man who has been successful within mainstream white America at some cost to his believability among certain groups of African-Americans. In particular, I observe that his own scholarly interest in an African trickster, Esu, is most interesting given that a part of the accusatory discourse aimed at him refers to *him* as a trickster. The notions of trickery and opportunism among Africans and African-Americans, and their place in recovery rhetoric, cannot be overemphasized; and although this particular study does not include an extended discussion of it, I would like to connect this national rhetorical challenge to the larger Pan-African context. An excellent vehicle for this is found in a critical essay by Marie Linton Umeh (1986). Umeh's essay is about Buchi Emecheta's *Double Yoke,* a book about the dilemmas and contradictions of educated Nigerian women and their efforts to resolve romantic confrontations and entanglements. Umeh observes, however:

> There is satire too in *Double Yoke.* . . . In the character of Reverend Professor Ikot, pretentious and immoral university professors in Nigeria are attacked. Ikot, like the true trickster figure, is shrewd, cunning and loquacious. Posing as a religious leader and educator, he dupes others but is rarely duped himself. His strong archetypal appeal, an ability to outwit others and articulate his ideas, enables him to exercise power and control over people. Even when caught in the act, he exploits the situation and emerges a winner. . . . Ikot preoccupies himself with "getting a piece of the cake." (p. 178)

The point is not so much that either Judge Thomas or Professor Gates is truly like this fictional character as it is that African tradition, especially under conditions of immense contradictions that seem insurmountable, often takes on a survivalist pragmatism that already had a privileged, in the sense of archetypal, place within the folkways. Thus, a potent rhetorical ploy — for white and Black alike — is the attempt to induce Black adaptation by appealing to Black pragmatism. This point is taken up in chapter 10 of the present study. To complete the point here of Black and white convergence of motive around recovery, I will mention a particularly powerful instance of such rhetorical activity. During Jesse Jackson's 1984 campaign for president, the *New York Times* printed an article entitled "Black Democrats in a Poll Prefer Mondale to Jackson as Nominee." In this article, and again in several companion pieces, the *Times* wrote: "Although three-quarters of the Blacks who voted in the Democratic Presidential primaries this year voted for the Rev. Jesse Jackson, Black Democrats prefer Walter F. Mondale. . . . Politicians interviewed by the Times said the poll findings meant that Blacks were putting pragmatism ahead of pride" (*New York Times,* July 10, 1984, p. 1).

11. For a more comprehensive study of the oppositional nature of Black heroism, see John Roberts (1989).

4: Monique: The Self-Metaphor in Narrative Discourse

1. Monique later changed her attitude in this regard after an opportunity to talk about her feelings openly and monitor what she was saying. This is what one might call the deprivatization process, or co-constructing a shared perspective. The notion of dialectics implies precisely this type of shift in perspective through collective exposure of the contradictions in a given perspective or situation.

2. Monique recently completed her undergraduate training in education despite efforts of the father of her son, a clinical psychologist, to sabotage her progress in a series of financial and legal maneuvers. Monique works hard and is an excellent model of a committed student. She works equally hard to give her son all of the social and cultural benefits — scouts, camp, music lessons — one might stereotypically identify with a two-parent professional family. Her estranged mate's efforts to get her to quit her last semester of school was intended, she believes, to prevent her from effectively maintaining her son and herself without his dominance. Education, then, is a discovery that allows recovery.

3. *"Human like them"*: an important statement. This is the rhetorical condition of Blacks and all other humans whose stigmata, however designated by society, becomes the full measure of their humanity. Recovery and its rhetoric emphasize the human side of the actor. Yet to say merely, "I am a human being," is insufficient. Even in Shakespeare's day, a Jew could not merely say, "I am human." Rather, Shylock, antihero of *The Merchant of Venice,* must utter: "Hath not a Jew eyes, ears, mouth? If you prick us, will we not bleed? And if you do us harm, will we not seek revenge?" Nor was Sojourner Truth, the great abolitionist and former slave, able merely to say, "I am human." She, we recall, like Shylock, declared, "Ain't I a woman?"

Monique, like Shylock and Sojourner, must say "I am human" in words more persuasive than the ones she used. She does this, functionally, when she brings white women to recognize her as a model. Thus, Monique's success in gaining her education is the fulfillment of her discovery of her "true worth." It represents her attainment of the respect she deserves. Likewise, it could be the possible measure of these white women's "true worth." Even though they have gone across racial lines, had biracial children, and know betrayal by their mates, these white women can attain an education.

4. Monique recently told me how the night before her college graduation, an older sister embarrassed her before a crowd of people in a neighborhood bar. This sister, a victim of drug addiction and the family scapegoat, told Monique that she had exploited the family, that she had used the family to raise her biracial son, while she went off to the university. Monique was understandably devastated by this encounter: she has been a primary emotional and economic support for the family, especially this sister. Monique described this encounter

as endemic in Black and other oppressed families, particularly when members leave to join the mainstream by education, marriage, and career. Monique also agreed with my suggestion that she had, for that very reason, this "verbal beating" coming, and that this sister was, in fact, the family and community voice: she said the things others felt but could not and would not verbalize. This incident also exposes the implicit betrayal Black women feel toward their sisters, daughters, and relatives who beget a "special breed" by miscegenation. Mary Helen Washington has discussed this very situation in her anthologies on Black women's literature, albeit from a different perspective.

5. Implicit in this account is a challenge to an important rhetorical argument in some Black men's claim that they would do better as Blacks and men if Black women were more like white women: docile. Monique's story is reminiscent of Linda White's comments at the opening of the chapter, notably this passage: "Black men . . . exaggerate their oppression in order to gain a woman's sympathy and exploit her emotions, transforming her into a passive shadow that ultimately is left alone to struggle, suffer, and weep. I and many other Black women cannot and will not get involved in these games. Why should we be condemned? To whom are we doing harm?"

6. Monique may feel for Black women with biracial children, but she does not identify with them as supports, as is frequently the case with mixed racial families. She does not have them as friends; nor does she seek out other biracial children as a support for her son. This fact forces us to consider another possibility: Monique does not primarily want to be white or to live exclusively in the white world; but she does want the prestige associated with being a special Black woman. We see here another aspect of her tension with other Black women: she cannot be special among other Black women with biracial sons.

7. I. Schiffer (1973, 171) has characterized the disillusionment of mass society with the leader in these terms:

The day must come when the process of disenchantment and the feeling of being left behind creep in. But our leader grows bigger and stronger and healthier and richer and much more dignified. He becomes the epitome of the traditional patriarch!

We realize that we are growing "down" and that all our dreams are fading of becoming a chief, of ending up free — free of the yoke of the "great man," free to transcend group psychology, free to possess the primal mother all to ourselves. Instead, we are drained, and "he" thrives.

8. Recent Black history has revealed this to be so for several Blacks including Vanessa Williams, the first Black Miss America, exposed by a white press and forced to resign her title. As she recalled, the Black community stood by her during her ordeal even though she had transcended traditional expectations by dating white, and her father had taken pride in the fact that she was raised outside of the provincialism of traditional racial expectations.

5: Eartha: Privatization in the Narrative Experience

1. From this viewpoint, Linda White (1977) used a "weapon" — choice of the white male — to remove the vanquished Black male's last vestige of pride and humanity: *the unconditional love of the Black female comrade.*

2. One sees here a young woman whose experience as the baby in the family took her along a predictable path, but with some interesting and not so predictable twists. One gets a sense of Eartha as a woman who sees herself standing outside of time and space, acting upon others. Once I counseled the family during a crisis: a sister was fleeing her violent husband with their two small children. The crisis had thrust the family back into the recollection of another sister whose husband had killed her some years earlier. At one point, Eartha, the eldest sister (a married woman with two teenage sons), and I were together in a room. The sister remarked that she was "tired of being the one to shoulder all of the family's burdens." She mentioned Eartha's reluctance to involve herself in family troubles. Eartha retorted, "I care about the family. I remember Pat's death. It hurts me too." She had, in fact, discussed the murder with me. Not only was she still grieving her sister's loss, but she was also ambivalent about Black men because of it. She told me, for example, how her first Black male friend had once attempted to beat her with his belt, and she had threatened to kill him. "He said I was crazy. But I wasn't going to let no man beat me with his belt after what happened to my sister. I would just have to go to jail."

Eartha feels uncomfortable with intense and long-term intimacy despite her claim to being a warm person. Her warmth is real enough, but it does not lead to extended emotional encounters. We see aspects of this reticence in her description of how she used her mother and sisters. They tie her down, as does the race. She wants to break with the earthbound.

3. The traditional tendency to associate spirituality with psychotic decompensation seems to distract one from some important developmental issues, especially among African-American and Puerto Rican clients. It is significant in a discussion of redemptive rhetoric that the availability of minority mental-health specialists in the inner-city has added insight into the recovery-of-voice process initiated in the radical therapy movements of the 1960s — movements associated with Frantz Fanon, R. D. Laing, Thomas Szasz, Phyllis Chesler, and others. I want to mention here, too, that Eartha's movement from Black to Puerto Rican and white mates might have been facilitated by the fact that her therapist was Puerto Rican. To suggest a transference of love from father to therapist and from Black boyfriend to non-Black boyfriend is not farfetched. For instance, Seymour Halleck (1971) argues that therapy will either bring one closer to liberation or encourage one to draw nearer to those ways of perceiving and feeling that enslave one. As a therapist, I have worked with several Black women who seemed best able to work with non-Black therapists, particularly when they were about to differentiate from the group. It is difficult to ask those you used to identify with to free you from this shared identification. That individual Blacks continue to experience psychotherapy (notably self-psychology) often as threatening is partially traceable to this rejection of "difference" as a sign of racial loyalty and commitment to collective liberation.

6: Akia: Narrative Construction as Heroic Recovery

1. I hasten to say that I do not seek to essentialize or totalize individual experience and agency by this formulation; the designation of Monique's and

Eartha's narratives as complex and confusing pertains to only those things we presume to share in the discourse as inherited elements of our past. Thus, the observation that many Blacks do not grow up in the working class or in the Pentecostal church misses the essential stigmata and stereotyping others place on all Blacks, and against which we all must resonate, even if it is to disavow recognition of "those Blacks." Additionally, I have in mind here a dynamic captured in the "convention of the street." In an outstanding dissertation on Afro-American fiction, Frank E. Dobson (1985, 14) cites a powerful passage from Sherley Ann Williams (1972, 60–61):

> There are several descriptions of street life but no real definitions. It is difficult to distill out of the complex patterns of interaction which occur in the Life, a simple statement which conveys the way in which the Life touches and affects the lives of most Black people in any given community. For the Life not only comprises the pimps, dope pushers, numbers runners, gamblers, stick-up-men and the "rowdies" who frequent the bars and joints and dance halls. Each church sister who plays a number with a local runner, each member of the Black bourgeois who buys a stolen stereo or dress or suit, each playboy — or girl — no matter what their profession or economic status, who attempts to use their sexual attractiveness as a means of manipulation and exploitation, participates in and supports the Life ethic, "Take what you can get when you can get it." For the Life is not so much a class phenomenon as it is a Black phenomenon.

It is precisely this "participation in the Life" that marks one most identifiably as "Black" and makes all Blacks vulnerable to confused and confusing racial narratives.

2. Indeed, while Akia had been experiencing some disappointment in aspects of her relationship with Black males as lovers and leaders of the race, she reveals more hurt at her loss with respect to Black women. Reflective of one tenet of Black feminist ideology, she sees Black males and white females as a problematic dyad and distinguishable from Black women insofar as race-gender identity and oppression are concerned.

3. Akia's words here remind me of Shirley Chisholm's departing sentiments with respect to the Black male congressional caucus. She felt they had failed to support her around a number of events, including her candidacy for president. In this context, we are reminded that various Black politicians have been candid about their belief in the need to distinguish symbolic gestures from pragmatics (see Gresson 1987). This thinking, however, is a part of the reason that the emergence of a rhetoric of self-recovery is held as both a counterrhetoric and a basis for disidentification in favor of new identity commitments. Commitment continuance in the face of contradictory evidence cannot be sustained if one wants psychological stability. I might add that those persons inclined to "keep the faith" under such conditions are likely to be precisely those "rugged individualists" who would not permit collective myths around racial loyalty to guide their behavior in the beginning. Of course, I intend this line of argument to be suggestive rather than definitive. Moreover, recalling the dialectical perspective, we have no reason to suspect that a rigorous logic underpins people's rationalizations on this topic.

4. Frantz Fanon (1967), on exploding lies, comes to mind here. He pointed out that Africans must ultimately root out all lies that engulf their lives. He suggested that even the oppressed learns to hold oppressive ideas. Identity may thus become tainted. Freud presumably understood this to be a part of the reason that a more authentic Jewish identity partly meant letting go of aspects of "Jewishness" (Gresson 1982). Such a break from the established beliefs — for example, that Blacks should conceal intragroup conflicts from whites — may be prompted or associated with loss of expected support from within the group. This is, of course, the message of Gates (1988), who has chosen to "reveal" or "recover" secrets and thereby "decollude" with one group (Blacks) as he "colludes" with another (whites). This is hardly a new experience for African-American people. We have considerable evidence that much of the so-called betrayal among African slaves was rooted in the fact that survival of one's own family might depend on exposing nonkin to the brutality of the white man (Gutman 1976).

5. The reference here to surrender as a feature of recovery derives from the necessity inherent in all recovery. From the earliest chronicles of human community and cooperation, surrender to something larger than self has been a perceived necessity. It is perhaps surprising, therefore, that both recovery rhetoric and the addiction recovery literature speak of the need to surrender. It is also important, and in keeping with a postmodernist vision, that some have tried to remove the "surrender" feature from recovery. For an illustration of this process, see Trish Hall (1990).

6. See Paul Newell Campbell (1972), esp. pp. 191–228, where he discusses the success and failure of rhetoric in terms of "honesty, in the sense of self-confrontation and self-revelation" (p. 226).

7. Women surrender to men. Women experience what men call surrender as growth. Although the alcoholism treatment field, through the guidance of Alcoholics Anonymous, has made the concept less problematic for men, it remains an essentially "secret" event connected to the deities (God) and the drug (alcohol). In short, men do not easily surrender, and, I believe, they do not easily experience growth. Here I want only to suggest that the language of surrender contains such notions as "tiredness" and "weary" and "beat." While I feel that we men are as tired and weary as women, we do not connect well with this idea. I am reminded of the perspective held by addiction experts such as Peter Bell; they point out that one reason Blacks get to the doctor late in the progression of their illness (excluding racism in health-care practice) is a greater tolerance for pain. We hold it in longer.

8. Lorde (1981, 729) elaborates on the meaning of this term:

The Black mother ... is the poet in every one of us.... [She is that part of us that knows that] the possible shapes of what has not been before exist only in the Black place [herself], where we keep those unnamed, untamed longings for something different and beyond what is now called possible, to which our analysis and our understanding can only build roads. But we have been taught to deny those fruitful areas of ourselves, which exist in every human being. I personally believe that those Black mothers exist more in women; yet that is the name for a humanity that men are not without. But they have taken a position against that piece of themselves, and it is a world position, a position throughout time.

Here Lorde reminds us of Mary Daly, discussed in chapter 7, above. The important ideas here are that, for men, recovery largely involves reconnecting with abandoned parts of themselves; whereas for women, it means permitting the vulnerability to guide them in their dealings. Again, I cite Lorde (1981, 728): "One thing has always kept me going — and it's not really courage or bravery, unless that's what courage or bravery is made up of — is a sense that there are so many ways in which I'm vulnerable and cannot help but be vulnerable, I'm not going to be vulnerable by putting weapons of silence in my enemies' hands."

9. This passage is reminiscent of Henry Louis Gates as "archaeologist," who appears in chapter 9 as the new Black culture hero of literary criticism.

10. Carol Pearson and Katherine Pope (1981, 15) tell us:

For male heroes not devoted to the macho heroic ideal, the experience is analogous. Both male and female heroes begin the quest for wholeness and selfhood by risking the violation of conventional norms, including conventions about appropriate sex-role behavior; both learn not to manipulate and restrain other people; and both reach accommodation with the best qualities associated with men and with women, integrating strength with humility, independence with empathy, rationality with intuition, and thought with emotion.

7: The Loss of Myth as Rhetorical Challenge

1. This idea of deliverance is the theme, for example, of many fairy tales as well as the basis for the deus ex machina, which was an interstitial prop in Greek plays. Perhaps one of the most beloved illustrations of this deliverance theme is the fable of "Sleeping Beauty." We recall that the wicked witch doomed the princess for her parents' slight, but that the good fairy godmother, after affirming (conceding) the pronouncement of the wicked witch, *transcended her by transforming the meaning and message of the spell*: the "death" was merely a "hundred-year sleep" from which everyone would awaken with their youth and happiness intact. I maintain that contemporary recovery discourse has a parallel function. Moreover, the rhetorical vehicles of the fairy tale, *myth and magic*, are important *topoi* of recovery discourse, which I will discuss more fully later.

2. Continuing the thought: "primogeniture" was a "group" power and reality whose end had come; symbolically, Jacob and the mother represented its demise. Isaac was therefore releasing Esau from the tyranny of the group and inviting him to recover his original powers, to accept his "true" birthright: heroism. The Book of Genesis is full of irony. And the story of Isaac, Esau, and Jacob exposes one of the most elemental examples: *he or she who loses self shall find self*. This is the discovery of the heroine.

3. It is presumed that their influence on the ever-present pursuit of new and different values, choices, and relationships yields a special type of individuation, one similar to but distinguishable from that described by developmental psychology.

4. Elsewhere, I developed a model that describes the ways in which people use public discourse, particularly its contradictory aspects, to renegotiate their commitments to racial identity (Gresson 1982). More recently, I reformulated this model to emphasize both the role of cultural contradictions in the recovery of personal choice among the oppressed and the psychodynamic process of separation involved in formulating nontraditional choices (Gresson 1985b).

5. She also identified three other representative *topoi* within contemporary Black women's literature: insanity, death, and lesbianism. Within this broader framework, "insanity," "death," and "lesbianism" are representative Black female tropes. Within the previously discussed context of Black privatization, each of these rhetorical choices constitutes a response to an exigency of intragroup violation and largely entail turning away from the Other into oneself.

Recent efforts to describe Black literature, particularly Black female literature, as either mystical (Morrison) or too white feminist (Walker) reflect the group's concern with this turning away from traditional racial heroism and are understandable from a pragmatic perspective. But the demands of a changing world, a world in which a Black is still most vulnerable, invite precisely such rhetorical choices. Such choices, moreover, do converge, in places, with the larger American recovery spirit, although Black rhetoric of recovery continues to focus largely on intragroup vulnerability to "white." A part of the reason for this continuity in the face of significant societal change is contemporary white recovery activity. White recovery, like Black recovery, is predicated on certain exigencies: namely, the loss of moral hegemony and the fear of domination by the once-dominated colored masses. This is, of course, a major current fear in South Africa.

6. This is a "freestyle" rendering of Perls's saying; like the Desiderata, it was a common/familiar icon of the 1960s and 1970s, being frequently used on posters, cards, and the like.

7. Could this be why "Black postmodernism" has come forth like the "Four Horsemen" to declare that "Blackness" is and has always been folly? and that the wisdom of African-American survival is adaptation? indeterminance? sham? In short, shall we have to pursue the possibility that Rudwick and Meier (1969) were correct when they argued that Blacks are ultimately realistic survivalists, aware and wary of the possibility of white rage and therefore, by inference, grateful for the chance to return to trickery?

8. One view of the conservative stance taken by Clarence Thomas is that he is taking a pragmatic posture, the only viable posture for a Black man who wants to rise to the top in contemporary America. This view, while superficially reasonable, might be usefully developed by further study of other Blacks who have risen to prominence during the past decade.

9. Self-recovery is itself a response, an imperfect self-awakening. In an interview with Adrienne Rich, Audre Lorde (1981) said that the reason Black women and men could not simply break all ties is that the race as race was forged through collusive bonds compelled by white racism. The history of ethnic group development supports this interpretation (Shibutani and Kwan 1975). But the emergence of repressive communication and the parallel experience of

alienative inner-discourse suggest that the collusive bonds have broken. Perhaps this is as it should be. The original racism has modified, though as Joel Kovel (1970) reveals in his psychohistory of racism, it is far from dead. The rhetoric of self-recovery suggests that we must define new formative images for relatedness (Gresson 1978). There is an even larger assignment: to forge a communion and a dialogue that allow for mutuality in equity.

8: White Recovery of Moral and Heroic Voice

1. Thus, we see, for example, the argument that women batter men as much as men batter women, and that men are wronged by a system that favors women's rights over those of the male. Then there is the racial parallel: Blacks on predominantly white campuses are the causes of the hostilities white students express toward them. This argument is, of course, a variant of the one used by Ivy League schools to rationalize the quotas they placed on American Jews in the 1920s. We will remember that Jews had gained an undesirable quantitative presence in the elite professions, and non-Jewish whites wanted *to recover their perceived losses.* (Something very much like this is taking place today at certain universities in California and New England where Asian-Americans enter these schools in ratios beyond their representation in the general population.)

2. The anthropological understanding of cannibalism is that it was a ritual aimed at gaining the strength (spirit) of the vanquished enemy, thereby enhancing one's own spirit. Some psychoanalytic scholars have seen it too as a means of resolving the difference between self and Other: by taking you into myself, you become a part of me, and I do not have to deal with you as a separate and possibly disagreeable entity. Of course, the connection with the current discussion is that the cannibalist, like the narrator, wants to tell a story for both self and Other. For a cogent study of cannibalism from this perspective, see Eli Sagan (1974).

3. The issue of sex between Blacks and whites has been discussed widely and requires little elaboration here. Interested readers may want to refer to Joel Kovel (1970). The more significant link I want to make here is that the use of sexual energy or affect to explore larger social matters is an important rhetorical breakthrough. For a major discussion of this dynamic in the cinema, see Thomas W. Benson (1980).

4. In this regard, too, Vanilla Ice is more like a warrior. Recall that "the Great White Hope" was to come forth and defeat the Black man, Jack Johnson, who had taken the heavyweight title, married a white woman, and taunted his white victims in the ring. After Johnson was destroyed, it would not be until Muhammad Ali that a Black man would again raise his voice in the ring: Joe Louis, Floyd Patterson, and Sugar Ray Robinson were all voiceless in this regard.

5. Allow me a personal story here. Recently at a neighborhood bar a young white male struck up a conversation with me. As the conversation progressed and he became more and more familiar, he began telling "Polack jokes," declaring himself part Polish. Eventually, he said, "I want to tell you this Black joke— over 95 percent of my buddies are nig——, uh, Blacks. I want to tell you this

joke. This cop stopped three Blacks in a car. He hit one over the head, and the Black guy asked, 'What did you do that for?' He proceeded to the second Black guy and bopped him over the head with the nightstick as he asked to see the vehicle's registration. Again, the second Black asked, 'What did you hit me for?' but got no answer. Then the cop hit the third Black, and when he asked 'Why?' he was informed, 'Because I was fulfilling your fantasy to be hit in the head.'" The young man's companion, an older white male, was growing more visibly anxious as the story progressed, but he seemed equally interested to see my reaction. When I commented that I had heard that one before, the tension dissipated and the conversation went back to this young man's Polish heritage. Perhaps because of his drinking and background this young man did not see that this joke was an aggressive story and that it was intended to be shared with other whites, not Blacks.

6. Justice Scalia belongs to the group of three new justices selected by conservative Republican presidents. While the battles in Congress regarding the partisan orientation each of these people represented mimic "fairness" (like the wrestling match), this is largely form: *it is understood that the justices will decide the legal tenor of the country for the duration of their lives — and they are chosen to represent the interests of the controlling president and party.* The choice of the three recent justices constitutes a recovery of white voice, a recovery of the concessions made during a radical period of the country's history. In this, the current series of events only replicates the Second Reconstruction of the late nineteenth century when Black progress was halted and the infamous Jim Crow laws were enacted to ensure that Blacks could not seriously challenge — through integration — the structural arrangement encoded in the Constitution and only partially offset by its amendments.

7. L. Althusser's "repressive state apparatus" is suggestive here. The idea he conveys is that various institutions play a coordinating role with regard to the perpetuation of certain role types and relational tensions. Of course, this is a pivotal theme of political communication study. On this, see Althusser (1970; 1971). For an application of Althusser's ideas to narrative in organizations, see Dennis K. Mumby (1988).

8. Several studies have shown a parallel tendency in the media. Specifically, these studies emphasize the media's ability to cue the reader to a particular view by the items they choose to report on and the extent and duration of their coverage. These include the important work of D. A. Graber (1976; 1984).

A notable recent instance of such cueing is described in a study by J. Gregory Payne (1989). His study of the *Los Angeles Times*'s handling of the 1984 gubernatorial campaign in California revealed a proclivity to highlight Mayor Bradley's race in campaign news stories. Furthermore, analysis of press coverage revealed both polls and voter interest focusing on race in a manner otherwise consistent with campaign coverage.

A related study was reported by C. Husband (1979). Husband studied press coverage of race relations in Britain during the 1960s and found that the press, in alliance with the politicians, operated with certain preconceptions that must be followed through in order for the reports to be intelligible to the masses. He also found that such formulations of the news are biased toward the elite. This was achieved partially by permitting certain politicians to dominate news coverage. It was also facilitated by reporting certain kinds of images of the "power elite" and the people it protected. For example, the British are felt to have a self-image as ultra-civilized and "fair," forever seeking to promote justice and harmonious relations. Husband concluded "that the potentially autonomous psychological dynamic of identity maintenance can no longer be left out of any mass media functioning within situations of intergroup contact" (p. 191).

Implicit in these studies is a collusive bond between the press and the established power. Together they seek to influence opinion through appealing to the already established values and emotions.

9: Henry Louis Gates's *The Signifying Monkey*

1. Thomas B. Farrell (1985) observes that narrative in conversation must differ from that in literature and other genres because of the roles of story and "action" in each and the constraint "time" introduces for each.

2. Molefi Asante is perhaps the principal literary proponent of the Afrocentric vision. In one place, he writes:

The Afrocentric method makes Afrological study. So one may study any subject and be an Afrologist as long as the subject is studied Afrocentrically. Everything is in relation to Africa, not in mere geographic terms but Africa as vision, ideal, and promontory.

Afrocentricity provides us with a counterbalance to the penetration of Eurocentric ideology and communication. Most doctrines of the Western world are meant to protect the status of the exploiter, the dominator, or if they were not so intended become the reality. Free flow of information, for example, strengthens the exploiter and keeps the weak nations weak. As a concept, free flow of information rises with American imperial expansion and global hegemony. Freedom for capital expansion was therefore appreciated as freedom for movement of information. My contention is that this view of the world haunts our theoretical positions on intercultural communication. (Asante 1983, 6)

And in another, though related, context, Asante adds:

Even rhetorical discourse among Africans in the Western world is polluted, distorted, and dismembered by the onslaught of European images and symbols. Sharing of images is reasonable, valuable, and positive; image domination, however, is the same as other colonial conquests, vile, repressive, and negative. Afrocentricity is the ideological centerpiece of human regeneration, systematizing our history and experience with our own culture at the core of existence. In its epistemic dimensions it is also a methodology for discovering the truth about intercultural communications. (Asante 1983, 7)

3. It is interesting to note that Houston A. Baker, Jr., does not actually disengage from the deconstructionist vision; the words in this case may be misleading. At the conclusion of his study, however, he is much clearer on the relevance of deconstructionism:

One way of considering the overall labor that needs to be performed is to see it as "reconstruction" in the manner of a recent group of African-American literary critics. It is essential, however, when talking of "reconstruction" to decide first any extant timber, or perhaps more aptly, any used crossties are worth salvaging in attempts to create a new perspective. It may ultimately prove the case that *deconstruction* is the best first step. (Baker 1984, 200)

4. Note here that Black scholarship is replete with instances of "failure" and "success" of this type. For example, Michele Wallace was punished for her volume *Black Macho and the Myth of Superwoman,* but Alice Walker got the Pulitzer Prize for *The Color Purple.* Harold Byrd got little for his volume *Can't Plead Black Anymore,* but William J. Wilson won a Spivack Award for *The Declining Significance of Race.* I am not comparing these works per se, merely indicating that seldom does the "first" person to introduce a theme get the honor; rather, it is the person who finds a way of conveying the message to the popular imagination of the ruling elites. This is precisely the thesis of an important book by W. Lawrence Hogue (1986).

5. I specify my world because different neighborhoods and regions possibly had different nuances of meaning and intention in the use of this concept.

6. This technique is actually a popular one among the elitist writers. In recent times it has become routine for the minority scholar to include pictures of artifacts, people, and events as an extension of the textual conversation and persuasion. This technique is prominent in Houston Baker (1984), who preceded Gates, and in Ramon Saldivar (1990), who acknowledges both Gates's and Baker's influence on his volume on Chicano narrative. This style has thick and elaborate prose, shows wide reading and familiarity with the classical tradition, and includes numerous pictures of art, especially from the author's own collection. In Gates's work, this goes beyond the photos of peasants and workers to include works from the archival collections of the elite schools with which he is associated. How can one not be impressed?

7. It is useful to recall that Jean-Paul Sartre's preface to Frantz Fanon's book was criticized by scholars like Hannah Arendt because it seemed he was condoning violence by Black revolutionaries. We should expect that Gates's sponsors would take an ideological stance similar to that he is projecting. In this sense, we need not demean Gates for having Derrida's support; rather, I want to indicate how this support does reflect the accuracy of the characterization by Baker (though he, too, remained implicated) that deconstructionist myths hasten one toward a nonself and a nonhistory. Unfortunately, those who criticize Gates for sleight of hand are probably in touch with something, but they also miss the point: Gates does see the place of Esu and the Monkey in the contemporary landscape; and the meaning of both tricksters does have a relevance to literary theory, Black and otherwise. The problem is that this tradition has been incorrectly detached from its real roots: conflict with self and conflict with the white man.

8. This is not mere speculation. The event Asante (1988a, b) tries to reverse is this loss of collusive bond. And nowhere is the theme more evident than in the literature on the Black middle-class versus the so-called Black under-

class (Glasgow 1980; Marable 1980; Wilson 1978). Manning Marable nicely summarized the basic contradiction and its psychopolitical dimensions:

> To be [an activist] within a capitalist society is to question or to react negatively to the basic social values of the society. The new Black elite who have opted for social status and economic mobility have not yet begun to question the character of the cultural and economic system which they have assimilated into. Yet to attempt an honest analysis on this question for the Black petty bourgeoisie would mean increased psychological crisis and "class suicide." (Marable 1980, 128)

Bibliography

Ali, S. 1989. *The Blackman's Guide to Understanding the Blackwoman.* Philadelphia: Civilized Publications.

Althusser, L. 1970. *For Marx.* Translated by B. Brewster. New York: Vintage.

——. 1971. *Lenin and Philosophy.* Translated by B. Brewster. New York: Monthly Review Press.

Arcilla, R. V. 1990. "Edification, Conversation, and Narrative: Rortyan Motifs for Philosophy of Education." *Educational Theory* 40 (winter): 35–40.

Arieti, S. 1972. *The Will to Be Human.* New York: Delta.

Armstrong, R. R. 1987. "Book Review." *Western Journal of Black Studies* 11:149.

Asante, M. K. 1983. "The Ideological Significance of Afrocentricity in Intercultural Communication." *Journal of Black Studies* 14 (September): 3–19.

——. 1985. "Rhetorical Alliances in the Civil Rights Movement." *The Negro Educational Review* 34 (January): 12.

——. 1988a. *The Afrocentric Idea.* Philadelphia: Temple University Press.

——. 1988b. *Afrocentricity.* New Brunswick, N.J.: African World Press.

Asante, M. K., and D. Atwater. 1986. "The Rhetorical Condition as Symbolic Structure in Discourse." *Communication Quarterly* 34 (spring): 170–77.

Awkward, M. 1988. "Race, Gender, and the Politics of Reading." *Black American Literary Forum* 22, no. 1 (spring): 5–27.

Babid, E. Y., M. Birnbaum, and K. D. Benne. 1983. *The Social Self: Group Influences on Personal Identity.* Beverly Hills, Calif.: Sage.

Baker, H. A., Jr. 1984. *Blues, Ideology, and Afro-American Literature: A Vernacular Theory.* Chicago: University of Chicago Press.

Bambara, T. C. 1979. Review of *Black Macho and the Myth of the Superwoman,* by Michelle Wallace. *Washington Post,* February 7, sec. B, pp. 1, 2.

——, ed. 1970. *The Black Woman: An Anthology.* New York: Bantam.

Banks, W. C. 1979. "White Preferences in Blacks: A Paradigm in Search of a Phenomenon." *Psychological Bulletin* 83:1179–86.

Barnes, J. 1972. "The Black Community as the Source of Positive Self-Concept for Black Children: A Theoretical Perspective." In *Black Psychology,* edited by R. L. Jones. New York: Harper & Row.

Barnett, R. C., and G. K. Baruch. 1978. "Women in the Middle Years: A Critique of Research and Theory." *Psychology of Women Quarterly* 32:187–97.

Barthes, R. 1970. *S/Z*. Translated by Richard Miller. New York: Farrar, Straus & Giroux.

———. 1972. *Mythologies*. New York: Hill & Wang.

Baughman, E. E. 1971. *Black Americans: A Psychological Analysis*. New York: Academic Press.

Becker, E. 1969. *Beyond Alienation: A Philosophy of Education for the Crisis of the Democracy*. New York: Free Press.

———. 1971. *The Birth and Death of Meaning: A Perspective in Psychiatry and Anthropology*. New York: Free Press.

———. 1974. *The Denial of Death*. New York: Vintage.

Becker, H. S. 1960. "Notes on the Concept of Commitment." *American Journal of Sociology* 66:32–40.

Begley, A. 1990. "Henry Louis Gates, Jr.: Black Studies' New Star." *New York Times Magazine*, April 1, p. 49.

Bell, B. W. 1988. *The Afro-American Novel and Its Tradition*. Amherst: University of Massachusetts Press.

Bell, D. 1976. *The Cultural Contradictions of Capitalism*. New York: Basic.

Bell-King, B. 1978. "A Symbolic Interactionist Approach to the Social World of Women." Ph.D. diss., U.S. International University.

Benson, T. W. 1974. " Rhetoric and Autobiography: The Case of Malcolm X." *Quarterly Journal of Speech* 60 (February): 1–13.

———. 1980. "The Rhetorical Structure of Frederick Wiseman's *High School*." *Communication Monographs* 47:233–61. Reprinted in *Rhetorical Dimensions in Media: A Critical Casebook,* edited by Martin J. Medhurst and Thomas W. Benson. Dubuque, Iowa: Kendall/Hunt, 1984.

———. 1989. "Rhetoric as a Way of Being." In *American Rhetoric: Context and Criticism,* edited by Thomas W. Benson. Carbondale: Southern Illinois University Press.

Berger, P. 1970. *A Rumor of Angels: Modern Society and the Rediscovery of the Supernatural*. Garden City, N.Y.: Doubleday.

Berger, P., and T. Luckmann. 1968. *The Social Construction of Reality: A Treatise in the Sociology of Knowledge*. New York: Doubleday.

Bethel, L., and B. Smith, eds. 1979. "The Black Women's Issue." *Conditions* 5.

Billig, M. 1982. *Ideology and Social Psychology: Extremism, Moderation and Contradiction*. New York: St. Martin's.

Billigheimer, R. V. 1987. "Blake's 'Eyes of God': Cycles to Apocalypse and Redemption." *Philological Quarterly* 66 (spring): 231–58.

Billingsley, A. 1969. *Black Families in White America*. Englewood Cliffs, N.J.: Prentice-Hall.

Bitzer, L. F. 1980. "Functional Communication: A Situational Perspective." In *Rhetoric in Transition: Studies in the Nature and Uses of Rhetoric,* edited by E. E. White. University Park: Pennsylvania State University Press.

Blair, T. L. 1977. *Retreat to the Ghetto: The End of a Dream?* New York: Hill & Wang.

Blanck, G., and R. Blanck. 1974. *Ego Psychology*. New York: Columbia University Press.

———. 1979. *Ego Psychology II*. New York: Columbia University Press.

Blauner, R. 1964. *Alienation and Freedom*. Chicago: University of Chicago Press.

Block, C. B. 1981. "Black Americans and the Cross-Cultural Counseling and Psychotherapy Experience." In *Cross-Cultural Counseling and Psychotherapy*, edited by A. J. Marsella and P. B. Pedersen. Elmsford, N.Y.: Pergamon.

Bly, R. 1992. *Iron John: A Book about Men*. New York: Random House.

Bordin, E. S. 1955. "Ambiguity as a Therapeutic Variable." *Journal of Consulting Psychology* 19:9–15.

Boykin, A. W., A. J. Franklin, and J. F. Yates, eds. 1979. *Research Directions of Black Psychologists*. New York: Harper & Row.

Boszormenyi-Nagy, I., and G. M. Sparks. 1973. *Invisible Loyalties: Reciprocity in Intergenerational Family Therapy*. New York: Harper & Row.

Bowen, M. 1978. *Family Therapy in Clinical Practice*. New York: Jason Aronson.

Branden, N. 1969. *The Psychology of Self-Esteem*. New York: Bantam.

Breen, M. 1965. "Culture and Schizophrenia: A Study of Negro and Jewish Schizophrenics." Ph.D. diss., Brandeis University.

Breger, L. 1974. *From Instinct to Identity*. Englewood Cliffs, N.J.: Prentice-Hall.

Brody, E. M., P. T. Johnson, M. C. Falcomer, and A. M. Lang. 1983. "Women's Changing Roles and Help to Elderly Parents: Attitudes of Three Generations of Women." *Journal of Gerontology* 38:597–607.

Brown, D. R., and W. F. Anderson. 1978. "A Survey of the Black Woman and the Persuasion Process: The Study of Strategies of Identification and Resistance." *Journal of Black Studies* 9:233–48.

Brown, R. 1987. *Society as Text*. Chicago: University of Chicago Press.

Bulhan, H. A. 1976. "Dialectics of Reactive Identification and the Formation of African Intellectuals: A Study of Somali Students." Ph.D. diss., Boston University.

———. 1980. "Dynamics of Cultural In-Betweenity: An Empirical Study." *International Journal of Psychology* 15:105–21.

———. 1985. *Frantz Fanon and the Psychology of Oppression*. New York: Plenum.

Burgest, D. R. 1980. "Black Awareness and Authentic Black/Black Relations." In *Contemporary Black Thought*, edited by M. K. Asante and A. S. Vandi. Beverly Hills, Calif.: Sage.

Burke, K. 1968. *A Rhetoric of Motive*. Berkeley: University of California Press.

———. 1970. *The Rhetoric of Religion: Studies in Logology*. Berkeley: University of California Press.

Buss, A. R. 1975. "The Emerging Field of the Sociology of Psychologizing Knowledge." *American Psychologist* 30:988–1002.

———. 1979. *A Dialectical Psychology*. New York: Wiley.

Butler, J. 1993. "Endangered/Endangering: Schematic Racism and White Paranoia." In *Reading Rodney King: Reading Urban Uprising*, edited by R. Gooding-Williams. New York: Routledge.

Buvinic, M., M. A. Lycette, and W. P. McGreevey, eds. 1983. *Women and Poverty in the Third World.* Baltimore: Johns Hopkins University Press.

Byrd, H. 1978. *Can't Plead Black Anymore.* Los Angeles: Byrd.

Campbell, J. 1968. *The Hero with a Thousand Faces.* 2d ed. Princeton, N.J.: Princeton University Press.

Campbell, P. N. 1972. *Rhetoric: A Study of the Communicative Aesthetic Dimensions of Language.* Belmont, Calif.: Dickenson.

Carlson, R. 1972. "Understanding Women: Implications for Personality Theory and Research." *Journal of Social Issues* 28:17–32.

Carrington, C. H. 1980. "Depression in Black Women: A Theoretical Appraisal." In *The Black Woman,* edited by L. R. Rose. Beverly Hills, Calif.: Sage.

Carter, K., and C. Spitzack, eds. 1989. *Doing Research on Women's Communications: Perspectives on Theory and Method.* Norwood, N.J.: Ablex.

Chesler, P. 1972. *Women and Madness.* New York: Avon.

Chodorow, N. 1974. "Family Structure and Feminine Personality." In *Women, Culture and Society,* edited by M. Z. Rosaldo and L. Lamhere. Stanford, Calif.: Stanford University Press.

———. 1978. *The Reproduction of Mothering.* Berkeley: University of California Press.

Chrissinger, M. S. 1980. "Factors Affecting Employment of Welfare Mothers." *Social Work* 25, no. 1 (January): 52–56.

Christian, B. 1985. *Black Feminist Criticism: Perspectives on Black Women Writers.* New York: Pergamon.

Cohen, D. K. 1976. "Loss as a Theme in Social Policy." *Harvard Education Review* 46, no. 4 (November): 553–71.

Coles, R. 1964. "Social Struggle and Weariness." *Psychiatry* 27:305–15.

Collins, P. H. 1991. *Black Feminist Thought: Knowledge, Consciousness, and the Politics of Empowerment.* New York: Routledge.

Condit, C. M. 1987. "Crafting Virtue: The Rhetorical Construction of Public Morality." *Quarterly Journal of Speech* 73:79–94.

Conklin, N. F., B. McCallum, and M. Wade. 1983. *The Culture of Southern Black Women: Approaches and Materials.* Huntsville: University of Alabama Press.

Contratto, S. 1987. "Father Presence in Women's Psychological Development." In *Advances in Psychoanalytic Sociology,* edited by J. Rabow, G. M. Platt, and M. S. Goldman. Malabar, Fla.: Robert E. Krieger.

Coser, L. A. 1974. *Greedy Institutions: Patterns of Undivided Commitment.* New York: Free Press.

Cox, S. 1976. *Female Psychology: The Emerging Self.* Chicago: Science Research Associates.

Cross, W. E. 1971. "The Negro-to-Black Conversion Experience." *Black World* 20:13–27.

———. 1980. "Black Identity: Rediscovering the Distinction between Personal Identity and Reference-Group Orientation." Paper presented to the Research in Child Development Study Group, Atlanta, Georgia.

Cruse, H. 1967. *The Crisis of the Negro Intellectual.* New York: Morrow.

Cummings, J., and E. Cummings. 1965. "On the Stigma of Mental Illness." *Community Mental Health Journal* 1:135–43.

Daly, M. 1978. *Gyn/Ecology: The Metaethics of Radical Feminism*. Boston: Beacon.

Davis, F. J. 1991. *Who Is Black? One Nation's Definition*. University Park: Pennsylvania State University Press.

Davis, G., and G. Watson. 1982. *Black Life in Corporate America: Swimming in the Mainstream*. New York: Doubleday.

De La Cancela, V. 1981. "Towards a Critical Psychological Analysis of Machismo: Puerto Ricans and Mental Health." Ph.D. diss., City University of New York.

de Lauretis, T. 1987. "Feminist Studies/Critical Studies: Issues, Terms, and Contexts." In *Feminist Studies/Critical Studies*, edited by T. de Lauretis. Bloomington: Indiana University Press.

Devereaux, G. 1967. *From Anxiety to Behavioral Science Method*. New York: Mouton.

Dixon, V., and B. Foster, eds. 1971. *Beyond Black or White*. Boston: Little, Brown & Co.

Dobson, F. E. 1985. "The Use of Oral Tradition and Ritual in Afro-American Fiction." Ph.D. diss., Bowling Green State University.

Dube, S. C. 1983. *On Crisis and Commitment in the Social Sciences*. New York: Humanities Press.

Dumas, R. G. 1980. "Dilemmas of Black Females in Leadership." In *The Black Woman*, edited by L. Rodgers-Rose. Beverly Hills, Calif.: Sage.

Duncan, H. D. 1962. *Communication and Social Order*. New York: Oxford University Press.

Dworkin, A. 1974. *Woman Hating*. New York: Dutton.

Dyson, M. E. 1993. *Reflecting Black: African-American Cultural Criticism*. Minneapolis: University of Minnesota Press.

Edelman, M. 1977. *Political Languages: Words That Succeed and Policies That Fail*. New York: Academic Press.

Edwards, H. 1979. "A Time to Listen." *The Black Scholar* 10:59–61.

Edwards, M. I., and M. Duleu, eds. 1983. *The Cross-Cultural Study of Women*. New York: Feminist Press.

Eisenstein, Z. 1979. *The Radical Future of Liberal Feminism*. New York: Monthly Review Press.

Eko, E. 1986. "Oral Tradition: The Bridge to Africa in Paule Marshall's *Praisesong for the Widow*." *Western Journal of Black Studies* 10:143.

Engram, E. 1980. "Role Transition in Early Adulthood: Orientations of Young Black Women." In *The Black Woman*, edited by L. Rodgers-Rose. Beverly Hills, Calif.: Sage.

———. 1982. *Science, Myth and Reality: The Black Family in One Half Century of Research*. Westport, Conn.: Greenwood.

Erikson, E. H. 1950. *Childhood and Society*. New York: Norton.

———. 1954. "On the Sense of Inner Identity." In *Psychoanalytic Psychiatry and Psychology*, vol. 1. New York: International Universities Press.

———. 1956. "The Problem of Ego Identity." *Journal of the American Psychoanalytic Association* 4:56–121.

———. 1968. *Identity, Youth and Crisis.* New York: Norton.

Evans, S. 1979. *Personal Politics: The Roots of Women's Liberation in the Civil Rights Movement.* New York: Knopf.

Farber, M. D. 1979. "The Metaphors of Marx: A Literary-Psychological View of 'Das Kapital.'" *Psychocultural Review* 3:39–58.

Fanon, F. 1967. *Black Skin, White Masks.* New York: Grove.

———. 1968. *The Wretched of the Earth.* New York: Grove.

Farrell, T. B. 1985. "Narrative in Natural Discourse: On Conversation and Rhetoric." *Journal of Communication* 35 (autumn): 110–11.

Feldman, K. A. 1965. "Family Antecedents of Commitment to Social Norms." Ph.D. diss., University of Michigan.

Fisher, W. R. 1987. *Human Communication as Narration: Toward a Philosophy of Reason, Value, and Action.* Columbia: University of South Carolina Press.

Fiske, M. 1980. "Changing Hierarchies of Commitment in Adulthood." In *Themes of Work and Love in Adulthood,* edited by N. Smesler and E. H. Erikson. Cambridge, Mass.: Harvard University Press.

Foster, F. S. 1983. "Changing Concepts of the Black Woman." *Journal of Black Studies* 3:433–54.

Frank, A. 1989. "The Rhetoric of Healing and Cancer Self-Help Patients." Paper presented at the International Conference on the Rhetoric of Social Science, University of Maryland, College Park, April.

Freire, P. 1970. *Pedagogy of the Oppressed.* New York: Seabury.

Gardner, J. A., and C. W. Thomas. 1970. Interview. "Different Strokes for Different Folks." *Psychology Today* (September): 45–49, 79–80.

Gary, L. E., ed. 1981. *Black Men.* Beverly Hills, Calif.: Sage.

Gates, H. L., Jr. 1985. "Writing, Race, and the Difference It Makes." *Critical Inquiry* (autumn): 10–11.

———. 1988. *The Signifying Monkey: A Theory of African-American Literary Criticism.* New York: Oxford University Press.

Gibbs, J. T., ed. 1988. *Young, Black, and Male in America: An Endangered Species.* Dover, Mass.: Auburn House.

Giele, J. Z. 1980. "Adulthood as Transcendence of Age and Sex." In *Themes of Work and Love in Adulthood,* edited by N. Smesler and E. H. Erikson. Cambridge, Mass.: Harvard University Press.

Gil, D. G. 1983. "Dialectics of Individual Development and Global Social Welfare." *Humanity and Society* 7, no. 1 (February): 37–75.

Gilkes, C. T. 1979. "Living and Working in a World of Trouble: The Emergent Career of the Black Woman Community Worker." Ph.D. diss., Northeastern University.

———. 1980. "'Holding Back the Ocean with a Broom': Black Women and Their Community Work." In *The Black Woman,* edited by L. Rodgers-Rose. Beverly Hills, Calif.: Sage.

———. 1982. "Successful Rebellious Professionals: The Black Woman's Professional Identity and Community Commitment." *Psychology of Women Quarterly* 6:289–311.

Gilligan, C. 1982. *In a Different Voice: Psychological Theory and Women's Development*. Cambridge, Mass.: Harvard University Press.

Glaser, B., and A. Strauss. 1967. *The Discovery of Grounded Theory: Strategies for Qualitative Research*. Chicago: Aldine.

Glasgow, D. C. 1980. *The Black Underclass: Poverty, Unemployment, Entrapment of Ghetto Youth*. San Francisco: Jossey-Bass.

Godell, H. P. 1968. "A Study of Commitment to a Profession: An Application of Becker's Concept to Classroom Teachers in Selected Elementary Schools." Ph.D. diss., Columbia University.

Goffman, E. 1963. *Stigma*. Englewood Cliffs, N.J.: Prentice-Hall.

Goldman, R. M., and W. D. Crano. 1976. "Black Boy and Man-Child in the Promised Land: Content Analysis in the Study of Value Change over Time." *Journal of Black Studies* 7:169–80.

Gooding-Williams, R., ed. 1993. *Reading Rodney King: Reading Urban Uprising*. New York: Routledge.

Gordon, M. M. 1978. *Human Nature, Class and Ethnicity*. New York: Oxford University Press.

Gould, R. L. 1978. *Transformations: Growth and Change in Adult Life*. New York: Simon & Schuster.

Graber, D. A. 1976. *Verbal Behavior and Politics*. Urbana: University of Illinois Press.

———. 1984. *Processing the News: How People Tame the Information Tide*. New York: Longman.

Gregg, R. B. 1989. "The Rhetoric of Denial and Alternity." In *American Rhetoric: Context and Criticism*, edited by Thomas W. Benson. Carbondale: Southern Illinois University Press.

Gresson, A. D. 1977. "Minority Epistemology and the Rhetoric of Creation." *Philosophy and Rhetoric* 10:244–62.

———. 1978. "Phenomenology and the Rhetoric of Identification: A Neglected Dimension of Coalition Communication." *Communication Quarterly* 26:14–23.

———. 1982. *The Dialectics of Betrayal: Sacrifice, Violation, and the Oppressed*. Norwood, N.J.: Ablex.

———. 1985a. "Beyond Selves Deferred: Langston Hughes' Style and the Psychology of Black Selfhood." *The Langston Hughes Review* 4, no. 1 (spring): 47–54.

———. 1985b. "Individuation and the Psychology of Black Women: Toward a Theory of Commitment." Ph.D. diss., Boston College.

———. 1987. "Transitional Metaphors and the Political Psychology of Identity Maintenance." In *Cognition and Symbolic Structures: The Psychology of Metaphoric Transformation*, edited by R. E. Haskell. Norwood, N.J.: Ablex.

———. 1992. "African-Americans and the Pursuit of Wider Identities: Self–Other Understanding in Black Female Narratives." In *Lived Stories: Essays in the Psychology of Narration*, edited by R. Ochberg and G. Rosenwald. New Haven: Yale University Press.

Gurin, P., and E. G. Epps. 1975. *Black Consciousness, Identity, and Achievement*. New York: Wiley.

Gurin, P., G. Gurin, and B. M. Morrison. 1978. "Personal and Ideological Aspects of Internal and External Control." *Social Psychology* 41:275–96.

Guthrie, R. V. 1976. *Even the Rat Was White: A Historical View of Psychology*. New York: Harper & Row.

Gutman, H. G. 1976. *The Black Family in Slavery and Freedom, 1750–1925*. New York: Vintage.

Hall, S. 1990. "Cultural Identity and Diaspora." In *Identity, Community, Culture, Difference*, edited by J. Rutherford. London: Lawrence and Wishart.

Hall, T. 1990. "New Way to Treat Alcoholism Discards Spirituality of A.A." *New York Times*, December 24, 1990, sec. A, p. 1.

Halleck, S. 1971. *The Politics of Experience*. New York: Science House.

Hamilton, C. V. 1973. *The Black Experience in American Politics*. New York: Putnam's.

Hanna, T. 1962. *The Lyrical Existentialist*. New York: Athenaeum.

Hare, N. 1979. "The Relative Psycho–Socio-Economic Suppression of the Black Male. In *Reflections on Black Psychology*, edited by W. D. Smith et al. Washington, D.C.: U.P.A.

Hare, N., and J. Hare. 1970. "Black Women: 1970." *Transaction* 8:65–68.

Harley, S., and R. Terborg-Penn, eds. 1978. *The Afro-American Woman: Images and Struggles*. New York: Kennikat Press.

Hauser, S. 1971. *Black and White Identity Formation*. New York: Kreiger.

Henderson, M. 1989. "Speaking in Tongues: Dialogism, Dialectics, and the Black Woman Writer's Literary Tradition." In *Changing Our Own World: Essays on Criticism, Theory, and Writing by Black Women*, edited by C. A. Wall. New Brunswick, N.J.: Rutgers University Press.

Hoch, P. 1979. *White Hero, Black Beast: Racism, Sexism, and the Mask of Masculinity*. London: Pluto.

Hogue, W. L. 1986. *Discourse and the Other: The Production of the Afro-American Text*. Durham, N.C.: Duke University Press.

hooks, b. 1981. *Ain't I a Woman? Black Women and Feminism*. Boston: South End Press.

———. 1984. *Feminist Theory: From Margin to Center*. Boston: South End Press.

Horrocks, J. E., and D. W. Jackson. 1972. *Self and Role: A Theory of Self-Process and Role Behavior*. Boston: Houghton-Mifflin.

Hull, G., P. Scott, and B. Smith. 1982. *All the Women Are White, All the Blacks Are Men, but Some of Us Are Brave: Black Women's Studies*. Old Westbury, N.Y.: Feminist Press.

Husband, C. 1979. "Social Identity and the Language of Race Relations." In *Language and Ethnic Relations*, edited by H. Giles and B. Saint-Jacques. New York: Pergamon.

Huston, P. 1979. *Third World Women Speak Out: Interviews in Six Countries on Change, Development, and Basic Needs.* New York: Praeger.

Hyde, J. S., and B. G. Rosenberg. 1976. *Half the Human Experience: The Psychology of Women.* Lexington, Mass.: Heath.

Ickes, W., and E. S. Knowles, eds. 1982. *Personality, Roles, and Social Behavior.* New York: Springer.

Isaacs, H. 1977. *Idols of the Tribe.* New York: Harper & Row.

Ivie, R. L. 1987. "Metaphor and the Rhetorical Invention of Cold War 'Idealists.'" *Communication Monographs* 54:165–82.

Jackson, A. 1979. "The Black Woman: A Look at the Effects of Race and Sex on Identity Formation and Motivation." In *Reflections on Black Psychology,* edited by W. D. Smith et al. Washington, D.C.: U.P.A.

Jackson, J. J. 1973. "Black Women in a Racist Society." In *Racism and Mental Health,* edited by C. V. Willie, B. M. Kramer, and B. S. Brown. Pittsburgh: University of Pittsburgh Press.

Jackson, J. S., L. M. Chalters, and H. W. Neighbors. 1982. "The Mental Health Status of Older Black Americans." *The Black Scholar* 13:21–35.

Jackson, J. S., W. R. McCullough, and C. Gurin. 1981. "Group Identity Development within Black Families." In *Black Families,* edited by H. P. McAdoo. Beverly Hills, Calif.: Sage.

Jackson, M. 1978. "Ambivalence and the Last-Born: Birth-Order Position in Convention and Myth." *Man* 13:341–61.

Jacoby, R. 1975. *Social Amnesia.* Boston: Beacon.

Jahoda, M. 1959. "Conformity and Independence: A Psychological Analysis." *Human Relations* 12:99–120.

Janeway, E. 1971. *Man's World, Woman's Place.* New York: Morrow.

Jenkins, A. M. 1980. *The Psychology of the Afro-American: A Humanistic Approach.* New York: Pergamon.

Johnson, B. 1984. "Metaphor, Metonymy, and Voice in *Their Eyes Were Watching God.*" In *Black Literature and Literary Theory,* edited by H. L. Gates, Jr. New York: Methuen.

Jones, R. L., ed. 1972. *Black Psychology.* New York: Harper & Row.

———, ed. 1980. *Black Psychology.* 2d ed. New York: Harper & Row.

Jones, R. S. 1978. "History, Social Structure, and Psyche: Toward a Black Social Psychology." *Pan African Study Society Journal* 2:18–25.

———. 1980. "Finding the Black Self: A Humanistic Strategy." *Journal of Black Psychology* 7:17–26.

———. 1981. "Identity, Self-Concept, and Shifting Political Allegiance of Blacks in the Colonial Americas: Maroons against Black Shot." *Western Journal of Black Studies* 5:61–74.

———. 1983. "The Self-Perception of Black Folk." In *Themes in African American Reflectivity,* edited by R. S. Jones and J. Rollins. Providence, R.I.: Providence Public Library.

———. 1988. "In the Absence of Ideology: Blacks in Colonial America and the Modern Black Experience." *Western Journal of Black Studies* 12:35.

———. Undated. "Black Political Psychology." Unpublished manuscript.

Josselson, R. L. 1983. "Psychodynamic Aspects of Identity Formation in College Women." *Journal of Youth and Adolescence* 2:3–52.

Kamau-Collier, M. A. Z. 1990. *Phoenix Arising*. Baltimore: Trans Press.

Kanter, R. M. 1968. "Commitment and Social Organization." *American Sociological Review* 33:499–517.

Kaplan, A. G., and T. P. Bean. 1976. *Beyond Sex-Role Stereotypes: Readings Toward a Psychology of Androgyny*. Boston: Little, Brown & Co.

Karenga, M. 1982. "The Crisis of Black Middle Class Leadership: A Critical Analysis." *The Black Scholar* 13:16–36.

Karenga, R. 1979. "On Wallace's Myth: Wading Thru Troubled Waters." *The Black Scholar* 10:36–39.

Katz, I., and R. G. Hass. 1988. "Racial Ambivalence and American Value Conflict: Correlational and Priming Studies of Dual Cognitive Structures." *Journal of Personality and Social Psychology* 55:893–905.

Keen, S. *Fire in the Belly*. 1991. New York: Bantam.

Kellerman, H., ed. 1981. *Group Cohesion: Theoretical and Clinical Perspectives*. New York: Grune and Stratton.

Keniston, K. 1970. "Stranded in the Present." In *Confrontation*, edited by M. Wertheimer. Glenview, Ill.: Scott Foresman.

Kiesler, C. A. 1971. *The Psychology of Commitment: Experiments Linking Behavior to Belief*. New York: Academic Press.

Kilpatrick, W. 1975. *Identity and Intimacy*. New York: Delta.

King, M. C. 1982. "The Politics of Sexual Stereotypes." *The Black Scholar* 13, nos. 4 and 5 (summer): 2–13.

Klapp, O. 1969. *The Collective Search for Identity*. New York: Holt, Rinehart & Winston.

Kleiber, D. H. 1983. "Sport and Human Development: A Dialectical Interpretation." *Journal of Humanistic Psychology* 24:76–95.

Klein, J. 1980. *Jewish Identity and Ethnotherapy*. New York: Center for Studies in Pluralism.

Klemesrud, J. 1979. "She's Confronting the Tensions between Black Men and Women." *New York Times*, January 12, sec. A, p. 21.

Klumpp, J. F., and T. A. Hollihan. 1979. "Debunking the Resignation of Earl Butz: Sacrificing an Official Racist." *Quarterly Journal of Speech* 65:1–11.

Kohut, H. 1971. *The Analysis of the Self: A Systematic Approach to the Psychoanalytic Treatment of Narcissistic Personality Disorders*. New York: International Universities Press.

———. 1977. *The Restoration of the Self*. New York: International Universities Press.

Komarovsky, M. 1946. "Cultural Contradictions and Sex Roles." *American Journal of Sociology* 52:184–89.

Kovel, J. 1970. *White Racism: A Psychohistory*. New York: Vintage.

Kramarae, C., and M. M. Jenkins. 1987. "Women Take Back the Talk." In *Women and Language in Transition*, edited by J. Penfield. Albany: State University of New York Press.

Ladner, J. 1971. *Tomorrow: The Black Woman*. New York: Doubleday.

———. 1978. *Mixed Families*. New York: Doubleday.

Laing, R. D. 1967. *The Politics of Experience.* New York: Ballantine.

Lambert, K. 1981. *Analysis, Repair, and Individuation.* New York: Academic Press.

Lasch, C. 1976. "The Narcissist Society." *New York Review of Books* 23, no. 15 (September 30): 5, 8, 10–13.

———. 1984. *The Minimal Self: Psychic Survival in Troubled Times.* New York: Norton.

Lee, B. J. 1990. "The Only Survivable World: A Postmodern Systems Approach to a Religious Intuition." In *Sacred Inter-Connections: Postmodern Spirituality, Political Economy and Art,* edited by David Ray Griffin. Albany: State University of New York Press.

Lemert, E. 1951. *Social Pathology.* New York: McGraw-Hill.

Lerner, B. 1972. *Therapy in the Ghetto: Political Impotence and Personal Disintegration.* Baltimore: Johns Hopkins University Press.

Lerner, L., ed. 1982. *Women and Individuation.* Special issue of *The Psychoanalytic Review* 69, no. 1 (spring).

Lester, J. 1982. "The Black Writer." *The New England Journal of Black Studies* 2:82–85.

Levinson, D. J. 1978. *The Seasons of a Man's Life.* New York: Ballantine.

Lewin, K. 1948. *Resolving Social Conflicts.* New York: Harper & Row.

Lewis, D. 1977. "A Response to Inequality: Black Women, Racism, and Sexism." *Signs* 3:339–61.

Lewis, W. F. 1987. "Telling America's Story: Narrative Form and the Reagan Presidency." *Quarterly Journal of Speech* 73 (August): 280–302.

Lichtenberg, J. D. 1983. *Psychoanalysis and Infant Research.* Hillsdale, N.J.: Erlbaum.

Lichtenstein, H. 1977. *The Dilemma of Human Identity.* New York: Jason Aronson.

Lindsay, B., ed. 1980. *Comparative Perspectives of Third World Women: The Impact of Race, Sex, and Class.* New York: Praeger.

Lopata, J. 1969. "Social Psychological Aspects of Role Involvement." *Sociology and Social Research* 53, no. 3: 285–98.

Lorde, A. 1979. "The Great American Disease." *The Black Scholar* 10:16–20.

———. 1981. "Interview with Adrienne Rich." *Signs* 6:734–35.

Lowenthal, M. F. 1975. "Psychosocial Variations across the Adult Life Course: Frontiers for Research and Policy." *The Gerontologist* 15:6–12.

Lucaites, J. L., and C. M. Condit. 1985. "Re-constructing Narrative Theory: A Functional Perspective." *Journal of Communication* 35 (autumn): 90–108.

Lynch, F. R. 1989. *Invisible Victims: White Males and the Crisis of Affirmative Action.* Westport, Conn.: Greenwood Press.

Mackey, R. A. 1984. *Ego-Psychology and Clinical Practice.* New York: Gardner.

McAdoo, H. P. 1976. "The Development of Self-Concept and Race Attitudes in Young Black Children over Time." Paper presented at the Third Conference on Empirical Research in Black Psychology, Cornell University, Ithaca, N.Y., October.

———, ed. 1980. *Black Families.* Beverly Hills, Calif.: Sage.

McCloskey, D. N. 1985. *The Rhetoric of Economics*. Madison: University of Wisconsin Press.

McCray, C. A. 1980. "The Black Woman and Family Roles." In *The Black Woman,* edited by L. Rodgers-Rose. Beverly Hills, Calif: Sage.

McGee, M., and J. S. Nelson. 1985. "Narrative Reason in Public Argument." *Journal of Communication* 35 (autumn): 152.

Madhubuti, H. R., ed. 1990. *Confusion by Any Other Name: Essays Exploring the Negative Impact of "The Blackman's Guide to Understanding the Blackwoman."* Chicago: Third World Press.

Magen, Z. 1983. "Transpersonal Commitments in Adolescence: A Cross-Cultural Perspective." *Journal of Humanistic Psychology* 23:96–112.

Mahler, M. S. 1967. "On Human Symbiosis and the Vicissitudes of Individuation." *Journal of American Psychoanalytic Association* 15:740–63.

Mahler, M. S., F. Pine, and A. Bergman. 1975. *The Psychological Birth of the Human Infant: Symbiosis and Individuation*. New York: Basic.

Malcolm X. 1970. *Malcolm X on Afro-American History*. New York: Pathfinder.

Malvereaux, J. 1970. "The Sexual Politics of Black People: Angry Black Women, Angry Black Men." *The Black Scholar* 10:32–34.

Marable, M. 1980. *From the Grassroots: Social and Political Essays Towards Afro-American Liberation*. Boston: South End Press.

———. 1982. "Reaganism, Racism and Reaction: Black Political Realignment in the 1980's." *The Black Scholar* 13:2–15.

Marcia, J. 1966. "Development and Validation of Ego-Identity Status." *Journal of Personality and Social Psychology* 34:551–58.

Mead, M. 1978. *Culture and Commitment: The New Relationships between the Generations in the 1970's*. New York: Columbia University Press.

Memmi, A. 1968. *Dominated Man: Notes Towards a Portrait*. Boston: Beacon.

Merriam, S. B. 1988. *Case Study Research in Education: A Qualitative Approach*. San Francisco: Jossey Bass.

Miller, J. B. 1973. *Toward a New Psychology of Women*. Boston: Beacon.

———. 1982. *Women and Power: Work in Progress*. Wellesley, Mass.: Wellesley College Press.

Minuchin, S. 1982. *Families and Family Therapy*. Cambridge, Mass.: Harvard University Press.

Mischel, T., ed. 1977. *The Self*. Oxford: Basil Blackwell.

Modleski, T. 1991. *Feminism without Women: Culture and Criticism in a "Postfeminist" Age*. New York: Routledge.

Mogul, K. 1971. "Women in Midlife: Decisions, Rewards and Conflicts Related to Work and Careers." *American Journal of Psychiatry* 136:1139–43.

Moon, T. 1991. "What Remains of Vanilla Ice If You Melt Cool Exterior?" *Centre Daily Times* (State College, Pa.), February 8.

Moore, M. 1978. "The Mental Health Problems and Treatment of Black Women in an Urban Community Mental Health Center." Ph.D. diss., Brandeis University.

Moses, W. 1981. "Individualism in America and Afro-America." In *Reflections: On Oneness and Other Curious Things, 1970–1980*. Providence, R.I.: Black Studies Program of Brown University.

———. 1982. *Black Messiahs and Uncle Toms: Social and Literary Manipulations of a Religious Myth*. University Park: Pennsylvania State University Press.

Mosley, M. H. 1979. "Self-Perception of Roles of Black and White Female College Students." In *Reflections on Black Psychology*, edited by W. D. Smith et al. Washington, D.C.: U.P.A.

Motte, M. 1972. "Study of Commitment in a Religious Organization." Ph.D. diss., Boston College.

Mumby, D. K. 1988. *Communication and Power in Organizations: Discourse, Ideology and Domination*. Norwood, N.J.: Ablex.

Murray, S., and M. Mednick. 1977. "Black Women's Achievement Orientation: Motivational and Cognitive Factors." *Psychology of Women Quarterly* 1:247–59.

Myers, L. 1980. *Black Women: Do They Cope Better?* Englewood Cliffs, N.J.: Prentice-Hall.

Nandy, A. 1983. *The Intimate Enemy: Loss and Recovery of Self under Colonialism*. New Delhi, India: Oxford University Press.

Naylor, G. 1988. *Mama Day*. New York: Ticknor and Fields.

Noble, J. 1978. *Beautiful Also Are the Souls of My Black Sisters: A History of the Black Woman in America*. Englewood Cliffs, N.J.: Prentice-Hall.

Nobles, W. 1981. "African-American Family Life: An Instrument of Culture." In *Black Families*, edited by H. P. McAdoo. Beverly Hills, Calif: Sage.

Noschis, K. 1982. "Identity and Habitat: A Psycho-Sociological Methodology." *Cahiers Internationaux de Socilogie* 29:33–54.

O'Banion, J. B. 1992. *Reorienting Rhetoric: The Dialectic of List and Story*. University Park: Pennsylvania State University Press.

O'Neale, S. 1987. "Inhibiting Midwives, Usurping Creators: The Struggling Emergence of Black Women in American Fiction." In *Feminist Studies/Critical Studies*, edited by T. de Lauretis. Bloomington: Indiana University Press.

Parkes, C. M. 1973. "Psychosocial Transitions: A Field for Study." *Social Science and Medicine* 5:101–15.

Parsons, T. 1964. *Social Structure and Personality*. New York: Free Press.

Payne, D. 1989. *Coping with Failure: The Therapeutic Uses of Rhetoric*. Columbia: University of South Carolina Press.

Payne, J. G. 1988. "Shaping the Race Issue: A Special Kind of Journalism." *Political Communication and Persuasion* 5:145–60.

Pearson, C., and K. Pope. 1981. *The Female Hero in American and British Literature*. New York: Bowker.

Pinderhughes, E. 1982a. "Family Therapy with Afro-Americans: A System Perspective." In *Ethnicity and Family Therapy*, edited by M. McGoldrick and J. Pearce. New York: Guilford.

———. 1982b. "Family Functioning of Afro-Americans." *Social Work* 27:91–96.

————. 1982c. "Black Genealogy: Self-Liberator and Therapeutic Tool." *Smith College Studies in Social Work* 52:93–106.

————. 1983. "Empowerment for Our Clients and for Ourselves." *Social Casework* 64, no. 6 (June): 331–38.

Plumpp, S. 1976. *Black Rituals*. Chicago: Third World Press.

Potkay, C. R. 1983. "The Role of Personality History Data in Clinical Judgment: A Selective Focus." *Journal of Personality Assessment* 37:200–210.

Puryear, G. R. 1980. "The Black Woman: Liberated or Oppressed?" In *Comparative Perspective of Third World Women,* edited by B. Lindsay. New York: Praeger.

Ramirez, M. 1983. *Psychology of the Americas: Mestizo Perspectives on Personality and Mental Health*. New York: Pergamon.

Riediger, D. R. 1991. *The Wages of Whiteness: Race and the Making of the American Working Class*. London and New York: Verso.

Rieff, P. 1959. *Freud: Mind of the Moralist*. Chicago: University of Chicago Press.

————. 1968. *The Triumph of the Therapeutic: Uses of Faith after Freud*. New York: Harper & Row.

Riegel, K. F. 1976a. "The Dialectics of Human Development." *American Psychologist* 31:689–700.

————. 1976b. *Psychology of Development and History*. New York: Plenum.

Roberts, J. 1989. *From Trickster to Badman*. Philadelphia: University of Pennsylvania Press.

Rodgers-Rose, L., ed. 1980. *The Black Woman*. Beverly Hills, Calif.: Sage.

Rosenberg, S. S. 1978. "Frederick Perls." In *Existential-Phenomenological Alternatives for Psychology,* edited by R. S. Valle and M. King. New York: Oxford University Press.

Rossi, A. 1972. "The Roots of Ambivalence in American Women." In *Readings in the Psychology of Women,* edited by H. Bardwick. New York: Harper & Row.

Rubin, I. 1975. *Compassion and Self-Hate*. New York: Ballantine.

Rudwick, E., and A. Meier. 1969. "Negro Retaliatory Violence in the Twentieth Century." In *The Making of Black America: Essays in Negro Life and History*. Vol. 2. New York: Antheneum.

Ryan, W. 1976. *Blaming the Victim*. New York: Random House.

Rychlak, J., ed. 1976. *Dialectic: Humanistic Rationale for Behavior and Development*. Basel: Karger.

Sagan, E. 1974. *Cannibalism: Human Aggression and Cultural Form*. New York: Harper & Row.

Saldivar, R. 1990. *Chicano Narrative*. Madison: University of Wisconsin Press.

Sampson, E. E. 1977. "Psychology and the American Ideal." *Journal of Personality and Social Psychology* 35:767–82.

————. 1978. "Scientific Paradigms and Social Values: Wanted — a Scientific Revolution." *Journal of Personality and Social Psychology* 36:1332–43.

————. 1981. "Cognitive Psychology of Ideology." *American Psychologist* 36:730–43.

Sanchez, A. R., and D. R. Atkinson. 1983. "Mexican-American Cultural Commitment, Preference for Counselor Ethnicity, and Willingness to Use Counseling." *Journal of Counseling Psychology* 30:215–20.

Santee, R., and S. Jackson. 1979. "Commitment to Self-Identification: A Sociopsychological Approach to Personality." *Human Relations* 32:141–58.

Scheler, M. 1961. *Ressentiment*. Translated by William W. Holdheim. New York: Free Press.

Schiele, D. T., and L. T. Osaki. 1976. "The Double-Bind: A Dilemma for People of Color." *Journal of Afro-American Issues* 4:16–20.

Schiffer, I. 1973. *Charisma: A Psychoanalytic Look at Mass Society*. New York: Free Press.

Schilder, P. 1937. "The Social Neuroses." *Psycho-Analytical Review* 25:1–19.

Sennett, R., and J. Cobb. 1972. *The Hidden Injuries of Class*. New York: Vintage.

Shange, N. 1977. *For Colored Girls Who Have Considered Suicide When the Rainbow Was Enuf*. New York: Macmillan.

Sherif, M., and H. Cantril. 1947. *The Psychology of Ego-Involvements: Social Attitudes and Identification*. New York: Wiley.

Sherman, J. A. 1981. *On the Psychology of Women: A Survey of Empirical Studies*. Springfield, Ill.: Charles C. Thomas.

Shibutani, T., and M. Kwan. 1975. *Ethnic Stratifications: A Comparative Approach*. New York: Macmillan.

Sloan, T. S. 1987. *Deciding: Self-Deception in Life Choices*. New York: Methuen.

Smith, M. B., J. S. Bruner, and R. W. White. 1963. *Opinions and Personality*. New York: Wiley.

Smith, S. A. 1985. *Myth, Media, and the Southern Mind*. Fayetteville: University of Arkansas Press.

Smith, V. 1989. "Black Feminist Theory and the Representation of the 'Other.' " In *Changing Our Own Words: Essays on Criticism, Theory, and Writing by Black Women,* edited by C. A. Wall. New Brunswick, N.J.: Rutgers University Press.

Sowell, T. 1990. *Preferential Policies: An International Perspective*. New York: Morrow.

Staples, R. 1973. *The Black Woman in America*. Chicago: Nelson-Hall.

———. 1979. "A Rejoinder: Black Feminism and the Cult of Masculinity: The Danger Within." *The Black Scholar* 10 (May/June): 63.

———. 1981. *The World of Black Singles: Changing Patterns of Male-Female Relations*. Westport, Conn.: Greenwood Press.

———. 1983. *Black Masculinity*. San Francisco: Black Scholar Press.

———, ed. 1971. *The Black Family: Essays and Studies*. Belmont, Calif.: Wadsworth.

Stebbins, R. A. 1971. *Commitment to Deviance: The Non-professional Criminal in the Community*. Westport, Conn.: Greenwood Press.

Steele, S. 1990. *The Content of Our Character*. New York: St. Martin's.

Stewart, J. B. 1979. "Relationships between Black Males and Females in Rhythm and Blues Music of the 1960s and 1970s." *Western Journal of Black Studies* 3 (fall): 186–96.

Strauss, M. D. 1971. "Women about Women: A Descriptive Study of the Psychological Impact of the Feminine Sex-Role Stereotype." Ph.D. diss., University of Texas at Austin.

Swidler, A. 1980. "Love and Work in Adulthood." In *Themes of Work and Love in Adulthood,* edited by N. Smesler and E. H. Erikson. Cambridge, Mass.: Harvard University Press.

Taylor, R. L. 1976. "Black Youth and Psychosocial Development: A Conceptual Framework." *Journal of Black Studies* 6:353–72.

Taylor, S. 1981. "Seven Lives: Women's Life Structure Evolution in Early Adulthood." Ph.D. diss., City University of New York.

Tomer, J. W. 1975. "Beyond Being Black: Identification Alone Is Not Enough." *Journal of Negro Education* 49:184–99.

Tomkins, S. 1964. *Affect, Imagery, Consciousness.* New York: Springer.

Turbayne, C. M. 1970. *The Myth of Metaphor.* Rev. ed. Columbia: University of South Carolina Press.

Turner, J. 1971. "Identity in Transition: A Theory of Black Militancy." In *The New American Revolution,* edited by R. Aya and N. Millers. New York: Free Press.

Umeh, M. L. 1986. "Reintegration with the Lost Self: A Study of Buchi Emecheta's *Double Yoke.*" In *Ngambika Studies of Women in African Literature,* edited by C. B. Davies and A. A. Graves. Trenton, N.J.: African World Press.

Veroff, J., et al. 1981. *The Inner American: A Self-Portrait from 1957 to 1976.* New York: Basic.

Vincent, C. E. 1976. "Historical and Theoretical Perspectives: Sex, Love, and Commitment Revisited." *Journal of Sex and Marital Therapy* 2:265–72.

Walker, A. 1982. *The Color Purple.* New York: Harcourt Brace Jovanovich.

———. 1990. *The Temple of My Familiar.* New York: Pocket Books.

Walker, W. R. 1980. "A Study of Black Consciousness as a Model for Examining the Relationship between Self-Perceived Status (SPS) and Ethnocentrism in Black Social Workers." Ph.D. diss., Howard University.

Wall, C. A., ed. 1989. *Changing Our Own Words: Essays on Criticism, Theory, and Writing by Black Women.* New Brunswick, N.J.: Rutgers University Press.

Wallace, M. 1978. *Black Macho and the Myth of Superwoman.* New York: Dial Press.

Washington, M. H., ed. 1975. *Black-Eyed Susans: Classic Stories by and about Black Women.* Garden City, N.Y.: Anchor/Doubleday.

———, ed. 1980. *Midnight Birds: Stories of Contemporary Black Women Writers.* New York: Doubleday.

Weinstein, F. 1980. *Nazism: The Dynamics of Leadership and the Holocaust.* New York: Academic Press.

Weinstein, F., and G. Platt. 1969. *The Wish to Be Free.* Berkeley: University of California Press.

————. 1973. *Psychoanalytic Sociology*. Baltimore: Johns Hopkins University Press.

White, C. L., and C. A. Dobris. 1990. "The Rhetorical Construction of Identity in Black Feminist Fiction: A Case Analysis of Gloria Naylor's *Mama Day*." Paper presented to the Eastern Communication Association Convention, Philadelphia, April 10.

White, E. E. 1980. "Rhetoric as Historical Configuration." In *Rhetoric in Transition: Studies in the Nature and Uses of Rhetoric,* edited by E. E. White. University Park: Pennsylvania State University Press.

White, L. 1977. "Comment." *Essence*: 26.

White, M. J. 1977. "Counternormative Behavior as Influenced by Deindividuating Conditions." *The Journal of Social Psychology* 103:75–90.

Williams, S. A. 1972. *Give Birth to Brightness*. New York: Dial Press.

————. 1979. "Comment on the Curb." *The Black Scholar* 10 (May/June): 51.

Williamson, J. 1980. *New People: Miscegenation and Mulattoes in the United States*. New York: Free Press.

Willis, S. 1987. *Specifying: Black Women Writing the American Experience*. Madison: University of Wisconsin Press.

Wilson, W. J. 1978. *The Declining Significance of Race*. Chicago: University of Chicago Press.

Winkler, K. J. 1990. "Proponents of 'Multicultural' Humanities Research Call for a Critical Look at Its Achievements." *Chronicle of Higher Education* (November 28): A5, 8, 9.

————. 1991. "While Concern over Race Relations Has Lessened among Whites, Sociologists Say Racism Is Taking New Forms, Not Disappearing." *Chronicle of Higher Education* (September 11): A8, 10, 11.

Winnicott, D. 1953. "Transitional Objects and Transitional Phenomena: A Study of the First Not-Me Possession." *International Journal of Psychoanalysis* 34:1–25.

Wortham, A. 1981. *The Other Side of Racism*. Columbus: Ohio State University Press.

Young, A., ed. 1972. *Black Experience: Analysis and Synthesis*. San Rafael, Calif.: Leswing Press.

Zaretsky, E. 1976. *Capitalism, the Family, and Personal Life*. New York: Harper & Row.

Ziller, R. C. 1964. "Individuation and Socialization: A Theory of Assimilation in Large Organizations." *Human Relations* 17:314–59.

Zimbardo, P. C. 1969. "The Human Choice: Individuation, Reason, and Order." In *Nebraska Symposium on Motivation,* edited by W. J. Arnold and D. Levine. Lincoln: University of Nebraska Press.

Zweig, P. 1970. *The Heresy of Self-Love: A Study of Subversive Individualism*. New York: Harper & Row.

Index

❖

Aaron Gresson is currently Associate Professor of Education and Professor-in-Charge of the Program in Educational Theory and Policy at Pennsylvania State University. He is the author of *The Dialectics of Betrayal: Sacrifice, Violation, and the Oppressed* (1982) and *Black Amnesia* (1990), as well as various articles on rhetoric, minority epistemology, political psychology, and mental health.